HARLEY-DAVIDSON
MOTORCYCLES

BILL STERMER

MOTORBOOKS

DEDICATION

I dedicate this book to Margery, Paul, and Julia. You make life so enjoyable!

ACKNOWLEDGEMENTS

I want to thank all those who had a hand in making this book possible:

Buzz Buzzelli, Editor of *American Rider* magazine

Mark Tuttle Jr., Editor of *Rider* magazine

Darrell LaRose, Parts Manager of Ventura Harley-Davidson/Buell

Jason Barresi, General Manager of Ventura Harley-Davidson/Buell

Jon Johnston, Service Manager of V-Twins 101

Jim Michels, my editor at Motorbooks

And of course Cook Neilson, former editor of *Cycle* magazine, who gave me my start

First published in 2007 by Motorbooks, an imprint of MBI Publishing Company LLC, Galtier Plaza, Suite 200, 380 Jackson Street, St. Paul, MN 55101 USA

Copyright © 2007 by Bill Stermer

Motorbooks titles are also available at discounts in bulk quantity for industrial or sales-promotional use. For details write to Special Sales Manager at MBI Publishing Company, Galtier Plaza, Suite 200, 380 Jackson Street, St. Paul, MN 55101 USA.

To find out more about our books, join us online at www.motorbooks.com.

About the author:

Bill Stermer is former editorial director of *Rider* magazine and a contributor to numerous motorcycling publications, including *Robb Report MotorCycling*. He lives in Camarillo, California.

On the cover:

This Softail Deluxe combines classic Harley styling with their patented rear suspension design.

On the frontispiece:

Lou Kimzey was one of the founders of *Easyriders*, the lifestyle magazine that has been the voice of the biker community for more than 35 years. *Paisano Publications*

On the title pages:

Left: This 1911 7D V-twin displaced 50 cubic inches, featured a pocket-valve design, and proved rugged and reliable. *Jim Englund*

Middle left: The infamous 1971 "boat-tail" Super Glide was Willie G. Davidson's first styling exercise, but it was not embraced by the Harley faithful. It was powered by a Shovelhead. *Bob Clark*

Middle right:
The Electra Glide is a very enjoyable and capable luxury tourer. *Buzz Buzzelli*

Right: Those who want to ride a Harley, but don't care for the "low-tech" inferences, can get comfortable with a V-Rod.

On the back cover:

Left: Want to see a lot of accessories? If so, head for upstate New York in early June to the Americade rally. It's a great opportunity to see thousands of accessorized bikes.

Right: Monty, a tech at Ventura Harley-Davidson/Buell, installs a handlebar for a customer. Before tackling any mechanical job, be certain you have the proper tools, parts, and knowledge.

Library of Congress Cataloging-in-Publication Data

Stermer, Bill.
  Harley-Davidson motorcycles : everything you need to know / by Bill Stermer.
    p. cm.
  Includes index.
  ISBN-13: 978-0-7603-2810-1 (softbound)
  ISBN-10: 0-7603-2810-2 (softbound)
  1. Harley Davidson motorcycle. 2. Motorcycling. I. Title.
TL448.H3S74 2007
629.227'5--dc22

                         2007036989

Editor: James Manning Michels
Designer: Jennifer Bergstrom

Printed in China

CONTENTS

Preface

WHAT IS A HARLEY-DAVIDSON?

WHY HARLEYS ARE DIFFERENT

Back in the 1980s, Harley-Davidson ran an ad with a tagline that implied that Harleys were "more than" a motorcycle. That's always been one of the major reasons for owning one—the idea that owners were buying into something else, something more . . . a lifestyle. When you ride a Harley, you immediately become part of a band of brothers and sisters. You are perceived to be a little rougher, a little more daring, a bit more direct than those who don't ride Harleys. Even if you work in a high-rise office building and wear a suit every day, when you're on your bike people treat you differently . . . and usually you like the way you're treated.

H-D celebrated its 100th Anniversary in 2003, and was justifiably proud of doing so. Despite the fact that the Harley-Davidson Motor Company often points to its heritage (several models have carried the "Heritage" designation), it has never made a point of the fact that it is the oldest, continually-producing motorcycle company in the world. Some could interpret that to mean "old and stodgy," but there's nothing stodgy about the fact that there are more than 1.5 million registered Harley-Davidson motorcycles on the road today, and that The Motor Company builds more than 150,000 bikes annually.

By mining its rich heritage, Harley-Davidson has produced some classic-looking models that reflect the slower-paced life of the 1940s and '50s, and evoke a welcome refuge from today's frazzled pace and high technology. By doing so, The Motor Company goes its own way, cleverly sidestepping the highly competitive bigger/faster/more powerful whirlwind that seems to engulf other motorcycle companies. On a Harley, one has nothing to prove; let those other guys go blasting by on their multicolored buzz bombs. Of course, H-D also offers its four-valve, liquid-cooled V-Rod line, showing that Harley-Davidson can indeed offer a bike with power and technology when it wishes.

One reason for its success is that Harley-Davidson knows its customers very well. Its executives and marketing people ride, and they meet with their customers at events like Bike Week in Daytona Beach, Sturgis, Myrtle Beach, and Laughlin. Its district managers are in constant contact with its dealers. Willie G. Davidson, grandson of one of the founders, has become a spokesperson and figurehead for the company. Harley-Davidson's management understands that, while their customers want performance, they do not necessarily want the biggest engine or the highest level of technology. They want classic styling, a certain mechanical presence, and that wonderful "potato-potato-potato" sound.

People don't buy Harleys because they're the biggest or fastest—they aren't. They buy them because they're cool; they go their own way at their own unhurried pace. Harleys represent an attitude and an authenticity that competing brands cannot approach, and they continue to command a premium price with their perceived "real steel" value.

WHAT THIS BOOK IS ABOUT

If you're new to motorcycling—or new to Harley-Davidsons—this book's intent is to give you the necessary background to intelligently choose the right model of new or used Harley, to select the appropriate riding gear, and to be conversant with the marque's background. Show up for your first breakfast run attired in your skull do-rag, $200 shades, and biker wallet and you may score a few style points. However, if you express surprise that Harleys have been manufactured for more than a century, ask a fellow rider what he means when he says he has an "Evo," or suggest that the woman who has a problem with her knucklehead might consider divorcing him, and you'll likely be branded a novice—or worse. This book will give you the basics of Harley knowledge including:

- How the various Harley models differ
- Which Harley model is best for the type of riding you want to do
- The types of accessories to select for certain uses
- How to increase your bike's performance without risk of damage
- What maintenance will be required
- What tools to carry
- How to go touring on your Harley
- What type of oil to run in your Harley
- Some suggestions on customizing your bike
- The pros and cons of leather and textile riding gear
- The pros and cons of the various types of helmets
- What you should know about tires
- How to tune up your riding
- And on and on . . .

WHAT THIS BOOK IS NOT

The hard part of writing any book of this sort is in knowing when to stop. Entire books have been written about many specific aspects of Harley-Davidsons, so this book is intentionally broad rather than deep, a compendium of information to give new and returning riders an overview of the world of Harley-Davidson motorcycles. Properly prepared, you can then pursue in depth the aspects that most interest you. Do this by hanging out with other riders, by reading more books, and, most importantly, by riding. As a person who has written about and tested all brands of bikes for over thirty years, I highly recommend subscribing to motorcycle magazines and reading them thoroughly. There is a lot of information contained in them, and magazines remain current.

Keep in mind this is not a how-to-ride book, though some riding tips are included. There are many sources of information about riding. I strongly suggest that every new and returning rider take the Harley-Davidson "The Rider's Edge" course available through your dealer.

There are many books on basic riding skills (including those by David Hough and Pat Hahn, to name a couple) and on advanced performance riding (by Reg Pridmore, Nick Ienatsch, and Lee Parks). These gentlemen can tell you how to ride better on the street or track, and any or several of these books should be on your shelf.

KEEP IT FUN

The final thing to keep in mind is that motorcycling is fun. Lots of fun! The most fun you can have with your clothes on! Enjoy it. And don't wait until you get that certain better jacket or those bigger saddle-bags or the ideal bike—enjoy it now. It just gets better. Nobody ever had fun riding by sitting at home wishing they could have fun riding. Don't get bogged down in the details. Just do it!

Want to see a lot of accessories? If so, head to upstate New York in early June for the Americade rally. Watch the parade and you'll see thousands of riders streaming by on accessorized bikes.

HARLEY LORE
WHERE . . . AND HOW . . .
IT ALL BEGAN

HERE WE WILL COVER:

- **History of the Motor Company**

- **The Partnership**

- **The Competition**

- **The Models**

Back before Harley-Davidson began, early motorcycles were powered by steam or primitive gasoline engines. Gottlieb Daimler, who helped develop the four-stroke Otto-cycle engine, is credited with taking the first motorcycle ride. It took place in Germany in 1885. Shown are early steam motorcycles displayed in the Guggenheim Museum.

In order to understand Harley-Davidson motorcycles and their long heritage, one must first understand their background, history, and lore. Let's start with some Harley history.

A SHORT HISTORY OF THE MOTOR COMPANY

As the nineteenth turned to the twentieth century, the United States was undergoing an incredible transformation from agrarian to industrialized nation. German inventor Nicholas Otto had only recently developed the four-cycle internal-combustion engine, and in 1885 Gottlieb Daimler had cobbled together what many consider to be the first motorcycle. Daimler's Einspur ("one track") was propelled—slowly—by a one-half-horsepower, single-cylinder gasoline engine. It rolled on a

large pair of iron-rimmed wheels with a smaller pair of outrigger wheels to stabilize it. Its first ride was conducted in Germany on November 10, 1885, and you're welcome to celebrate this anniversary as you see fit. Despite the implications, Daimler never designed his machine to fulfill dreams of moonlit rides, wind in the hair, or races on the banking at the Daytona Motor Speedway. His reason for using a two-wheeled machine was simply that his primitive engine was not sufficiently powerful to propel a heavier four-wheeled carriage.

It was the age of innovation and invention, and in 1901 the Indian Motocycle Company was founded by George M. Hendee and Carl Oscar Hedstrom in Springfield, Massachusetts. That same year, many others were also dreaming of, designing, or building vehicles that were essentially powered bicycles. These vehicles quickly evolved from motorized bicycles to single-purpose vehicles that were designed from the ground up as motorcycles.

BILL HARLEY AND THE DAVIDSON BROTHERS

Marketers and sales personnel know the value of location, location, location. The Motor Company's roots owe much to this simple font of opportunity. William S. Harley and Arthur Davidson lived next door to each other in Milwaukee, Wisconsin. Harley was born in 1880 and Davidson in 1881. When the two friends came of age, they both took jobs at a local manufacturing plant—Harley as a draftsman and Davidson as a pattern maker. There, they decided to build their own internal-combustion bicycle motor. They befriended a co-worker—a German draftsman—who was familiar with the De Dion engine already popular in Europe. With his help, Harley and Davidson designed a small, air-cooled motor.

According to the 1900 census, Milwaukee was a bustling city of 285,315 inhabitants on Lake Michigan. Its name is derived from the Indian word *Millioke*, which means "The Good Land," or "Gathering place by the water." Many German immigrants settled in Wisconsin, bringing with them a heritage of brewing and manufacturing trade skills. The town came to be referred to as "Cream City," a reference to the locally quarried, cream-colored bricks used in many of the local buildings, and "Brew City" because of its beer brewing background. Frenchman Solomon Juneau came here in 1818, started a settlement, and became Milwaukee's first mayor. His name would eventually figure in Harley-Davidson lore, as you'll soon see.

This extremely rare single was a prototype for the first Indian motorcycle and was built in 1899. The humpbacked tank held fuel and oil, while the canister behind the front downtube held dry-cell batteries. *David Dewhurst*

Arthur's older brother, Walter Davidson, had moved to Kansas City, Kansas, where he worked as a railroad machinist. When he returned to Milwaukee to attend brother William's wedding, Arthur and William recruited him for their bicycle motor project. Soon the little gasoline engine, with a bore and stroke of just $2^1/8 \times 2^7/8$ inches, came together. According to legend, the carburetor was fashioned from a tomato can. Once the engine was completed, however, Harley and the Davidson brothers realized that their 10.2-cubic-inch creation was not powerful enough for their needs.

In 1902, the men designed a second engine. For this one they got help designing the carburetor from another mechanical talent whom good fortune had brought to the area—Ole Evinrude. (Yes, *that* Evinrude.) This powerplant had the same displacement as the previous bicycle motor but with a larger flywheel and over/under pocket valves; its three-horsepower output proved sufficient for their needs.

The first Harley-Davidson factory was nothing but a 10x15-foot wooden shed in the backyard of the Davidson

According to legend, the first H-D carburetor was fashioned from a tomato can.

Above: The rider started the engine of this 1907 strap-tank Harley single by pedaling. It displaced 26.8 cubic inches, made about 3.5 horsepower, and featured belt final drive. *Jim Englund*

Above Inset: The complex set of controls on the 1907 strap-tank single illustrates how difficult these early bikes must have been to ride. *Jim Englund*

In 1903, James Wyman rode a 1.5-horsepower California Motor Bicycle like this one from coast to coast. It was the first motorized vehicle to successfully complete that trek. *Jim Englund*

family's home on the southwest corner of 38th Street and Highland Boulevard in Milwaukee. It was built by the Davidsons' father, who learned carpentry in his native Scotland. Painted on the door was a name whose future the young inventors could not possibly have imagined: "Harley-Davidson Motor Co" (which, by the way, is always hyphenated).

In the third year of the century, the Wright Brothers made their famous powered flight, and Henry Ford started his fledgling automotive enterprise. That same year, the legend goes, Harley and the Davidsons built and sold their first motorcycles. They were powered by an engine with a bore and stroke of 3.0x3.5 inches and a displacement of 25 cubic inches. While their earlier engines had been designed for bicycle frames, for their first motorcycle the lads constructed a very stout, purpose-built frame. The official Harley-Davidson history asserts that The Motor Company built and sold three single-cylinder motorcycles in 1903, the first bike a gloss-black machine with a loop frame and belt final drive. They built and sold three additional motorcycles in '04. In the years that followed, sales, shall we say, picked up.

For years, The Motor Company has displayed what it contends is its first motorcycle from 1903, and officially recognizes this as its first year of production. It threw one heck of a party in Milwaukee in 2003 to commemorate the centennial of that event. Historian Herbert Wagner disputes this claim, however. In his book, *At the Creation*, he asserts that the first marketable Harley-Davidson was actually completed in 1904 but that bikes were not available for sale until 1905. According to Wagner, the original history of the company was altered after 1908, and a mythical history was substituted as an advertising strategy. As no photos or documents have been discovered from these earliest days, this mystery may forever be unsolved. With that said, Wagner's book still makes for fascinating reading.

Within a few years, the backyard factory building had tripled in size, and demand was so strong that the company quickly outgrew the facility. H-D purchased a large lot a block up 38th Street on the north side of Chestnut and, over the years and in many stages, the Harley-Davidson plant took shape. Chestnut was eventually renamed Juneau Avenue after the city's first mayor, and the main Harley-Davidson plant's address has been 3700 W. Juneau Avenue ever since. These early Harley-Davidson motorcycles—whenever they were actually first produced—had an adjustable baffle in the exhaust pipe that could be opened for more power out in the countryside or closed for quieter in-town use. The bikes were painted gray and came to be called "The Silent Gray Fellow."

THE FIRST V-TWIN: 1909

With the company's rapid expansion and the growth of competition, Harley-Davidson needed to develop a more powerful machine to keep pace with the market. The crude engines of the day subjected riders to extreme levels of vibration, and because so little was yet understood about valves, airflow, and metallurgy, they made very little power per unit of displacement. Another consideration was that fuel was so poor by today's standards, so low in octane, that the engines had to be low in compression or the fuel would detonate rather than burn in the combustion chamber.

Simply increasing the displacement of the single likely would have also exacerbated the vibration of these slow-turning engines. To avoid this, and to add power and smoothness without resorting to a higher-revving engine, the obvious solution was to add a second cylinder. The atmospheric valves of the day were not conducive to high revs. It took the development of the inlet camshaft to allow air to flow more quickly through the engine.

The first Harley-Davidson V-twin engine's cylinders were angled at 45 degrees, which has become a hallmark of Big Twins ever since. When constructing the V-twin, Harley-Davidson used what is called a knife-and-fork arrangement to link the connecting rods to the crankshaft at a common point. In order to do this, the big end of one of the connecting rods fits within the big end of the other, which straddles it. The double-throw crankshaft, in which each connecting rod bolts to its own throw of the crank-shaft, would not come into common usage for some time.

While most Harley-Davidson aficionados know that The Motor Company introduced its first V-twin in 1909, a Harley V-twin, probably a proto-type, showed up in July 1908 at a hill-climb sponsored by the Chicago Motorcycle Club in Algonquin, Illinois. There, according to an official Harley-Davidson publication, a man named

Harvey Bernard rode it in the 61-cubic-inch class and had the best time of the day.

While the first commercial Harley-Davidson V-twin in 1909 should have represented a significant step forward, unfortunately it was a failure. The bike had automatic intake valves, which had been used successfully on the singles but did not work well on the V-twin. The intake tract and carburetor were shared by both cylinders, which changed the flow characteristics and confused the atmospheric intake valves; it really needed an inlet cam. As a result, only a few dozen 1909 Harley-Davidson V-twins were produced, and the model was dropped for 1910. Still, the powers-that-were at Harley-Davidson realized that V-twins were the future of high-end motorcycling and forged ahead to redesign the engine. Its successor, which had mechanical intake valves and was set in a new frame, was introduced for 1911 and was indeed a success. Still, even at this point, the bike had to be pedaled to start the engine, as the "step starter" (kick starter) had not yet been introduced.

THE EARLY COMPETITION

It's said that the first motorcycle race took place when the second motorcycle

Its first V-twin was a failure in 1909, so Harley-Davidson redesigned it. This 1911 7D V-twin displaced 50 cubic inches, featured a pocket-valve design, and proved rugged and reliable. *Jim Englund*

This 1915 Silent Gray Fellow F-head V-twin produced about 11 horsepower and is now part of the Ron Paugh (of Paughco fame) Collection. *Bob Clark*

The new class of smaller dirt-track racing machines grew from an effort to slow the speeds of bikes that had claimed several lives in the teens and '20s. This 1927 Harley "Peashooter" is a 21-cubic-inch machine owned by Ron Paugh. *Bob Clark*

This 1938 ULH 80-cubic-inch flathead with its springer front end has been fully restored, and is still a sweet runner today. *Glenn Bator, Bator International*

Serious V-twin board-track racers, such as this 1927, 61-cubic-inch model with eight valves, could attain speeds of well over 100 miles per hour—with no brakes! *Bob Clark*

was built. With the number of manufacturers burgeoning, bikes like Cyclone, Indian, and The Flying Merkel were all vying for favorable publicity and a larger slice of the oily motorcycle sales pie. Starting in 1914, Harley-Davidson fielded its own race team and was hugely successful in board-track and flat-track racing, but World War I interrupted the fun. Many young men went off to the war, and Harley-Davidson did its part by manufacturing specialized military motorcycles. By war's end in 1918, all of Harley-Davidson's production was going to the war effort.

KNUCKLES, SHOVELS, PANS, EVOS, AND MORE: A BRIEF HISTORY OF HARLEY-DAVIDSON MOTORCYCLE MODELS

This chapter sets forth a brief historical overview of the company and its machines to give you some background when you're hanging out with your riding buddies. With that in mind, let's touch on the significant engine families through the years.

Though their motors have grown in displacement and sophistication, improved and evolved, the Big Twins have always shared certain features. For nearly a century all Big-Twin Harleys have been air-cooled, longitudinally-mounted, 45-degree V-twins with displacements that have earned them the "Big" designation in all their variations. There have been other short-lived models with different engine configurations, but they have not been Big Twins. And, of course, the Sportster, a smaller-displacement twin, has been around now for more than 50 years.

Some of the Big-Twin engines have become known by colloquial nicknames based upon some aspect of their appearance, while others have become known by their official factory names.

F-Head (1911–1929): These were the very early V-twins. The name refers to the shape of the intake tract as necessitated by the location of the valves.

Flathead (1929–1939): Introduced for 1929, the 45-cubic-inch WL sidevalve with its twin bullet headlights sold well. But for 1930 the VL got the big 74-cubic-inch version. A flathead (also called a "sidevalve") has no valves in the cylinder head. They're set off to the side, which makes for rather tortuous airflow into and out of the engine. In Harley lore, the look or shape of the tops of the cylinders contributed to the colorful nicknames (as opposed to the official names from the factory) of some models. On the

Despite its Knucklehead name, the EL engine was a thing of beauty (as this cutaway of the first-year 1936, 61-cubic-inch engine shows). *Bob Clark*

Powered by the flathead engine, Harley's three-wheeled Servicars are only occasionally seen today.

flathead, for instance, the heads are flat on top.

H-D continued to use the flathead engine to power the three-wheeled Servicar until 1974. The Servicar had a large box on the back between the wheels and was used by small businesses for deliveries. This was probably the last flathead engine in general use in anything larger than a lawnmower.

Knucklehead (1936–1947): Okay, no brother-in-law jokes here. In 1936, Harley-Davidson brought out a new model called the EL, its first production bike with overhead valves and a recirculating oil system. The first knucklehead engine displaced 61 cubic inches; this grew to 74 cubic inches in 1941. The UL and ULH got an 80-cubic-inch engine from 1936–1945. How'd the knucklehead get its nickname? Clench your fist and notice the curves of your knuckles. Now look at the rocker covers of this engine. Enough said.

Another offshoot was the XA, a unique 45-cubic-inch military Harley that had a horizontally opposed twin-cylinder engine and driveshaft. It was developed for desert duty in North Africa, where the sand would eat chains

and cooling would be an issue. Only about 1,000 were made.

Panhead (1948–1965): America was home from World War II, and the former GIs were looking for transportation and women—not necessarily in that order. While much of the wartime production had been given over to military machines, Harley-Davidson was finally ready to introduce the next generation of Big Twins for civilians. The Panhead engine retained the overhead valves of its predecessor but now featured aluminum cylinder heads and hydraulic valve lifters. It was also offered in both 61- and 74-cubic-inch versions. As for how the bike got its colloquial nickname, visualize a pair of baking pans. Now look at the valve covers. You got it!

Kick . . . dang! Kick . . . damn! After more than 60 years of kick starting, Harley-Davidson fitted an electric starter to the 1965 Electra Glide, which was the last year of the Panhead. This convenience eventually spread throughout the line.

Shovelhead (1966–1985): Every decade or so, Harley-Davidson upgraded its engines, and the Shovelhead debuted

In 1954, this Anniversary Edition Panhead was still a hardtail; it did not yet have a rear suspension. *Bob Clark*

Along with his two riding buddies, Wayne Willcuts purchased a new 74-inch Shovelhead Electra Glide in 1967 and picked it up at the factory in Milwaukee. When it was stolen years later, he purchased one of his buddies' bikes and continued riding. After 10 years of storage, the bike was lovingly restored in 2006. *Wayne Willcuts*

in 1966. It was the first major redesign since just after WWII. Lay a coal shovel face-down on the ground and peruse it from the side. Now look at the shape of this engine's cylinder heads. That's why it's called a shovelhead. Originally 74 cubic inches, some models grew to 80 inches in 1979.

The rocker boxes were made of cast aluminum, replacing the leaky sheetmetal of the Panhead. It had the new Tilotson carburetor and the "PowerPak" heads that gave it a claimed 15 percent increase in power

Two significant advances occurred in 1980. One, the Sturgis was the first modern Harley model to be offered with belt final drive, which was quieter than chain, lasted longer, and required fewer adjustments and no lubrication. Second, the engine on the new FLT Tour Glide was suspended by three elastomer rubber mounts. These allowed the engine to shake all it wanted while isolating the vibration from the frame and rider. It was a major advance in comfort.

Evolution (1984–1999): By 1984, it was time once again for a new version of the signature V-twin, so Harley-Davidson introduced the Evolution engine. It displaced 80 cubic inches (1340cc) but sported steel-lined alloy cylinders with new pushrods, pistons, and cylinder heads. The Motor Company claimed that it generated 10 percent more horsepower and 15 percent more torque than its predecessor, though it had the same displacement. The new valve covers were rather blocky, and some riders referred to it originally as the "Blockhead," but "Evo" is the name that stuck. The engine proved itself not only extremely reliable, but it also lent itself very well to hopping up. In every sense, it was the engine that saved Harley-Davidson.

Twin Cam 88 (1999–2006): When released for the 1999 model year, the 88-cubic-inch (1450cc) Twin Cam engine featured two camshafts and was available in the FL and Dyna models, where it was rubber mounted to isolate its vibration from the rider. A year later, H-D introduced the 88B version, which was available only in the Softail models. It utilized twin counterbalancers (weights that rotate opposite the engine's crankshaft) that cancel out much of the engine's vibration before it even reaches the frame, which is much easier on both components—and riders. Because of the counterbalancers, the engine can be mounted solidly to the frame, strengthening the frame considerably. With rubber mounting, the frame must be slightly larger to accommodate the engine's movements. Counterbalance the engine, however, and the frame can be fit more tightly around it for a more classic look.

The V-Rod (2002–present): As the twenty-first century began, most members of the Baby Boom generation were in their 40s and 50s. Despite the huge success Harley-Davidson had been enjoying for the past 20 years, the

The predecessors to the Sportster, these Harley K-models can be seen on display at the Wheels Through Time Museum in Maggie Valley, North Carolina.

When the Topper scooter was introduced, it was a white-tie-and-tails affair. *Dudley Perkins Harley-Davidson*

In the 1960s and 1970s, The Motor Company offered a complete line of two- and four-stroke singles made by Aermacchi and sold under the Harley-Davidson nameplate. These tiddlers were both street and off-road bikes.

company realized it was still possible for its products to get the reputation of being an "old man's motorcycle." To counter this, H-D teamed with automaker Porsche and utilized their formidable motor technology to help develop a totally new V-twin. In 2002 Harley-Davidson introduced the result: the V-Rod, a total departure from anything The Motor Company had done in the past.

The V-Rod was a V-twin all right, but what was that hanging out front . . . a radiator? And what's with those cylinders being splayed 60 degrees apart rather than the traditional 45 degrees? A wider cylinder angle allows longer, lower motorcycle design, and it also creates more space between the cylinders for mounting fuel injectors and the airbox. Its very modern styling was certainly a departure, and it displaced only 1130cc, while the Big Twins had 1450cc. Though it was dynoed at an impressive 106 rear-wheel horsepower, the torque on the 1130cc V-Rod was only 72 lb-ft, which meant it was a revving engine rather than a torque engine, as Big Twins have always been. For the 2007 model year, some V-Rod models were bumped up to 1250cc.

Twin Cam 96 (2007–present): After eight successful years with the Twin Cam 88, for 2007 H-D increased displacement to 96 cubic inches (1584cc) and released what was essentially a new engine, though its cylinders and heads appeared identical to those of its predecessor. The bump in displacement was achieved by increasing the stroke from 101.5 to 111.25mm (4.0 to 4.38 inches) while using the same 95.2mm bore. This move also increased the compression ratio from 8.9 to 9.2:1. All Big Twins also got the new six-speed Cruise Drive transmission that had been introduced on the previous year's Dyna series, replacing the old five-speed. And, finally, all Harley-Davidson models became fuel injected for 2007.

The K-Models: American troops abroad during WWII had become acquainted with the lighter, quicker bikes designed for Europe's twisty roads. Many GIs who had been stationed in England took a liking to British bikes, which were more agile and handled better than most of their U.S. counterparts, had swinging-arm rear suspensions, and utilized hand and foot controls that were easier to operate.

Harley-Davidson's XR750s virtually owned dirt-track racing for many years. In the background here, at Ron Paugh's collection, is a single-cylinder 1999 Rotax/Harley-Davidson military scout bike. *Bob Clark*

The Evolution motor helped save Harley-Davidson in the 1980s and led the company back to prosperity. It was powerful and reliable, and it responded well to modification.

In response, for 1952, Harley-Davidson introduced the K-model, a sportier machine with a 45-cubic-inch (750cc) flathead, sidevalve V-twin engine. The bike featured a swingarm suspension with shock absorbers, plus a hand clutch and foot shift. It also had an integral gearbox, rather than a separate unit as used on the Big Twins. It was a fairly modern design except for its flathead cylinders. A year later Indian, Harley's main rival, went out of business, leaving The Motor Company as the sole American manufacturer of large-displacement motorcycles. Unfortunately, this was not where long-term growth would soon be in the motorcycle market.

With the British bringing their more modern, high-performance bikes into the U.S. in growing numbers, H-D countered two years later with a 54-cubic-inch (883cc) version of the K-model dubbed the KH. An even sportier version, the KHK, was introduced for 1955 with hotter cams, polished ports, and a roller-bearing bottom end. Still, these were stop-gaps, as Harley-Davidson was busy refining a more modern, sportier bike that was signifi-

cantly different and could more successfully counter the bikes from overseas.

Sportster: To compete with the British invasion, Harley-Davidson dealers were asking for a more powerful version of the KH. The flatheads were underpowered and H-D was working on aluminum heads, but the development process was riddled with problems. In an effort to git 'er done, H-D's top brass told its engineers to put a set of iron overhead-valve heads on the new model and get it into production.

H-D released the new Sportster in 1957 which, with its overhead valves, 883cc displacement, and (of course) 45-degree cylinder angle, made good power. Sportsters have two cams because of their sidevalve heritage. To support its contention that it made sporty machines, Harley-Davidson had remained heavily involved in racing and won the AMA Grand National Championship with the KR model in 1954, and the following year a KR won the Daytona 200, the most important motorcycle race in the United States. Both series were dominated by Harleys for the next six years. The Sportster sold well and got a reputation as fitting competition for the Triumph Bonnevilles of the day, as the H-D carried a significant displacement advantage.

Over the years the Sportster evolved, losing its "iron-head" roots in 1986 when it adopted an Evolution-based motor with aluminum heads. There were now two versions of the Sportster, an 883 and a 1200.

Topper Scooter: From 1960 to '65, Harley-Davidson built a two-stroke, 165cc scooter called the Topper to appeal to a new generation of post-war kids who would eventually come to be known as the Baby Boomers. The leading edge of this generation had just turned 14 in 1960, and they were clamoring for transportation. The Topper was rather squarish looking, but the advantage was that most parents—and young riders—were not intimidated by a docile-looking scooter.

Aermacchi: In 1960, in a further attempt to address this market of young consumers, Harley-Davidson purchased a half-interest in an Italian company called Aeronautica-Macchi, which was abbreviated as Aermacchi. This company produced a line of small, single-cylinder motorcycles in its plant in Varese, Italy. Over the years they manufactured two-stroke dirt and dual-sport bikes, and four-stroke 250 and 350cc street singles called Sprints, all under the Harley-Davidson name. Don't be shocked if, at a swap meet, you see a dirt bike with "Harley-Davidson" on the tank. H-D sold this division in 1978.

The AMF Years: If your family has a black sheep, you can appreciate how Harley-Davidson feels about an interlude that is known simply as "The AMF years." It all began in the early 1960s as a tide of smaller, less-expensive, and very competent motorcycles from Japan began deluging the American market. With the Baby Boomers in their college years— more or less—and wanting inexpensive transportation, they snapped up these little bikes and largely ignored the old-line machines. Then, with the advent of the full-size Honda CB750 four-cylinder in 1969, the moribund British motorcycle companies began to die off, and Harley-Davidson was feeling the heat, too. It was making big, heavy, expensive machines with slow-turning engines, while the Baby Boomers were looking for something quite different. In an attempt to bring in fresh capital, the Motor Company merged with American Machine and Foundry (AMF), which manufactured bowling and other sporting equipment.

The 1970s were hard times, as H-D found itself controlled by a parent company whose principals were not motorcycle people. New product development suffered, as did quality control, and, compared with the high-tech machines from Japan, the Harleys of the time seemed like dinosaurs. However, some dedicated motorcycle people were left in charge of the H-D division, and they began developing the new Evolution engine.

While H-D did not exactly thrive under AMF management, to AMF's credit this interlude did help H-D weather the economic storms of the '70s and survive. A core group of top H-D management, led by Vaughn Beals, bought the company back from AMF in 1981. The buyout team also included the recently retired Jeff Bleustein, Willie G. Davidson (grandson of one of the founders), Charlie Thompson, Jim Paterson, David Caruso, Timothy Hoelter, and David Lickerman, among others. The company introduced the Evolution engine in 1984 and has never looked back.

The Buell: Back in the 1970s, Erik Buell was a Superbike racer who went to work for Harley-Davidson as a chassis engineer. He left the company in 1982 and, in 1987, created a line of American sportbikes powered by Harley-Davidson motors. With Erik's eye toward technical innovation, Buells were the first production motorcycles to be equipped with such features as male-slider forks, perimeter brakes, and braided-steel brake lines.

Harley-Davidson, in an attempt to broaden its appeal to younger riders, in bought 49 percent of the Buell Motorcycle Company in February 1994; it picked up another 49 percent in 1998 while retaining Erik Buell's services. Over the years, the Buell division has developed its own 984cc and 1,203cc V-twin engines and is no longer powered by H-D iron.

New for 1999, the Twin Cam 88 was the successor to the Evo. It received a second camshaft and an eight-inch boost in displacement. This is the Electra Glide version.

Low, mean, and powerful, with four valves per cylinder and liquid cooling, the V-Rod is much more technically advanced than air-cooled Harley-Davidsons. In stock form, it produces about 106 rear-wheel horsepower.

Former roadracer Erik Buell designed the Buell sportbike and originally powered it with an air-cooled Harley V-twin. The brand is now owned by Harley-Davidson and often sold in Harley dealerships.

When introduced for 2007, the Twin Cam 96 offered many advances over its predecessor, including increased displacement, a compression boost from 8.9 to 9.2:1, an improved driveline, reduced clutch effort, simplification of maintenance, and an automatic adjuster that eliminated primary chain adjustments.

As of this writing, the Buell factory in East Troy, Wisconsin, employs more than 200 people and builds more than 10,000 bikes per year. While there is not much physical carryover between the brands, Buells are unique and functional air-cooled V-twin sportbikes marketed through Harley-Davidson dealerships.

Hollister: Over the 4th of July weekend in 1947, an AMA Gypsy Tour converged on Hollister, California, for a rally and a little fun. Well, things got a bit out of hand on this second Independence Day after WWII as some of the 4,000 participants engaged in some excessive drinking, reckless riding, and destruction of property. There'd been some racing at the local fairgrounds, but the activities spilled over into the town where riders raced up and down the streets, rode their bikes into bars, and threw "barrages" of beer bottles from windows. Some 40 state troopers were called in to help control the festivities. Nearly 60 people were injured and more than 50 jailed.

A *Life* magazine photographer was on hand, and among the photos he took were several of a rather inebriated-looking young man sitting on a bike with a bottle in hand and a collection of empties piled around him. Of course, no self-respecting biker would actually pile many pounds of glass around his bike—the shot was obviously staged. When several shots of this type appeared in *Life* magazine, well, the public was outraged and motorcyclists of all sorts got a bad rep. The Hollister incident served as inspiration for the Marlon Brando movie *The Wild One*, which further confirmed the "bad biker" image to the American public. Just for the record, Brando rode a Triumph in the movie.

Easy Rider *and* **Easyriders**: Another bit of biker lore concerns the 1969 movie *Easy Rider*, starring Peter Fonda, Dennis Hopper, and Jack Nicholson. The movie concerned Wyatt and Billy (Fonda and Hopper), a couple of long-haired bikers riding cross-country on Panhead choppers. They'd scored some drugs in Los Angeles and were heading for Mardi Gras in New Orleans. Along the way, they encounter a cast of characters that includes ranchers, hippies, hookers, and rednecks. Nicholson portrays George Hansen, a down-and-out loner who joins them but is soon beaten to death by a group of nasty locals. The film's violent ending is a commentary on freedom in late-1960s America.

Out in Southern California in 1972, Lou Kimzey and Joe Teresi started a magazine for bikers. They were inspired by *Easy Rider*, but Kimzey once told me that they named their magazine *Easyriders* because they were concerned about legal problems with the movie studio if their magazine's name was exactly the same. They held their breath, nothing happened, and this hard-core monthly biker lifestyle magazine is still going strong more than 35 years later.

The movie *Easy Rider* became a biker cult classic after its release in 1970. Unfortunately, the actual bike used in the movie was stolen and never recovered. Here's a modern reproduction of the 74-cubic-inch "Captain America" Panhead chopper popularized in the film. *Bob Clark*

Lou Kimzey was one of the founders of *Easyriders*, the lifestyle magazine that has been the voice of the biker community for more than 35 years. *Paisano Publications*

The Clubs: You've no doubt heard of them: Clubs with such names as The Hells Angels, Satan's Slaves, Devil's Disciples, and others. While the great majority of clubs that involve motorcycling consist of pretty decent individuals out for a little riding and fun, others have the taint of unnecessary roughness. The American Motorcyclist Association once stated that it was only 1 percent of the riders who were causing all the trouble. Soon after that, those who saw themselves as trouble-makers sported patches that proclaimed "1%er." In any case, the point is, whatever their activity, all of these groups wish to be referred to as motorcycle clubs, not "gangs." Calling some groups the latter may cause you to wish you hadn't.

Back in 1978, when I started writing for motorcycle magazines, Harley-Davidson was very negative about "hog" or "hawg" being used as any type of reference to the company, even though it was a nickname for a big ol' motorcycle. When top management bought the motorcycle division back from AMF, all that changed, and the new company regained its sense of humor. This change was so dramatic that, when the Harley-Davidson Motor Company started an officially sanctioned owners' club in 1983, it called it the Harley Owners Group, or HOG. Buy a new Harley and you'll get a free one-year membership in the HOG Club. The HOG Club has more than a million members worldwide, is the world's largest factory-supported owners' club, and is a key marketing element.

The American Motorcyclist Association once stated that it was only 1 percent of the riders who were causing all the trouble.

Chapter 2

THE BIKE
CHOOSING THE RIGHT TOOL FOR YOUR JOB

The infamous 1971 "boat-tail" Super Glide was Willie G. Davidson's first styling exercise, but it was not embraced by the Harley faithful. It was powered by a Shovelhead engine. *Bob Clark*

ON HARLEYS AND BIKERS: WHY HARLEYS ARE DIFFERENT

Have you ever noticed that Harley-Davidson motorcycles are different from other brands, and the people who ride them tend to be a little different, too? In the first place, Harleys have a heritage that stretches back to 1903, and, in the second, they have always been associated with rebels and loners. What's different, then, is that the motorcycle is not just a means of getting from place to place—it's an item of personal expression. As the saying goes, there's no such thing as a stock Harley. And as H-D stated in an advertisement some years ago, it's "More than a Motorcycle."

While other brands seem to get caught up in the endless spiral of *bigger, faster, more powerful*, H-D has sidestepped that whole business, delivering bikes that are heavier, slower, and less powerful than what most other manufacturers are offering, yet selling as many of them as they can make. How? Because H-D riders aren't just buying a machine, they're buying a lifestyle. It's all about self-expression and brotherhood, hanging out with friends and travelin' easy.

CHOOSING YOUR HARLEY: THE FACTS TO CONSIDER

If you're reading this book, chances are you either own a Harley-Davidson motorcycle or wish to. If you own a Harley, you may already be thinking about your next one. In any case, let's take a quick look at the Harley-Davidson family of current-model motorcycles and consider their particular uses.

First of all, whatever brand you favor, consider that a motorcycle is a tool for a job. In order to decide upon the tool, first you need to define the job. In carpentry, for example, if you wish to turn a screw, drive a nail, or make one long piece of wood into two shorter ones, you need to select the proper tool. Granted, you could pound a nail with a screwdriver or break a piece of wood in two with a hammer, and you might even enjoy it—for a while. But, after three hours of trying to turn screws with a handsaw, you'll most likely wish you'd chosen a screwdriver instead.

Motorcycles also have jobs to perform, and different kinds and types of them perform certain jobs more or less efficiently than others. Define the job you wish it to do, and that will point toward the type of motorcycle you will need to perform that job.

Let's take a look at the Harley-Davidson motorcycle family from the point of view of six different riders, all of whom have a slightly different job in mind. Once they have defined their particular job, they can consider what specific model they need. The question to each of them is, "What job do you want your motorcycle to perform?"

Rider One: "I'm not an experienced rider, don't want to spend a huge amount of money, and kind of want to feel my way around motorcycling before I really commit to it. I'd like a Harley because some of my buddies have them, and I really respect and appreciate the fact they're American made and have been around for more than a century. I'd like to get in for a minimum amount of money and commitment at first to see if I like it, but I still really want to become a part of the Harley-Davidson experience."

Rider Two: "I want something really cool. Give me a bike with a lot of heritage, great style, something I can customize and really make my own. I'd get some custom wheels and aftermarket brakes, a nice seat, have the bike

custom painted. I want to get into the engine, put in a cam and some pipes so it really moves, get some mellow sound so people pay attention. When I go down to the restaurant and park that bike, I want there to be ten people coming up to me saying, 'Hey man, nice ride!'"

Rider Three: "Since I got out of the service many years ago, I've had this dream of getting on a bike and going off to see the country. I wanted to do it on a chopper originally, but then marriage, a family, and career intervened. Now that the kids are grown, I've got the where-withal and time, and I still want to live that dream. My wife will be on the back, and we want to go at our leisure on something with a decent amount of comfort and luggage-carrying capacity."

Rider Four: "When I go on group rides, why does everybody have to ride so darned slow? I still want the heritage of the air-cooled motor but want to get out there and go, lean it over in the turns until things drag, make riding more active! I don't want to just cruise."

Rider Five: "I'm a younger guy, have owned several other brands of

Though they're lighter, have smaller displacement engines, and are less expensive, Sportsters have a good bit of performance and handle pretty well. An easy way to differentiate the major Harley air-cooled models is that a Sportster has its belt final drive on the right side, while a Big Twin's is on the left. *Buzz Buzzelli*

Harley's Road King is a nice compromise—an FL touring bike with rubber-mounted engine and standard saddlebags but with a windshield rather than a heavy fairing. *Buzz Buzzelli*

Why Harleys Never Seem to Change

By Buzz Buzzelli, editor of *American Rider* magazine

Year after year, Harley-Davidson introduces new models, which turn out to be nothing more than new iterations of the same old bike. This prompts many questions, including why do Harleys always look the same? Why doesn't the company restyle them? And why doesn't Harley build more "modern" motorcycles?

There is a very simple answer: because the customers won't let the factory change. The motorcycles are what they are because if the styling changes too radically from its traditional appearance, customers revolt by staying away in droves. There are many historical examples of this. In 1971, when Willie G. Davidson (grandson of one of the founders) first joined the company as its chief stylist, his first styling exercise was the FX Super Glide's infamous "boat-tail" rear fender treatment. This fiberglass nacelle was a combination fender and seat with a molded-in tail lamp and license plate holder. In an era when Edsels had sucky-mouth front ends and Cadillacs had swoopy fins, the boat tail was a very well conceived design . . . except for one thing: it didn't look like it belonged on a Harley. In order to sell these non-traditional bikes, dealers promptly removed the boat tails and tossed them into the rafters, installing standard steel rear fenders and seats. It was a lesson that Willie G. will never forget.

Then there was the Siamese exhaust system on the 1977-era Sportsters. Not only did this exhaust system look extremely un-Harley, but its name also had a distinctly foreign quality. Loyal Harley customers who wanted strictly American motorcycles revolted and rejected these pipes. As a result, dealer and customer rafters were soon garnished with these exhaust systems as they were swapped for pipes with a more traditional appearance.

When the 1977 XLCR Cafe Racer was introduced, its frame had a triangulated rear section supporting the shocks and seat. From an engineering perspective it was a success: it was stronger, stiffer and lighter than previous designs. However, it had an appearance usually seen on European and Japanese imports. Unfortunately for Harley, all this technologically improved frame brought the Sportster over the next three years was a layer of dust, as buyers wouldn't touch them. In 1981 a new frame with a more traditional appearance restored sales to previous levels.

The Cafe Racer was an attempt to appeal to the performance-minded buyer, but the machine was heavy and underpowered, and was perceived as a "sheep in wolf's clothing." Although this model eventually became a desirable cult bike in later years, it was originally a marketing flop and sales languished. Harley learned an important lesson: never compete head-on with other high-performance bikes; instead, rely on the company's heritage and traditional styling appeal. Customers wanted a motorcycle that looked all-American.

All this didn't stop Harley's engineers from advancing the product technologically. New and updated engineering designs, materials, and manufacturing processes have continued to improve Harley performance, reliability and durability—all while retaining traditional outward appearances. As *Cycle* magazine editor Phil Schilling once put it, "It's like taking an orange, scraping out the inside, and installing an apple."

motorcycles, yet have always appreciated the heritage and American-made aspect of Harley-Davidsons. However, once you've ridden bikes with four-valve heads, high-revving multiple-cylinder engines and 100 rear-wheel horsepower, well, you're not as satisfied with an old two-valve, air-cooled design that only makes about 65 horsepower. I want something that looks cool, has some high technology behind it, and really hauls!"

Rider Six: "I've been around, have had several Harleys, love them, and have customized a few. However, I've been through all the problems you get with a custom, like having to make components built by one manufacturer fit those built by another, or trying to fit a huge rear tire to a given frame, or building a motor to make around 100 horsepower and then having to deal with upgrading the suspension, brakes, and handling to make it rideable. All the changes void the warranty, then you try to license and insure and eventually sell your custom, and it's a real problem because no one knows exactly what it is or how much it's worth. If I could just go into a shop and order a cool custom Harley off the floor, for a set price, and with a warranty, I'd be a happy man."

CHOOSING THE TOOL

Now let's say you ride a Harley, know these six people well, and, over the course of a few months, have heard the above statements from them. Let's look at the job each wants the motorcycle to do and the corresponding tool in the Harley-Davidson lineup.

Rider One: This guy wants in for a minimum of money and commitment, so he's a prime candidate for a Harley Sportster. They're smaller, lighter, and less expensive than the Big Twins, yet have a similar style and are powered by air-cooled, two-valve-per-cylinder, 45-degree V-twins of 883 or 1,200cc displacement. The 883s are the least expensive Harleys, and the lightest. They represent a lot of value for the money yet don't skimp on that all-important heritage. "Sporties" first appeared in 1957 and have been around now for half a century.

With the 2004 model year, the Sportster line was completely redesigned and updated. They were given new cylinders and heads, and their pistons and connecting rods were lightened. Along with many other engine changes, perhaps the most significant change was that all Sportsters were given a new frame with rubber engine mounts, which really controlled vibration from off idle until about 4,500 rpm. For anyone who wants all the Sportster sound and feel, but without the vibration, get on a 2004 or later model.

Rider Two: Much of what this guy is saying could apply to any Harley, but the

key is his remark about "heritage." Sure, the Harley-Davidson Motor Company has a heritage stretching back more than 100 years, but the bikes in one model family really can be made to look like classics, and one is actually named "Heritage." They are the Softails, and their name comes from the fact that the rear portion of their frame is designed to resemble a hard-tail (or rigid) machine that has no rear suspension. However, Softails actually have a pair of rear shock absorbers running horizontally, hidden beneath the engine. As a result, although the back end looks like the rigid triangle of a hard-tail, it actually moves up and down to absorb impact. Starting with the Twin Cam 88B in 2000, Softail engines were counterbalanced for smoothness.

Most Softails are classically styled with heavily valanced fenders, deep seats, and ornate touches. They are unquestionably the most customized of Harley models. With the proper amount of chrome, style of pipes, and other amenities, they can be made to look like they just rolled off the showroom floor . . . in about 1949, or whatever era you prefer. And, as you wish, Harley-Davidson and

A rolling lap of luxury, the Electra Glide Classic comes with the bat-wing fairing, hard saddlebags, and TourPak trunk. _Scott Hirko Photography_

One of the most classic, recognizable lines in all of motorcycling, the Electra Glide fairing provides decent wind protection, especially when combined with lowers.

Despite its classic lines, the Electra Glide fairing features a full complement of gauges including speedometer, tachometer, fuel gauge, oil pressure, voltmeter, and ambient air temperature.

Harley's hard bags are long and deep, but not very wide. They lock, the lids are tethered by that cloth hinge on the right, and they're easily removable via the internal fasteners.

the aftermarket offer many additional accessories that can enhance the style and performance of these and other Harley model families.

Rider Three: Let's see . . . "comfort and luggage-carrying capacity" . . . that would be the FL touring series. The FLH Road King carries a set of large saddlebags and a simple windshield. Next are the Electra Glides with hard, locking, and color-matched saddlebags and fork-mounted fairings. Depending upon the model, the FL-series Harleys may come standard with huge TourPak trunks and lower leg protectors that include built-in storage areas. If these items are not standard on a particular touring model, they're always optional.

Finally, there's the FLT Road Glide, another touring model with a fairing, but it's frame-mounted so it does not turn with the fork. It could be considered a slightly sportier dresser. If choosing between the two, note that the FLH's fork-mounted fairing turns with the handlebars, and as a result the bike will have heavier steering. The FLT Road Glide's fairing is mounted to the frame, rather than the fork, and does not turn with the handlebar. The result is steering that feels lighter.

Touring Harleys are designed to take one or two people and their luggage in comfort anywhere they wish to go. Some models also come with an air suspension, and complete sound systems, including AM/FM radio, CD player, rider-passenger intercom, and even satellite radio, are available. The FL family's engines are rubber mounted for smoothness. While the 2006 model year and earlier carried five-speed transmissions, starting with the 2007 models, all were given the Cruise Drive six-speed transmission.

Rider Four: Here's a guy who wants a little sportier ride but wants to stay within the air-cooled engine family

with its heritage. He would likely be happiest with the FXD Dyna family of Harleys. H-D sees its Dynas as simple and raw-boned, more primal and basic. The Dyna frame is different from that of the other models; it's characterized by two exposed rear shock absorbers, and the engine is rubber mounted. It's the sportiest of the Big Twin models. Another possibility for this rider is the Sportster. Or, if he's really serious about handling and performance, his dealer will likely walk him over to the other side of the shop (if he's so equipped) and show him the Buell motorcycle lineup.

Rider Five: You don't have to be a younger rider to want a high-tech, powerful bike, but if you want that in a Harley the obvious choice is the VRSC V-Rod. Introduced for the 2002 model year, the V-Rod was designed in conjunction with Porsche. It features a liquid-cooled, 60-degree V-twin engine with dual-overhead cams and four valves per cylinder. I've seen stock V-Rods put out 106 rear-wheel horsepower on the dynamometer, but only about 72 lb-ft of torque. That's considerably more horsepower than a Big Twin Harley, yet a bit less torque.

Because of the high horsepower and relatively low torque, the V-Rod is a very different ride from the Big Twins and Sportsters. The engine likes to rev, yet the bike carries a mostly cruiser-style chassis that sits low and does not offer a lot of cornering clearance for the types of speeds the bike can generate. It will flat smoke stock air-cooled Harleys and most cruisers off the line and records impressive quarter-mile times, too. Of course, it doesn't sound like a typical Big-Twin, and it revs to 9,000 rpm. While most V-Rods provide a feet-forward seating position, the Street Rod has the more common mid-placed controls that allow sportier riding.

Rider Six: What this guy wants to hear about is the Harley-Davidson Custom Vehicle Operations (CVO) program. Each year now, Harley-Davidson manufactures a select number (usually several thousand) of a few models (currently the Road King, Electra Glide, and V-Rod) with larger engine displacement, more horsepower and torque, and certain custom touches. They're available through Harley dealers, carry a full new-bike warranty, and many custom accessories are standard or available for them.

BUELL

This is the sport rider's Harley—only it's not a Harley. The Buell Motorcycle Company is a subsidiary of Harley-Davidson, Inc., and its bikes are powered by V-twin engines. Buell produces sport motorcycles, motorcycle parts, accessories, and apparel, and the bikes are a lot of fun to ride on a winding road. Buell motorcycles are sold by Buell dealers, which are often (but not always) part of a Harley-Davidson dealership. Because of their streetfighter attitude and sporting style, the powers-that-be tend to keep a slight distance between the Harley and Buell displays. Check on them at www.buell.com.

It's interesting to note that Buell engines are manufactured in a Harley-Davidson plant right beside the Sportster engine line. Although they're very different, there is some technological crossover. Current Sportster cylinder heads (starting with those in the 2004 rubber-mounted Sportster) are adaptations of the heads from the original carbureted Buells.

THE ALTERNATIVE AMERICAN V-TWIN MANUFACTURERS

Back in the early to middle 1990s, new Harleys were in short supply, and dealers were selling them for well over

suggested retail price. Several entrepreneurs realized that if they purchased frames from various aftermarket manufacturers, V-twin engines from others, and additional components like wheels, brakes, and exhausts from others still, they could offer custom bikes that strongly resembled Harleys but were brand new and offered complete warranties and U.S. Department of Transportation (DOT) certification. Today, dozens of companies are manufacturing big-inch, air-cooled, custom-look V-twin-powered motorcycles in the United States. Most purchase powerplants from companies like S&S, TP Engineering, RevTech, Harley-Davidson, and others, and a few build their own proprietary engines. And of course, most make considerably more power than a stock Big Twin Harley.

Wait a minute, if a person can purchase a new Harley for about $13,000 to $20,000, why would they spend that much or more on some brand they'd never heard of? Well, consider what most people do with their new Harleys once they buy them: they install a set of pipes, a performance cam, and an ignition module, and they revise the carburetor (or injectors) to enhance performance. Even more involved riders

The Dyna series consists of bikes with rubber-mounted engines and exposed shocks. They're the sportier of the Big Twins. *Eaglerider*

For those on a budget, the best introduction to the Harley-Davidson motorcycle family is the Sportster. They're relatively inexpensive, quick enough, and certainly competent. Their heritage now extends back more than 50 years—to 1957.

"CVO" stands for Custom Vehicle Operation, a division of The Motor Company that offers what are essentially custom Harleys right from the factory with greater power, a full warranty, and full emissions compliance. Shown is a 2004 CVO Deuce FXSTDSE2 Twin Cam from the Ron Paugh collection. *Bob Clark*

Okay, it's not a Harley, but Buell is owned by Harley-Davidson, and its bikes are often sold from Harley dealerships. Buells make good power, have great brakes, handle very well, and give the rider a sporting option.

The Big Dog is not a Harley either, but rather an alternative American V-twin that's available as a factory custom. In a way, they correspond to Harley CVOs, as this model offers a custom frame, fork, stretched tank, trick wheels, custom fenders, and the rest. *Buzz Buzzelli*

Fairings and Windshields

The relentless windblast as we ride can be cold, wet, and tiring. For that reason, some riders prefer bikes with fairings and windshields. A fairing is a formed shell made of fiberglass or some form of plastic that's designed to deflect the wind from the rider. It usually flares out to the sides for hand protection and carries a windshield at the top. Harley fairings since the early 1990s have been made of an inner and outer shell, between which can be mounted sound systems and other electronics, and the Road Glide fairing carries a pair of small storage pockets. Fairings may be used in concert with wind deflectors for the legs, known as *lowers,* that may also incorporate storage pockets.

I had mentioned above that the Electra Glides have fork-mounted fairings, while the Road Glide's is mounted to the frame. Keep in mind that if your Electra Glide is carrying 40 pounds of fairing and electronics (including a sound system, GPS, and a radar detector) on the fork, you will have to move that additional weight every time you turn the handlebars. With the Road Glide, that weight is distributed to the frame, and the steering has a lighter feel.

A windshield is a flat or slightly curved section of clear or tinted plastic that fits to the front of a motorcycle. It usually does not flare out to the sides, and has a flatter shape than the fairing. Harley-Davidson's Detachables series offers windshields that can be removed and replaced in seconds without tools; some aftermarket windshield companies offer similar products. Most other shields can be removed or replaced in minutes with simple hand tools.

The fairing's advantages include (usually) superior wind protection and storage capability, with the ability to house a sound system, GPS, and other accessories. It can also be color-matched to the bike. On the other hand, it's heavier and costs more. The windshield's advantages include lightness, a lower price, and easy removal. However, it usually doesn't block the wind as well as a fairing and has no storage capability.

Saddlebags: Hard and Leather—and Both

Some late-model Harley-Davidsons come with hard, composite saddlebags, while others come with softer leather bags. And some come with hard bags that have been covered in leather for that classic look. Here's what to know about each type.

For many years, the Electra Glides have come with hard, color-matched saddlebags. Originally their lids detached entirely; occasionally, such lids appear in a ditch—the price paid by a rider for neglecting to close them properly. In later years, however, those lids have been attached with soft hinges that act as tethers, and they no longer separate. These hard bags are long but not very wide and have helped a lot of people get on the road. They're weather-tight in most situations and can be locked.

Traditional leather saddlebags are available in a variety of sizes, have a classic look, and are certainly cool, espe-cially on Softails and other models. However, soft bags that close with buckles cannot be locked, and the leather requires some care. They may require a heavy framework so they don't slump and may not be as weathertight as hard bags. Fussing with a pair of buckles each time you want to get into the bags is annoying, so in later years H-D has hidden a pair of quick-release buckles behind the traditional ones. Just squeeze to release and insert them with a snap to keep the bags closed.

Another type of saddlebag is a hard bag that's covered with leather. It combines the advantages of lockability and weather tightness with the undeniably classy look of leather. Yes, the leather needs to be cleaned and moisturized and eventually deteriorates over time, but if you want that classic look with more function, it may be the ideal combination.

may install big-inch pistons and cylinders, and perhaps an aftermarket transmission. Some will buy new fenders, a tank, and more, have it custom painted, add after-market brakes, seat, and a huge rear tire. In the end, if you're going to make your bike run better than stock and customize it to some extent, four things will happen: you will spend a lot of money; the process will take months; you will void your factory warranty; and all the parts you take off will collect dust in your garage rafters—or go on eBay.

The reason people buy V-twin bikes from these smaller, alternative manufac-turers is because they sidestep many of the problems cited above. According to the manufacturers, they meet all DOT and Environmental Protection Agency (EPA) mandates, and therefore you shouldn't get any tickets for excessive noise or equip-ment violations—so long as you leave them stock. They often have huge engines (100 cubic inches and more) and make huge power (90 or 100 horses and more is common). Rather than having rafters full of stock Harley parts gathering dust, you can choose the exact seat and fork you want, wheels and engine, brakes and fenders and pipes—even custom paint—right from the manufacturer.

When these smaller manufacturers first started up in the early 1990s, the bikes they made were at first dismissed as "Harley clones." Of course, that was a misnomer, as a clone is essentially a copy, and why would anyone buy a copy of a Harley if it cost more, yet didn't have that famous name? No, what these manufac-turers were offering was greater perform-ance and a level of stock "customization" that H-D simply couldn't match at the time— and with a full warranty. Harley's later Custom Vehicle Operations (CVO) program was a response to these companies.

When these smaller manufacturers first started up in the early 1990s, the bikes they made were at first dismissed as "Harley clones."

This American Ironhorse Tejas, for example, comes with a rigid frame, 280mm rear tire, stretched tank, and a 111-inch S&S engine making 105 horsepower, options not available from Harley-Davidson. *American Ironhorse*

Big bikes need big motors. Shown is the 117-inch S&S, which is available on all American Ironhorse motorcycles. It makes 115 horsepower with 120 lb-ft of torque. Here it is in the Outlaw model. *American Ironhorse*

A big rear tire, like the 300mm on this American Ironhorse Slammer, suggests power, style, and hooliganism. Such tires can be adapted to Harleys, but it will require a new swingarm and frame. *American Ironhorse*

If you've ever tried to mount an aftermarket accessory to a bike and had trouble making it fit, you can appreciate the problems a bike builder may have if it buys frames from one company, engines from another, forks from a third, wheels from a fourth, and so on, as a customizer would. That's why it's always a plus when a manufacturer makes the majority of its parts in-house. Some of the major alternative manufacturers include Big Dog, American Ironhorse, and Ultra. Victory Motorcycles, which is a subsidiary of Polaris Industries, Inc., and is based in Minnesota, is another major American manufacturer in its own right. Unlike most of the other American V-twin manufacturers who use engines that are mostly adaptations and refinements of the Harley Evolution engine, the Victory motor is a totally proprietary engine that utilizes four valve heads and a single overhead cam per cylinder.

Unlike custom builders, these alternative manufacturers build from several dozen to several thousand machines a year, so you can be assured they have some experience producing a raked fork, mounting a wide tire, and much more. You can walk into a showroom, discuss what you want, and perhaps even take a

test ride. Instead of waiting months for a custom to be completed, you may be able to ride off on your own custom-look bike immediately. Because these machines are from actual manufacturers, there should be no problem financing, insuring, or licensing them. When you wish to sell, the NADA Blue Book should help legitimize your asking price.

How do bikes from these small manufacturers differ from those made in Milwaukee? Let me count the ways: At this writing Harley won't sell you a hard-tail bike, a bike with a 250-series or larger rear tire, or a stock, air-cooled engine thumping out 100 horsepower or more from well over 100 cubic inches. However, Harley's Custom Vehicle Operations (CVO) now makes engines that displace up to 110 cubic inches. H-D doesn't do rake or stretch or "overs." H-D doesn't do open primaries. The list goes on and on.

Get your Harley crankin' out 85 or 100 horsepower and you may well void the factory warranty—unless you had a Harley Screamin' Eagle kit installed by a dealer, or bought a CVO bike. Many of these alternative bikes crank out 100 horses or more while fully covered by a factory warranty. In fact, it may actually cost *less* to have a bike done by a manufacturer than to build it up piecemeal

Is Wider Better?

The biggest trend in custom bikes is to fit ever wider rear tires. At present, the widest tires being manufactured are the monster 330- and 350-series (their width in millimeters), and larger may be coming! These require wheels that are around a foot wide, which is wider than a lot of automobile tires.

No stock motorcycle from a major manufacturer can handle such a meaty tire, as they're too wide to fit within stock wheels and swingarms. Therefore, the biggest tires are being fitted to aftermarket wheels, frames, and swingarms. The 130- and 150-series rear tires that were common a few years ago are being phased out by ever larger tires and wheels from the aftermarket, and for the 2007 model year Harley-Davidson started offering 240-series tires on its stock VRSCX V-Rod. On any bike it is often possible to fit a tire one size larger than stock, but only if you check with the dealer and carefully evaluate that it will not rub on the swingarm or other parts.

Why are riders fitting ever larger rear tires to their bikes? *Primarily because they're cool!* Other than somewhat longer wear and a little more rubber on the road for better grip, there is no practical reason for running rear tires larger than about a 250 series . . . other than possibly winning trophies at bike shows.

Fitting wider rear tires can lead to headaches. On a stock Harley, beyond a certain size, a larger rear tire will crowd the belt final drive, and some riders will convert to chain drive, which is narrower. Getting even wider moves the tire's center point farther left, and eventually the bike can become unbalanced; the center points of its front and rear tires no longer align. The aftermarket has responded to this problem with kits to offset the transmission, convert to right-side drive, or use a swingarm-mounted intermediate shaft ("jack shaft") with a gear on one end to receive power from the drive gear, and a gear on the other end to send that power to the rear wheel.

There is another complication. Motorcycles turn by leaning. As a result, the typical motorcycle tire has a rounded tread surface for seamless transitions across the full range of lean. This design also keeps the distance from the contact point with the road to the center of the axle roughly constant. But a low-profile tire and large-diameter wheel is part of the wide-tire look. The result is that a very wide tire is flatter (has a less curved tread surface) than a stock motorcycle tire. This flatter tread resists leaning, causing steering that feels heavy.

Because the tread-to-axle distance changes on these wide, low-profile tires, leaning also causes the rear of the bike to rise, creating further steering anomalies. The fact that the front tire with this new look tends to stay narrow, with a typical tread design, doesn't help consistency or predictability as you lean and corner. In short, while mass production manufacturers spend a lot of time ensuring that their bikes steer and handle well, custom builders put their efforts into making their bikes look really cool. Sometimes what looks cool can be a handful to ride. If you get on a wide-tire machine, go easy until you learn how its ride differs from your regular bike.

Finally, a big ol' tire and wheel is going to be heavy, and it's all unsprung weight, along with the braking components attached to that wheel. The difference between "sprung" and "unsprung" weight is important to handling, which is why the terms often come up in racing discussions. Sprung weight—the weight above and supported by the springs—pushes the tires down onto the ground. Sprung weight helps traction. But unsprung weight—below the springs—is the weight your suspension has to force back down onto the road after a bump pitches it upward. When a heavy wheel gets bumped up, it's harder for the springs to push it back down than if the wheel (and tire and braking components) is light. You can't regulate speed or direction through a tire that is not in good contact with the road. Because wide wheels and tires weigh more than narrow ones, they produce a less comfortable, less precise ride—though on level pavement, they offer loads of straight-line traction.

---

yourself, and it will certainly be done in less time.

But you need to be cautious. Around 2000, many bike enthusiasts were excited that the renewed Indian and Excelsior-Henderson motorcycle companies were serious efforts cranking out new motorcycles with classic names and styling. Each had the advantages of major finan- cial backing and a memorable history— yet each failed. At this writing, Indian is trying to make a comeback once again with a new owner. Keep this in mind when dealing with small manufacturers. Investigate. Do your research. Talk to owners of the brand. Even the very best warranty won't do you much good if the company goes out of business.

Your dealer should have a good selection of used bikes on hand, including lots of Harleys. Ask about the Harley-Davidson Remanufacturing Program for used Evolution or Twin Cam machines. The program refurbishes these models for a reasonable fee.

Here's a nice-looking classic bike that really isn't. This Softail Springer has been accessorized to look like a vintage bike. It actually belongs to the parts manager at Ventura Harley-Davidson/Buell in Camarillo, California.

The Road Glide and Electra Glide are both touring bikes, but the Road Glide has a frame-mounted fairing. This means that the weight of the fairing is not fed directly into the fork as it is with the Electra Glide, which has a fork-mounted fairing. This promotes improved handling. *Scott Hirko Photography*

CUSTOM MOTORCYCLES

Another possibility is to have a bike built for you by a custom shop. A true one-off involves an extraordinary amount of handwork, and that's going to be expensive. With an alternative V-twin manufacturer, economies of scale can bring the price much lower than a custom builder can offer. Also, while we usually equate handwork with quality, that quality can vary from one customizer to another. The quality can also vary within a customizer's own line of bikes.

Order up your custom and prepare to sit back awhile—it will take some months to get it done exactly the way

you want it. Once it's done, it may not comply with all the U.S. Department of Transportation regulations regarding lights, brakes, mirrors, and the rest. And it may not comply with the Environmental Protection Agency's dictates regarding noise and exhaust emissions, either. These may not be an issue to you, but tell it to the judge if you're ticketed for violations of any of these statutes. See the sidebar at the end of this chapter about custom bikes and the EPA. At least it should be exactly what you want, and make a stunning personal statement.

Finally, there's the matter of sympathy. When it comes to financing a one-off custom, is your banker going to be sympathetic when you tell him you want to borrow $25,000 to purchase what he only sees as an outrageously weird motorcycle? ("Hey, it doesn't even have a rear suspension!") Will the Department of Motor Vehicles (DMV) be sympathetic to licensing a "Special Construction" machine that does not seem to comply with many DOT and EPA dictates? Will your insurance agent be sympathetic to the idea that such a spare-looking motorcycle should be insured for $35,000? Finally, when you eventually want to sell it, will potential buyers be sympathetic to

With its smoother lines and dual headlights, the Road Glide fairing has a more modern look. It also has fairing pockets, which the Electra Glide does not offer.

the idea that you were really into flaming skulls as a theme, while they actually prefer teddy bears?

USED HARLEY BIG TWINS: WHAT TO LOOK FOR

Harley Big Twins have been offered in only three engine families since 1966—Shovelheads, Evos, and Twin Cams. When the Shovels came out in the mid-1960s, they were a step up from the old Panheads but were not a major advance in terms of technology. Rather, it was the Evolution engine in 1983 that introduced aluminum heads and numerous other advances. In short, the Evo was the engine that saved Harley-Davidson.

Today, in terms of a used motorcycle, I would suggest considering a Shovel or earlier model only in terms of restoring it as a classic. If you want to tinker, and don't mind dealing with the inherent problems of an older bike, a Shovel is fine. However, if you're looking for a daily or serious weekend runner, the Evo is a vastly superior performing engine, and much more reliable. Also, Harley dealers no longer stock major parts for the pre-Evo bikes, though they're still readily available as special orders or through the aftermarket and swap meets. The last one's a major reason why it's such a kick to restore an old Harley.

Another major benefit to buying a used Evolution or Twin Cam is Harley-Davidson's Remanufacturing Program. This is a program that applies to used 1340cc Evolution and Twin Cam 88, 88B, and 95 Engines. Bring your bike to a Harley-Davidson dealer and they will remove the engine and send it to the H-D Capitol Drive facility in Milwaukee. It will be disassembled by factory techs who will rebuild it to stock specs, repaint, and test it. Keep in mind that any hop-up parts you installed will be replaced but not returned. Your remanufactured engine will be returned to your dealer in approximately two

weeks, where it will be reinstalled in your bike. So long as it is removed and installed by an authorized Harley-Davidson dealer, a remanufactured engine will carry a 12-month unlimited mileage limited warranty.

Customs, Kit Bikes, and the EPA

What you need to know about the legality of your custom or kit bike:

In July 2006, in response to a request by the American Motorcyclist Association (AMA), the United States Environmental Protection Agency issued a "Letter of Guidance" on the subject of motorcycle emissions regulations in order to clarify its rules regarding "kit" and "custom" motorcycles. Previously, there had been some haziness on this subject regarding noise and other emissions. According to a release by the AMA, which defined the EPA's letter, "Kit bikes are motorcycles typically built by individuals using off-the-shelf components, while custom bikes are generally show bikes built by a business and sold to a customer." Here's a brief look at the EPA's letter . . . .

"Under the regulations, a person is allowed only one kit motorcycle in their lifetime that is exempt from meeting EPA emissions requirements.

"For custom motorcycles, a builder may create and sell up to 24 bikes a year that don't meet EPA emissions requirements, but those machines must be labeled as exempt and are show bikes that only rarely may be ridden."

However, if an individual uses an EPA-certified engine, that "individual will, in fact, be permitted to build a kit motorcycle without invoking the 'one per lifetime' rule, subject to restrictions on exhaust systems, carburetors, fuel injection, and certain other components."

According to the EPA Letter of Guidance, "New highway motorcycles certified in this manner may be operated or re-sold without restriction, as long as all requirements of this procedure are met and the anti-tampering requirements of the federal Clean Air Act (42 U.S. C. sec. 203(a)) are met." The AMA pointed out that before the EPA adopted these rules in 2004, "it was illegal for anyone to ride a street motorcycle built in 1980 or later if it didn't meet EPA emissions requirements."

When do these rules go into effect? "The EPA rules adopted in 2004 require new road motorcycles sold nationwide beginning with the 2006 model year to meet strict emissions standards adopted earlier by California. The first phase of the California standards went into effect with model year 2004, with a second tier scheduled to go into effect with model year 2008. The EPA adopted the same standards but with a two-year delay, meaning the first phase took effect with the 2006 model year, and the second phase will take effect in model year 2010."

What, specifically, are the emissions rules? "New motorcycles sold in California beginning with the 2004 model year, and nationwide beginning with the 2006 model year, may not emit more than 1.4 grams per kilometer of hydrocarbons and nitrogen oxides, and 12 grams per kilometer of carbon monoxide.

"The California standard gets tougher in model year 2008, with a limit of 0.8 grams per kilometer of hydrocarbons and nitrogen oxides, and 12 grams per kilometer of carbon monoxide. The federal standard that goes in effect in model year 2010 is the same."

For a look at the complete EPA Letter of Guidance, it is posted on the agency's website at http://www.epa.gov/oms/cert/dearmfr/cisd0615.pdf.

Chapter 3

PERSONALIZING AND CUSTOMIZING:
ACCESSORIES FOR YOUR HARLEY

Accessories allow us to personalize our bikes and make them more usable and comfortable. Here's a bike that makes an unmistakable impression.

Darn-near every hard part is available chromed for your Harley, or can be chromed. Have at it, and add a little bling to your bike.

THINGS TO ADD TO YOUR HARLEY

There's a saying that there's no such thing as a stock Harley-Davidson motorcycle. That's because once they buy a bike, Harley owners tend to get serious about making it theirs, personalizing it, making it do the job they want it to do in the most precise manner possible. And to help them in their quest, Harley-Davidson and the aftermarket offer hundreds of thousands of items for motorcycles in general, and Harleys in particular. Any of them can make the bike more functional, more highly styled, or both. Also, as Harley-Davidson once said in one of its ads, "Fashion *is* function."

While there's no way we could possibly begin to cover even a significant percentage of the products available for Harley-Davidsons through H-D and the aftermarket, here's a quick rundown of some of the more popular types of items you may wish to consider adding to your Harley. Please note that since we devote a full chapter to performance products, and another to touring products, this chapter will address some of the "other" categories of products for Harleys. As for the term "aftermarket," it refers to products made or offered by companies other than Harley-Davidson.

CHROME

Everybody likes a little chrome, and most of us like lots of it. Darn-near every hard part is available chromed for your Harley, or can be chromed. Have at it, and add a little bling to your bike. My only admonition is that good taste knows when to stop. Then again, who cares?

ELECTRICAL ACCESSORIES
Lighting

Auxiliary Lighting: Lighting can be decorative, functional, or both. Decorative lighting includes such items as strip lights (low-wattage lights designed to make the motorcycle more visible or to decorate it, rather than to project illumination down the road) and neon. Decorative lighting tends to be so specialized it's beyond the scope of this book. However, let's delve a bit into functional lighting.

Motorcycles lean when they corner, which creates all sorts of illumination problems. Headlight bulbs come with shields over them that are designed as a cutoff to prevent the light from blinding oncoming motorists. The problem is, when motorcycles lean into left turns (in countries in which traffic travels to the right), they are essentially riding into the blind spot created by this cutoff.

Pencil beam driving lamps send a well-focused beam of light a long way ahead and are best for use on relatively quiet, straight roads in the countryside. Wide beams, or "floods," pour light into the near area to supplement the low beam. They're useful for spotting gravel, potholes, and oil, and they help fill in that blind spot in turns. Other lights are for medium-range illumination.

Halogen and Xenon Lighting: Back in the late 1970s and early '80s, quartz-halogen lights became all the rage and soon became standard equipment on cars and motorcycles. They offer a much brighter, whiter light than the weak, yellowish sealed-beam headlights, as they burn at a higher temperature. They utilize sealed bulbs filled with an inert halogen gas that, when excited by electricity, allows the filament to glow brightly but not burn. The quartz glass lenses are designed to handle the additional heat they generate.

A generation later, the new technology is xenon HID (high-intensity

discharge) lights. HID lamps utilize an arc of electricity passing between two anodes (rather than a filament) housed in a bulb filled with xenon gas. Xenon gas is used because of its ability to promote ignition very quickly; without it, an HID light would not reach operating luminosity for several minutes. These lights can be quite expensive.

An HID light with xenon bulb may provide more than twice as much light as a modern H7 halogen bulb. The color temperature of the light emitted by the xenon bulb is more similar to daylight, which is why they appear blue to oncoming traffic. Because an HID light requires a lot of voltage to initiate the arc, it has a ballast that must be located near the bulb. While it may put out $2^{1}/_2$ times as much light as a halogen, the xenon light will actually use a little less power (depending upon application) to maintain the arc.

Please note that optics are designed to fit a given light source, so do not attempt to place xenon HID lighting systems in housings and lenses designed for standard halogen bulbs, or to modify xenon bulbs to fit in these housings. Such conversions would change the photometrics. So long as the entire lighting unit is

---

TIP

Auxiliary functional lights not only illuminate the road, but also make your bike more visible to others. They can allow other motorists to get a better "read" on your speed and location, which helps with depth perception at night, making it less likely they'll pull out in front of you.

Shedding Light on Xenon

Now that xenon has become a buzzword equated with brighter headlights, beware of imitators. Some bargain basement companies offer xenon-filled halogen-style filament bulbs to which a blue film has been applied. They are marketed as xenon bulbs, and while this may have some technical legitimacy, it is misleading. These bulbs will produce no more light than a standard halogen, and perhaps less because of the blue coating.

Light rays are bent as they pass through the faceted lens of a standard headlight, which allows less of the light energy to illuminate the road. The hot thing in illumination optics today is to pair a clear lens with a faceted reflector. This is a late-model Harley headlight, with matching light bar.

This small door with the Harley logo pivots upward to reveal the CD player. Always pull off the road and stop the bike before changing the CD or operating the player. Never attempt to do this while riding!

Power Draw

Because a pair of auxiliary halogen lights will likely add 70 to 100 watts of draw to your electrical system, they should not present a power problem for most motorcycles. Try not to use them for long periods at low speeds, or in conjunction with heated garments. Xenon lights, however, often draw less power than the lights they replace. If in doubt, ask your dealer.

changed together (light source, reflector, and lens), all should be well.

Another major trend in headlights, for both autos and motorcycles, is to run clear lenses with faceted reflectors rather than the fluted, prismed lenses with parabolic reflectors of recent times. The fluting in a lens is designed to direct and disperse the light, but when light is bent in this manner, it loses some of its power and whiteness. A faceted reflector with clear lens can better direct and spread the light, which results in greater focus, power, and whiteness. More of the light energy reaches the road.

Most state laws require that driving lights be mounted no higher than the headlight, as lights mounted high tend to reflect back into the rider's eyes in foggy conditions and may bother oncoming motorists. Mounting areas abound: fairings, light bars, crash bars, forks, mirror stems, engine cases. Do not mount lights too far outboard, as they could be damaged in a tip-over.

Most companies that offer auxiliary lighting provide brackets for them, but often only for specific models. Be certain to order the correct mounting brackets for your particular Harley model.

SOUND SYSTEMS

Harley-Davidson's Electra Glide and Road Glide dressers can be equipped with sound systems, but motorcycles in general have notoriously lousy acoustics because of wind and other ambient noise. When fairings and windshields block some of the wind and ambient noise, sound systems are somewhat more practical.

Sun, wind, rain, and vibration all play havoc with sensitive sound systems, so it is imperative that your components be well sealed from the elements. If your bike did not come with one of the factory's excellent sound systems, they can be retrofitted. Aftermarket sound systems are also available. Be certain to use high-quality components specifically designed for motorcycle use. And, regardless of your sound system, for safety's sake always stay focused on the road. When using headphones, check local laws, as some do not allow sound to be introduced into both ears. Do not have the volume so high that you cannot hear emergency vehicles and other traffic around you. No matter how big your Harley is, in most any collision, you lose.

Radio: AM/FM radio is the most basic type of sound system. It keeps you in touch with local weather and traffic conditions, but you're at the mercy of reception quality, which changes as you ride.

Satellite radio became available from your Harley dealer in 2006. It not only offers a wealth of specific channels, but also should not fade with distance because the signal comes from a satellite. The first portable XM unit exclusively designed for many 1996 and later Harley models—the handlebar-mounted Road Tech AL20—is available through the Harley-Davidson Parts and Accessories program for around $259. It provides more than 170 channels and comes with an automobile mounting bracket that, with the additional purchase of an automobile kit from XM, allows the radio to be transferred to a four-wheeler. I tested the H-D system and found that the only time I lost the satellite signal was when riding beside a rock wall or tall building.

Cassette Tape Players: While stereo cassette tape players solve the problem of hearing what you want to hear when you want to hear it, they are old technology and are being replaced by compact disc (CD) players. Cassette tapes function best in a clean environment and are susceptible to dirt and wear. Handle and store tapes with care, and keep your system as clean as possible.

Compact Disc Players: CDs are played by a laser beam rather than a needle but can skip when the bike hits a bump. Because only a beam of light touches the disc's surface under normal circumstances, it should not be harmed by a minimal amount of bouncing. However, severe bumps may cause the disc to contact something hard while it's spinning, which can damage it. Another potential problem is that the delicate internal workings of the CD player itself may suffer in an environment that includes extreme temperature

changes, dust, and vibration. Again, if you want an aftermarket system, choose one specifically designed and sealed for motorcycle use. Also, though CDs themselves were touted as near indestructible when introduced, scratch them up and they play poorly, so factor proper storage into your sound system.

MP3 Players: MP3 players are tiny but can hold hundreds or even thousands of songs and can be plugged into some sound systems. Because they usually have their own battery power, they can be plugged directly into headphones and kept in a pocket. With MP3 players there's no need for a heavy, expensive sound system that's built into the bike.

Citizens Band Radios: CB radios have a range of several mile and allow the operator to communicate with other motorists or anyone else with a CB radio within range. They're especially useful for learning about road, weather, and traffic conditions, fuel availability, speed traps, and where to find the best food. CBs are now being used by guided motorcycle tour operators to provide a running commentary about scenery and historic sights.

CB radios are offered both as standard and optional equipment on some Harley dressers, and as accessories in the aftermarket. It's important to select a CB specifically designed for motorcycle use, as they provide better weather and vibration resistance than non-motorcycle units.

Helmet Speakers and Microphones: Helmet speakers are the best means of overcoming wind and other ambient noise so rider and passenger can hear well while riding. They often mount under the helmet's comfort liner with hook-and-loop fasteners, or in special indents within the helmet, and are quite

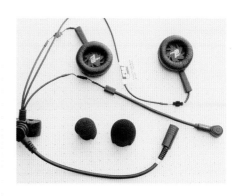

The best way to hear a sound system while riding is through helmet speakers. These, by J&M, plug into the bike's sound system. Wireless systems are also available.

One of the first wireless systems was the Nolan helmet with Bluetooth technology. By operating the buttons on the side, the rider can talk with the passenger or other riders. *Cima International*

Remember, though, that riding a bike takes even more concentration than driving a car, and talking on a mobile phone while driving a car can lead to some serious errors in judgment.

light. Factory sound systems are usually switched so the sound can be directed through either the helmet or the dashboard speakers.

Note: Check local laws regarding the legality of using speakers inside your helmet.

Microphones are available that attach either inside the chinbar of a full-face helmet or on a stalk mounted on the side of an open-face helmet. These can be used as part of an intercom system. Wind noise can be a problem on the more exposed stalk-mounted mics.

Intercoms: These systems allow the rider and passenger to speak directly to each other via microphones and helmet speakers. They are usually hard-wired together, though wireless Bluetooth systems are now available. Intercoms are a major improvement over shouting into the wind.

Intercoms are available as part of a Harley-Davidson sound system; they're also available as aftermarket accessory units independent of the bike and powered by their own batteries. The better systems will have separate volume controls for rider and passenger, and they usually work well. Use independent battery systems judiciously, as leaving them turned on constantly will shorten battery life.

The drawback for any hard-wired system is that it must be plugged in for use and unplugged each time the riders dismount. Check that they have sturdy plugs and that the wires are not susceptible to tangling while in use.

Mobile Phones: It is now possible to plug a mobile phone into a sound system so it can be used hands-free. Set your mobile phone to auto-answer so it will pick up all calls as you're riding. Depending upon your phone, it may be necessary to push a button to hang up. Bluetooth Technology headsets are now available for helmets, so the rider

no longer has to hard-wire the mobile phone to the headset.

Remember, though, that riding a bike takes even more concentration than driving a car, and talking on a mobile phone while driving a car can lead to some serious errors in judgment. Everybody thinks they do just fine, it's everyone else who can't talk and drive at the same time. This is rarely true. Regardless, if riding a bike is more user intensive than driving a car, and driving a car and talking on a mobile phone can cause problems, well, you do the math.

Radar Detectors: If you wish to run a radar detector, its audible warning signal can also be wired into a speaker system. With various audio inputs coming into the helmet, some systems allow the rider to prioritize the signals, so some signals mute when others are received. For example, many systems will mute the music when they receive a mobile phone call, or if the radar detector picks up a signal.

49 Megahertz: This bike-to-bike system is similar to the CB radio but operates on a 49-megahertz frequency and is powered by AA batteries. Effective range is only about 2/10 of a mile, in line of sight only. They're designed for two or more bikes traveling together and riding within a few hundred feet of each other. They're also useful for keeping in touch with the rest of your group when you're not on the bikes but, say, walking around a rally. Depending on bike, helmet, and wind conditions, and whether the bikes are equipped with windshields, 49MHz systems tend to be overwhelmed by wind noise at higher speeds.

Family Radio: These sporty, hand-held, walkie-talkie-type radios are popular because of their broad range of use for hunting, fishing, hiking, skiing, etc., and have come to be known as "family" radios. In my experience, they can be adapted quite successfully to motorcycle use when teamed with the proper helmet speakers and push-to-talk equipment. They offer a range of about 2 miles over varied terrain, including around corners. When the ride is over, the additional equipment can be unplugged and hand-held for camping and other uses.

GPS

Why should car drivers have all the fun with Global Positioning System (GPS) receivers? A network of satellites sends signals to Earth that GPS units receive, and, through triangulation, these units can pinpoint their exact position on Earth to within a few feet. They're handy for directing a rider to an address or for finding gas stations, restaurants, motels, or pretty much anything else. They're especially good for finding your way in rough terrain or in remote areas. Talking GPS receivers can be wired into audio systems.

HEATED GRIPS AND SEATS

The first time I tried a bike with heated handgrips, I was sold! Not only are they a comfort on a cold day, but they're also a safety factor, as they allow the rider more precise control of the throttle, front brake, and clutch lever. Heated grips allow the rider to wear lighter gloves, which enhances feel for the controls. Some manufacturers (including Harley-Davidson) offer heated grips either stock or as an option. They're also available from the aftermarket.

Look for heated grips that offer at least two (high and low) temperature settings to allow for changing weather conditions, and in which the heating elements are built into the grips themselves. Some add-ons install over the existing grips and not only make the grips larger, but also can potentially slide or rotate, lessening control.

SECURITY

The characteristics that make motorcycles so desirable, their lightness and simplicity, work against them in terms of security. Motorcycles and their luggage are, by their very nature, vulnerable to theft. Because of their openness, there is little you can do to protect your bike fully from a determined thief. However, by doing enough, you can discourage a thief who is less than determined.

A Global Positioning Satellite system (GPS) allows the rider to know exactly where he or she is on the globe at any time. This is the Zumo system by Garmin. *Garmin*

Always use your fork lock to prevent theft of your bike. The addition of a U-lock provides that extra bit of security.

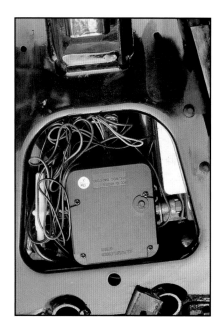

Unfortunately, it seems that no one pays attention to alarms any longer. However, a blaring alarm may so rattle a thief that he'll try for easier pickin's.

TIP

The alarm is only as effective as its electrical supply. It may attach directly to the battery or have its own independent power source. In either case, mount the alarm in such a way that it is difficult or impossible for its electrical connection to be severed.

Harley-Davidson's new security system utilizes an electronic alarm puck to disable the ignition system. It is activated whenever the puck is more than eight feet away from the bike.

The two issues here are how to discourage people from stealing things from your bike and from stealing the bike itself. Harley-Davidsons are frequently stolen, since there is such a huge market in used parts for them. Anything that slows a thief and exposes him to detection is a discouragement to his slimy operation. Park in a well-lit area with lots of foot traffic. In a city, a toll parking garage improves your chances. If there's a toll taker, ask permission to park your bike in his or her sight.

Soft luggage strapped to a bike is absurdly easy to steal, which is one reason I suggest using lockable hard bags, including the TourPak, if available. If you must use soft luggage, try to conceal the buckles from the mounting system under the body of the bags. Use a tether on a magnetic tank bag. Better yet, if your parked bike will not be in view, remove the soft luggage and carry it with you. In any case, your most valuable items (passport, laptop, journal, itinerary, money) should come with you.

Many bikes have leather saddlebags that bolt to the rear fender. They usually cannot be locked, but you can take steps to discourage a thief. Carry a supply of black tie-wraps and, if you'll be leaving the bike for a while, loop a tie-wrap around the buckles and insert it through a hole in the strap. These will be hard to see if it's dark, and very frustrating for the thief as they must be cut. When you return to the bike, cut them with your pocketknife and go on your way.

To discourage theft of the bike itself, utilize locks and alarms. Neither will absolutely protect your bike from a determined thief but again may cause him to shuffle off, looking for easier prey. As a first line of defense, always use the fork lock. When possible, lock the bike to a solid object, such as a lamppost, tree, or bench, with a sturdy, case-hardened chain and lock. Most bike chains are available in a plastic sleeve that protects the bike from being scratched. Try to mount the chain high and taut so it does not lie on the ground, as thieves who use bolt cutters like to place the tool on the ground and stand on the handle for additional leverage. I once considered a fork lock, or a U-lock that immobilized one wheel, to be pretty secure. Then I heard about a ring of young bike thieves who went around on skateboards. When they found a locked bike, they would hoist the immobile wheel onto a skateboard and wheel it to an accomplice's truck.

A bike alarm should be mounted in whatever location will allow it to be heard, and protect it from tampering. Under the seat is the preferred location, where the alarm will be out of sight and out of mind until a thief learns it's there the hard way.

Some alarms have a "warn-off" signal, something like an electronic growl that is activated when the bike is jostled or moved slightly. If the warn-off is triggered several times within a short time, the full alarm will sound.

Other desirable alarm features include an ignition disabler that automatically disables the ignition until a code is entered, and a pager that sends a signal to a hand-held device that alerts the owner the bike is being tampered with.

Recently, Harley-Davidson has come to offer a security system that consists of a black security box on the bike and a plastic key fob with matching electrics that the rider carries. When the fob is carried more than 8 feet from the bike, the ignition is automatically disabled, and the turn signals flash momentarily. If someone disturbs the bike, they flash again as a warning, and a full alarm siren can be added. Should you forget or lose your key fob, you can enter a code into the bike via the turn signal controls to allow you to ride it.

FITTING THE BIKE TO YOURSELF
Seats, Pegs, and Bars

If you intend to put some serious miles on your bike, it's important to fit it to yourself. Ride it awhile and note if any major problems arise in the comfort triangle of seat, pegs, and grips. Does something need to be higher, lower, softer, or farther forward? If so, much can be done by adjusting or changing the footpegs and controls, handlebars and seat.

***Aftermarket Seats*:** Each stock motorcycle seat is built within a budget to fit a universal human rear end. There's a pretty good chance your rear end is not universal. If that's the case, the stock seat probably won't fit you ideally. And it will look like everyone else's stock seat. In fact, seats are the third-most-common aftermarket accessory added to motorcycles, after chrome and an exhaust system.

If you wish to make your bike feel and look like *your* bike, an aftermarket seat is also a styling touch.

In selecting an aftermarket saddle, set your priorities. Why, exactly, are you changing it? If it hurts to ride the stock seat for any distance, you definitely need to look toward comfort. Do you want just a solo seat, or will you carry a

A custom seat provides a bike with a new look without making any body modifications. It also provides the rider with a more tailored ride. Here's a seat for a Softail by Mustang. *David Zemla*

How Seats Are Made

Seats are based upon a pan, or baseplate, that may be made of steel, fiberglass, or plastic. A heavy rider who complains that his seat is squirmy should note the composition of the baseplate and order a heavier version.

Seat foam starts as a two-part liquid polymer that is injected into a mold. The firmness can be regulated by varying the proportions of the two chemicals. This foam sets up in about 15 minutes to form the base, and then a layer of sheet foam is usually laid over the top. This dual-density approach allows the seat an initial softness when you sit down, yet it's supported by a firm base.

Stock seat covers are made of vinyl, a synthetic material that is durable and stretchy; it requires only soap and water for cleanup and virtually no other maintenance. Many riders are interested in custom leather seats. Leather can be tooled, stitched, and colored to make a great-looking seat, but it's less stretchy and therefore can feel stiffer than vinyl. Leather absorbs moisture, does not weather well, and (like leather boots and jackets) requires care. It's also a whole lot more expensive. Exotic animal skins like alligator, shark, emu, and others are available as inlays in custom seats. Consider the drawbacks and care required before you decide that you need a leather or exotic seat.

Leather looks great on a custom bike, but if you're going to use the bike as a daily rider, the leather will require a lot of attention. Perhaps the best option is to utilize a conventional seat for most of your riding, then install the custom for special occasions.

If you want an improved ride but don't wish to replace the entire seat, consider gel pads like these by Saddlemen. *Saddlemen*

Butt Buffer's seat cushion is constructed with a dry polymer core. It was developed for the medical industry to prevent bed sores and to eliminate painful pressure points. *Buzz Buzzelli*

One of the most luxurious items available for a passenger is the backrest of a TourPak trunk. It's not only wide and well padded, but the passenger can also place his or her elbows up on the sides for added comfort.

passenger? Do you want it thin and low-profile for a custom look or wide, dished, and well-padded for comfortable touring? Be careful not to create a problem where none exists—for example by trading out a comfortable seat for one that looks better but hurts your backside over the long rides you enjoy. If you have problems reaching the ground, you will definitely want to specify a thinner, lower seat. Often, a shorter rider will be better able to reach the ground if the seat tapers at the front.

Seats range from the all-comfort, mega-mile touring seats to the knock-your-boots-off, high-styled customs you won't want to ride for more than five miles at a time . . . and everything in between. And aftermarket seat makers are ready to make one to fit you if you make your needs known.

Aftermarket Seats vs. Custom Seats: If you go to your dealer or shop through a catalog and buy a mass-produced, aftermarket seat, you may be subjecting yourself to exactly the same kinds of problems that made you want to buy a new seat in the first place. Most seat manufacturers will happily build you a custom seat but will need your input. Seats can be matched to your height,

weight, inseam, width, and other needs, and can accommodate special problems. If you're short, for example, and have trouble getting your feet to the ground, the front of the seat can be narrowed. If your stock seat is too firm or too spongy, the manufacturer can custom blend the foam for both you and your passenger. If you're tall and need legroom, they can build you a higher seat, or you can have the dish area set farther back.

One of the hottest items is the so-called "gel" seat. The gel is a visco-elastic substance that feels something like a more solid form of Jell-O. It moves in a similar way and quivers slightly but won't leak or melt. The idea is that a block of gel inset into a seat will displace according to the unique contours of your backside, eliminating pressure points that lead to pain and tingling during longer rides.

The manufacturers who use gel tell me it allows a given amount of padding to offer greater comfort. Those who don't use it tell me it only works in high-pressure applications, like bicycle seats. They contend that it does not compress and say that if it were so good you would see it in office, tractor, and other seats. I have ridden on gel seats and find them a bit firm for my liking. Your liking may be different.

Seat Cushions: Rather than completely replacing your bike's seat in search of comfort, installing a seat cushion is an inexpensive and potentially more satisfying option. These items strap over the seat and are usually either inflatable or made of some type of gel or foam. They can be more satisfying because often there's some adjustment to them (in terms of air pressure), or they're available in various thicknesses or densities. There are also bead seat cushions that are designed for ventilation in hot weather.

Drawbacks are that they won't likely be as attractive as your seat, they'll add some height to what may already be a marginal perch for the rider, and you can lose them when you attend a race and decide your seat cushion would be the perfect thing to make the bleacher seat more comfortable—but forget to take it with you when you leave. This last drawback can make a person surprisingly grumpy—not that it's ever happened to anyone.

Seat cushions are available separately for the rider and passenger, so each can enjoy individual comfort. They're usually black and may become hot in the sun, and inflatables will need some sort of porous covering so they'll breathe.

Backrests: The single most important piece of equipment for keeping a passenger happy is a backrest. Without it, he or she must maintain constant muscle tension and can never fully relax on the back of the bike. Many bikes have small rear seats, some of which actually slope rearward. With a backrest, the passenger has something against which to lean and relax. As an added plus, if you get on the throttle too hard—accidentally, of course—a backrest will keep an unprepared passenger from dropping off the back of the bike.

Be certain the backrest is the correct model for your bike and that it

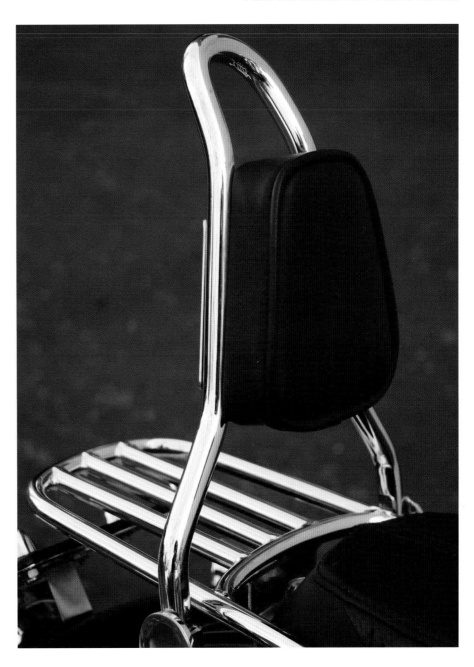

Combine a backrest with a luggage rack to increase your carrying capacity and provide your passenger with some welcome luxury.

Saddlemen's Explorer Rider Backrest improves rider comfort but makes throwing a leg over the seat more complicated. *Saddlemen*

comes with all appropriate hardware. Installation is usually simple and can be done by the home mechanic.

Forward controls allow the rider to stretch out without removing his or her feet from the controls. These Küryakyn 3¼-inch Extended Forward Controls are nicely polished and sculpted. *Küryakyn*

Highway pegs also allow the rider to stretch out but take the feet away from the controls. Küryakyn's Cruise Arm MKIII provides a pair of forward highway pegs that are insulation rubber mounted. *Küryakyn*

Rider backrests are available, but because the rider usually finds enough support and security by merely leaning forward and hanging onto the grips, they are not as much of a necessity. If your handlebar tilts you backward to the point you've got to struggle against the wind, you may be more comfortable with either a shorter bar or a backrest. Unless you're quite limber, a rider backrest will complicate swinging your leg over the bike.

Forward Foot Controls: Forward controls take the place of stock brake and shift levers, and their floorboards or pegs, and usually allow the rider to spread out more. They also add a bit of chrome dazzle up front. Installation will require utilizing the usual hand tools and likely a different length of hydraulic line if the rear brake is hydraulically actuated (this will necessitate bleeding the brake). You may also need to install a different-length linkage for the shift mechanism.

Grips and Levers: Most bikes come with perfectly adequate handgrips and clutch and brake levers, but replacing them with custom products makes your bike look cool. Levers are usually changed for style reasons, while grips are usually changed for comfort.

Installation is easy, as only the pivot bolt must be removed and replaced to change the levers. Sometimes, matching levers and foot controls are available. Grips are usually held on with adhesive and sometimes must be cut to be removed. Another method is to pry an opening between the grip and the bar with a screwdriver (be careful not to scratch the handlebar) and shoot compressed air into the opening. Once the old grips are off, remove any adhesive residue with acetone before applying a thin layer of rubber cement, or whatever else the grip manufacturer may specify. After you push on the new grips, twist them a little to help spread

the adhesive—then do not ride the bike until the adhesive is completely dry.

Handlebars: As you've seen on roads and at bike gatherings everywhere, changing the stock handlebars with an aftermarket unit is commonplace. This may be done to improve comfort, accommodate a new seat, or simply to change the bike's style. So long as the new handlebars are of the same diameter as stock, the bars should be able to utilize all existing brackets. You'll need to change the grips and reinstall clutch and brake lever housings, but the cables and wiring should not have to be removed or disturbed for bars of comparable height or length to stock. If all wiring is external, this operation should be easy. For wires routed inside the bars, it will take a little longer. Because the existing grips may have to be cut off, have a new set of grips handy for installation.

If the new handlebars are notably longer or higher than the ones they're replacing, it will likely be necessary to replace existing cables, wires, and hydraulic lines—both for aesthetics and to ensure the bars still turn freely lock to lock. This can run into money and a lot of extra work. Ask the handlebar manufacturer if the product will handle all stock hardware. If not, you'll need to know how much longer or shorter the cables and lines will need to be and order them in advance. Be very sure to tighten the handlebar clamps and other parts well and make certain cables and hoses don't bind once the new bars are in their final position. If you swap clip-ons on your Buell, make sure the new grips' position doesn't interfere with your fairing, gauges, or tank, or pinch your fingers in a tight turn.

Bars of much different dimension from stock can change your whole riding experience and affect comfort, control, and even how easy it is to fit your bike back into a tight garage.

When changing handlebars, the trend is to a clean installation in which all the wires are routed and hidden inside the bars. These are the Climax Hand Controls by Custom Cycle Control Systems. *Rick Raus*

Although custom bars are hot mods—T bars (typically narrow), "ape hangers" (tall and wide), beach bars (wide), etc.—don't make the change on looks alone. If you're considering a drastic swap, borrow a fellow enthusiast's bike outfitted with the bars you have in mind and put some miles on it. What feels good on a parked bike may not be comfortable for you at sustained highway speeds or in tight maneuvers at low speeds. Find this out before you invest good money and time.

WIND PROTECTION

Windshields and fairings need to be considered separately, as they're two very different items with a common purpose.

Windshields: With the popularity of touring on Harleys, including the Softail models, the traditional flat windshield has made a comeback. Most windshields mount with a set of handlebar and fork-tube clamps.

The rider should be able to look over the shield, as it can "white out" from oncoming headlights at night, and rain, dirt, and other debris can diminish visibility at any time. Even though the rider's eyes may be several inches above the shield, its angle will usually deflect the wind blast high enough to pass over the rider's head and keep bugs from smacking the face or helmet shield. If the rider is unable to look over the shield, it should be trimmed to proper length.

The rake of the shield should be similar to that of the fork. On bikes with rake in excess of 35 degrees, it's fine to angle the shield a little less.

Shield Height: To order a windshield of the proper height, sit on the bare bike and have a friend hold one end of a tape measure on the top of the headlight, where the shield will nearly rest. Look forward to a spot at which you can comfortably see the road . . . this will be about 15 to 20 feet ahead. Now have your friend measure straight up from the light to a point just below your line of sight. Record the measurement.

Now subtract an inch from this measurement because the shield will not actually rest on the headlight.

TIP

Before changing the handlebars, either remove the fuel tank or pad it with a cover (such as a thick towel) so it will not be damaged by dropped tools. If changing hydraulic lines, note that DOT 3, DOT 4, and DOT 5.1 brake fluid will destroy paint, but DOT 5 is less corrosive. Cover the tank with a layer of plastic over the padding and exercise extreme caution. In any case, always use the type of brake fluid that is specified in your owner's manual or on the master cylinder cover. Do not change fluid types, as some are not compatible with others.

Carrying Cameras and Laptops

If you carry electronic equipment like cameras and computers on your motorcycle, you must protect them from potential damage due to vibration. With the advent of small, simple, inexpensive digital cameras, most riders now simply pop their shooter into a jacket pocket to keep it handy. However, if you wish to carry a larger, more sophisticated camera, perhaps with additional lenses, here's what I have used.

When I had my film cameras, I carried two 35-millimeter bodies and four lenses safely on a motorcycle for more than 25 years in a standard camera bag. I first removed everything from the bag and filled it with two blocks of open-cell foam, one atop the other. After deciding where to locate the pieces (backup body in the bottom, heavy zoom lens close to the wearer's body), I hollowed out a little area for each body and lens with an electric knife. The shaped opening was slightly smaller than the piece so that the foam could grip it well. These nested easily, separated from each other by several inches of foam. For my digital camera, I'm able to utilize a much smaller foam-packed case for the single body and two zoom lenses.

A laptop computer is a much denser, heavier object than a camera. It should be carried in its own case, well padded, in a saddlebag or trunk. Or, it can be carried in a well-padded soft bag either slung over a shoulder or placed in a backpack equipped with a substantial harness. Slinging or backpacking virtually eliminates harmful vibration, but should the rider be thrown from the bike, the laptop will most certainly be destroyed—and could also injure the rider. Be sure to back up your drives if slinging a computer. Jump drives are especially handy for this, and they can be carried easily.

If placed vertically within a saddlebag, the laptop can be carried within a standard padded computer case; add bubble wrap as an extra precaution. If carried horizontally in a trunk, be certain nothing heavy is placed atop the computer.

TIP

If you're adding items in anticipation of a trip, do so a few days beforehand to allow time for any installation problems and for a shakedown run. Be certain you have all necessary tools, hardware, and expertise to install the products and that the instructions are adequate. Never is it more true that "A picture is worth ten thousand words" than when it comes to well-illustrated instructions. Items need to be tested and adjusted, and often there's some sorting out to do. Batteries need to be charged, and most jobs take longer than expected.

Subtract another inch because you don't want the edge of the shield in your sight line; if you're still not comfortable with it, subtract a third inch. If it doesn't seem right yet, go lower still. The shield should reach no higher above the headlight than this new figure.

While shield angle is the major adjustment, some windshields can slide up an inch or two from the headlight. If you're ordering a shield that comes in length increments of two inches (as is common), and your "ideal" length splits the difference, choose the shorter unit. A slightly too-tall shield is much more aggravating than one that's an inch or two shorter than ideal. Besides, the shield should not rest flush on the headlight but should have a slight gap. If the windshield is adjustable (most Harley shields are not), fine-tune its height by sliding it up or down in its mounting brackets.

Installation: Installation is simple and straightforward and can usually be done in a half hour or less with simple hand tools. With the mounting hardware loosely in place, set the shield on the bike and attach it to the mounting hardware. On most, the top brackets bolt to the handlebar and the lower to the fork legs above the lower triple clamp. Adjust everything and snug it down.

Go riding with the shield installed, and you'll notice much more sound being reflected back to you from the engine. In fact, it may seem as if someone has surreptitiously installed an aftermarket exhaust. You'll also notice that you'll feel wind gusts fed into the bike itself rather than buffeting you. With less wind reaching the rider, he or she will stay warmer, less frazzled, and more rested on longer trips. You may notice more inputs from side winds. As with any newly installed product, check all fittings for tightness and adjustment after about 100 miles.

Fairings: Harley-Davidson Electra Glides have used handlebar-mounted fairings since the 1970s. When Craig Vetter introduced his Windjammer frame-mounted fairing in the early '70s,

Top-line Electra Glide models come with lowers, which are wind protectors for the legs. They also include some minimal storage. These can be added at any time.

You can customize the cockpit of your Harley with a chrome master cylinder cover—or two.

Trimming a Windshield

Whoa! Put down that saw and listen to me! Before doing anything drastic, determine if trimming really is necessary. Loosen the adjustments and try to slide the shield down more, or angle it further back. If this won't work, determine how much needs to be trimmed and apply sufficient masking tape to cover the top of the shield, including the area to be trimmed. Mark off the amount you expect to trim by drawing on the tape (use a ruler or make a template for the best results), and then check again. Remember the carpenter's adage: "Measure twice, cut once." Once you're sure of the cut, remove the windshield and pad it so it won't be scratched by the saw table.

The safest tool for trimming is a band saw, as it makes a very even cut in one direction. I do not recommend reciprocating saber or jig saws, though they can work well so long as you have another person to help hold and steady the shield. Use a hacksaw if you must, but be very careful to not allow it to bind. Once the cut has been made, finish it off by sanding with 60- to 80-grit sandpaper or a coarse file to bevel the edges. A Surform or other drywall rasp will also smooth jagged edges.

TIP

Consider windshield models that are quickly detachable. You want the shield on the bike much of the time for touring, but once you reach Sturgis, Daytona, or the rally, you may wish to remove it for cruising around town. Once installed, most shields can be removed in a few minutes with minimal tools, leaving the mounting hardware in place. Harley-Davidson's Detachables windshields and backrests can be removed in seconds by hand with no tools required. The rider stands in front of the motorcycle, straddles the front fender, and grasps the shield from the front. Give it a tug up and forward, and it pulls free from its hardware. Several aftermarket companies also offer quick-detach shields. They go back on just as easily.

A lightly tinted shield can cut down daytime glare by perhaps 10 percent, as with a car windshield. At night it can also cut headlight glare. As for how much tint you can have legally, check state and local laws.

With a detachable shield, such as this one from National Cycle, it's possible to have wind protection on the way to the rally and then easily remove the shield for riding around town. Also ask your dealer about Harley-Davidson's Detachables series of accessories. *National Cycle*

TIP

Engine guards, forward controls, footboards, or other accessories that protrude from the sides of the bike can limit cornering clearance. Determine if this is the case before mounting the item. If a hard part bolted to the bike begins to drag in a turn, it can lever the tires off the pavement with further leaning. As soon as a tire's grip on the pavement is severed, that end of the bike comes unstuck and flies toward the outside of the turn, taking you and the bike with it—off the road or into oncoming traffic. Even when the bolt-on product seems to offer sufficient clearance, keep in mind that a dip or bump in a turn can compress the suspension and use up this little margin of safety.

---

it almost single-handedly introduced the touring revolution. Soon a dozen or so more manufacturers were offering both handlebar- and frame-mounted motorcycle fairings for all brands of bikes.

In the 1980s, purpose-built motorcycles with frame-mounted fairings and integrated, color-matched luggage, such as the Harley Road Glide, sounded the death knell for what had become a huge aftermarket for fairings and saddlebags. Today, most riders either purchase a bike with fairing and bags from the manufacturer or go without. Windshields and textile, leather, and hard-shell saddlebags are readily available for Harley-Davidsons, both from The Motor Company and the aftermarket. Also see Chapter Six on touring.

BIKE PROTECTION

Covers: If you keep your bike outside, I strongly recommend using a bike cover to protect it. These covers are usually made of nylon or canvas, either lightweight or heavy, and will keep off the sun, rain, and dust. However, the cover must not hold moisture against the bike, which promotes corrosion. For the same reason you would not

want to wear an impermeable rain suit on a humid day, the moisture inside a bike cover must be allowed to escape, either through vents or breathable fabric. And when you remove a damp cover, spread it out somewhere to dry so it doesn't develop mildew.

Be certain the cover fits tightly when stretched, as a loose-fitting cover can flutter in the wind, creating rub marks on painted surfaces over time. Look for covers that have a soft liner material where they contact the windshield. Secure the cover so it will not blow off.

Some covers have reinforced holes through which a cable lock may be passed to discourage theft. However, because they're made of cloth, covers can be cut or otherwise vandalized. Because they conceal the bike, the cover may discourage thieves intending to steal a specific make or model.

Engine Guards/Case Guards: Engine cases and covers can be damaged in a tip-over, so some riders bolt engine or case guards to their bikes. These are usually chromed tube-steel rails that can support the bike. Some riders bolt highway pegs to them so they can spread out on the road, but this often places their feet far from the controls. Another way to spread out is to install forward controls, which bring the feet and their controls out for comfort.

WHEELS
Going Wider
The obvious trend is toward ever-wider wheels for ever-wider rear tires. According to some riders and builders, they've now reached the point of near or absolute absurdity in terms of function. With that said, front wheels are following suit, but to a lesser degree. The widest rear tires currently available on stock bikes from the major manufacturers are in the 200- to 240-series range, but anything goes in the alternative V-twin and custom markets. The aftermarket keeps offering ever-wider hoops that are in the 330-series range, and still wider tires are certainly coming.

Do these extremely wide tires and wheels work? After a fashion. Returning to our "tool for a job" guiding principle, if your desire is to gain attention

with the old "mine is bigger than yours" school of thought, they certainly do work in that sense. However, these wider wheels and tires are heavy, which results in greater unsprung weight on suspended bikes, which will adversely affect the way the bike rides. The profile will affect how the bike leans into turns and may affect steering entering and leaving turns, too. It all becomes very complex.

I do not recommend utilizing automobile tires on motorcycles. Cars drive flat on the ground, riding on a flat tread supported by a perpendicular sidewall (more or less); motorcycles lean over a broad range, utilizing much of the exposed rubber, which is rounded for seamless transitions across the full leaning range. An automotive tire may wear like iron on a motorcycle, but its squared design will create handling anomalies as you lean through turns, and it may let go of the road if you go past the tread area onto the sidewall. Unless you only intend to ride in a straight line, stick with a tire made for a motorcycle. Safety is more important than money.

A full bike cover (like this one by Roadgear) is ideal for protecting your bike when it's kept outside. It's also useful for keeping dust (and cats) off when it's kept in the garage. They're a bit bulky for taking on the road, however. *Roadgear*

TIP

For a bike that is parked outside, the larger, heavier, full cover provides maximum coverage. For touring, or just to keep the cats and dust off a bike stored in the garage, choose a thinner, lighter cover that may only protect the upper part of the bike. They fold up much smaller and will at least prevent the seat from being wet in the morning if you park outside.

Wide rear tires are cool and imply that the bike makes such power that it needs a huge amount of rubber on the road. To go really wide, however, requires a modified swingarm and rear fender. *Dunlop Motorcycle Tires*

Wire wheels are traditional on Harleys; this is an aftermarket unit with many more spokes than stock.

The Diamond 3D Series of Forge-Tec wheels from Kim Suter includes the Creations 3, Creations 5, and Creations 7. The numbers refer to the number of spokes in the wheel. Matching rotors, pulleys, and sprockets are available as well. *Forge-Tec*

One of the hottest trends in customization today is for a bike to carry matching pulleys, wheels, and brake rotors. This Forge-Tec Deviate Wheel is rotary forged, utilizing a proprietary forge press and "virgin" aircraft grade 6061 aluminum. *Forge-Tec*

Bringing these wide tire/wheel combinations to market is no easy proposition, and requires an orchestrated dance among several related companies. First, the tire makers manufacture wider tires, then the aftermarket wheel makers have to come up with new tooling for wider wheels to fit them. Finally, the custom frame makers must develop the frames and swingarms to accommodate them. These enormous 300- and 330-series tires require wheels that are about $10^1/_2$ inches to a foot or more wide.

Eighteen inches is the predominant wheel diameter, as it shows more wheel and less tire. Some manufacturers have told me that right-side-drive systems for custom bikes have become popular for use with 300-series and larger wheels, as they're necessary to keep the bike balanced.

Wheel Basics

Cast Wheels: Cast aluminum wheels are formed by pouring molten metal into a mold. Gas pockets can form during the molding process, which can cause weak spots. As a result, these wheels are sometimes made thicker and heavier to compensate. If the casting contains trapped gas, it can work its way to the surface and cause the chromed finish to separate and peel off. Although better casting and chroming techniques have minimized this, cast wheels are still generally not as strong as forged wheels.

Forged Wheels: Forged wheels are created from a solid piece of metal, often of 6061 aluminum billet. They are heated until soft and malleable, then placed in forging dies and pressed under extreme pressure to finalize their shape. Forged wheels can be structurally sound and very strong, with no seams to potentially leak.

There are also one- and two-piece wheels: the one-piece is usually cast and weaker but also less expensive because it's easier to manufacture. The two-piece usually utilizes a cast outer section with a forged inner. The two-piece is

One advantage of matching pulleys to complement its wheels and rotors is that matched sets of Forge-Tec wheels are shipped with the rotors and pulley torqued to OEM specs. Shown is Forge-Tec's Deviate pulley. *Forge-Tec*

The 11.5-inch, one-piece Forge-Tec brake rotor is constructed from 400 Series stainless steel, polished to a mirror-like finish, and available for all of their styles and designs of wheels. Shown is the Deviate rotor. *Forge-Tec*

The purpose of engine guards and safety bars is to keep you—and your bike—up off the pavement should you go sliding. This safety bar will minimize damage in a tip-over but cannot save you from injury. It can also be used for mounting remote footpegs or auxiliary lights.

The ultimate in keeping your bike clean is a garage within a garage. The Bike Bubble is constructed of lightweight, durable plastic and kept inflated by a small fan to form a protective "bubble" around the bike. Electrical costs run pennies a day.

not only much stronger, but if either part breaks it can be replaced.

Wire Wheels: Wire spoke wheels are traditional on motorcycles and were universal until cast hoops appeared in the late 1970s. They're *de rigueur* on most choppers and classic-styled bikes, and they look great. Manufacturers are doing a lot with different spoke numbers and shapes. While cast and forged wheels require no maintenance, the spokes in wire wheels can loosen over time and require tightening.

Because the spokes penetrate the rim, they're difficult to seal, and these wheels must usually be used with tubes. Some wire-wheel manufacturers use a sealant material on the inside that they state will allow their wheels to be used with tubeless tires.

Tube vs. Tubeless Tires: If a nail punctures a tube, the tube will deflate immediately. Tubeless tires, on the other hand, may capture the nail and the tire will continue to hold air for some time,

allowing the rider to get home safely. If you find a nail head protruding from your tubeless tire, and it's still holding air, *do not remove it*. Get the bike to a shop where the tire may be repaired or replaced.

Another reason for not running tube-type tires is that Harleys don't have centerstands, which makes it virtually impossible to remove a wheel and repair it beside the road. While a tubeless tire can be plugged from the outside without removing it from the wheel, a tube-type cannot. That can be the difference between using a repair kit plug to get you on your way in 20 minutes, or losing hours waiting for the dealer to send a truck. To top it off, for the cost of the dealer service call to pick you up by the road with your flat tube-type tire, you could probably have paid for a new tubeless tire and been on your way hours ago.

Once the plug is in place, it's very important to understand that it's a temporary, emergency measure and your next stop should be at a dealership for a new tire or, at the very least, a proper patch.

APPAREL

HERE WE WILL COVER:

- **Leather Clothing**

- **Textile Clothing**

- **Clothing for Inclement Weather**

- **Boots and Gloves**

A full jacket display, like this one at Ventura Harley-Davidson/Buell in California, gives the customer a full selection from which to choose and allows for easy comparison among jackets.

Motorcycling is an exercise in versatility, both in terms of weather and in the types of roads we ride.

MOTORCYCLE CLOTHING

Motorcycling is an exercise in versatility, both in terms of weather and in the types of roads we ride. You start out on a spring morning in the city and the temperature is 45 degrees. Stop for lunch a few hours later in the flatlands and it's 75 degrees. By mid-afternoon you're in the mountains where the temperature has dropped to 60, then late in the day you're pulling into a motel at 6,500 feet and it's 40 degrees. Perhaps it's raining. How do you cope with all these extremes? By choosing the right riding gear.

Most apparel for motorcycle riders today is made of leather (usually cowhide and occasionally deerskin or kangaroo), textiles (usually some form of basket-weave ballistic nylon), or a combination of both. Both hides and textiles have advantages and disadvantages.

LEATHER CLOTHING

Cowhide leather, which has been traditional for the Harley rider for more than a century, makes for an excellent motorcycling garment. It is a natural, fibrous, porous material. This porosity allows it to breathe, and its fibers help it hold together for abrasion resistance. Leather is classy, has the heft and feel of quality, it wears well, and I love the way it creaks when you move. Its pleasant aroma ranks right up there with chocolate-chip cookies or a good steak. It's repairable and, if cared for properly, it may be possible to pass your leather garments on to your children.

Leather breaks the wind well but is not inherently warm, so leatherwear for motorcycling needs to be lined and insulated. Its only major drawback is that, if you're caught in the rain, leather will lose its natural oils and (unless it's been specially treated) turn stiff and discolor. Carry a rain suit.

When leather garments become lightly soiled from riding, wipe them down with a damp washcloth. After several such wipings, or anytime the leather begins to lose its suppleness, treat it with a commercial leather enhancer to replenish the essential oils. There are also leather cleaners, but many enhancers include cleaners. This is a simple process that usually involves first wiping down the leather as usual, rubbing on the enhancer, then several minutes later wiping it off with a dry rag.

With leather you can go wild. It is available simple, or with fringe and conchos and other embellishments. It can be made in colors. Custom-made leather garments can add style and function to your ride; best of all, they'll fit perfectly.

Deerskin is softer and more supple than cowhide, has greater abrasion resistance, and is not nearly as susceptible to damage by rain. It has also been my experience that deerskin garments retain heat better in the cold, yet also breathe better and are cooler in hot weather. The tradeoff is that deerskin is more expensive.

Kangaroo leather is said to be the most abrasion resistant. Whole suits are available, but they're quite expensive. Gloves that have kangaroo-leather palms, on the other hand, are a wonderful indulgence.

How Motorcycle Leather Is Different from Fashion Leather

You may be tempted to use a leather fashion jacket for motorcycling since perhaps you have one in the closet, but it's not likely to work nearly as well as true, purpose-built motorcycle clothing. Fashion leather is thinner, not sufficiently thick for serious wind or abrasion protection. The open design of fashion

The Harley-Davidson Cycle Champ is a police-style leather jacket with a classic look and a raft of features.

wear will allow wind to rush up your sleeves and waist while it's also coming in at the neck. The main zipper of a motorcycle jacket will be backed by a flap to prevent wind from coming through, but a fashion jacket may not have such a flap. Collars will wave madly in the wind, shoulders will bind, and sleeves will ride up as you reach for the grips.

Jackets designed for motorcycling have lengthened sleeves that have been rotated forward to accommodate your riding position. Often the back has been cut lower ("dropped") to protect the kidneys and provide added wind protection, and the extra pleat of material behind your shoulders that allows for greater reach and movement is called the "action back."

TIP

Wet leather must be allowed to air dry (do *not* put it into a dryer). Lay towels over and under it and squeeze the water into them. When it's relatively dry, treat it with a good leather restorer, or the garment will be ruined. If your boots get soaked, you can dry them more effectively by stuffing crumpled newspapers inside.

This textile Cayenne jacket from Rev'It features pockets galore. It also includes a zip-off fanny pack that contains several more pockets. Inside, it has a zip-out thermal liner as well as a waterproof liner.

Textile Clothing.

It's every rider's dream to have such a great riding suit that, no matter how the weather changes—whether it turns hot, cold, or wet—he would not need to stop to change clothing.

Also, as the temperature changes during a ride, you will be adding and subtracting clothing. To allow for expansion, many jackets have waist adjusters in the form of elastic, snap, lace-up, or hook-and-loop fasteners that fashion jackets do not offer. Of course, until you get a good leather or synthetic motorcycle jacket, wear the one you have now, or an army jacket, or anything else that will take the brunt of the friction if you slide across the pavement.

TEXTILE CLOTHING

It's every rider's dream to have such a great riding suit that, no matter how the weather changes—whether it turns hot, cold, or wet—he would not need to stop to change clothing, but could just keep riding. That's where textile fabrics come in. They're made of synthetic materials, such as nylon, often marketed under trade names like Cordura, Taslan, or Dynax, and are available in several weave thicknesses, expressed as "denier." For example, a good riding suit (such as those by Aerostich Riderwearhouse) will often use 500-denier ballistic nylon. Nylon is made from petroleum—oil—and therefore resists absorbing moisture. A water-resistant coating bonded to the nylon fabric renders it essentially impervious to weather, but water can come in through the stitch holes that pass through the fabric. Therefore, seams must be taped, treated with seam sealer, or protected with flaps.

If properly made, sealed, and insulated, a textile riding suit can allow you to just continue riding through light rain or cold weather, but it may eventually soak through. Add a waterproof, breathable membrane like Gore-Tex, Hipora, Reissa, or others, and you've got not only a pretty secure outfit but also one that can breathe and offer a wider range of comfort. It is possible that the outer shell can become soaked while the liner keeps the inside—and you—dry. This means that while you'll be physically dry, you'll still be encased in a cold, sodden envelope. The shell material does not breathe that well, and without proper venting, a textile garment may become stuffy in hot weather.

Sometimes you just have to ride in the rain because you're not where you need to be. For those times, having a good rain-repellent jacket and pants or bibs makes a world of difference. With a full-face helmet and a good rain suit, it's not much different from being in a car—albeit one with a none-too-spacious interior.

WHAT MAKES A GOOD RIDING JACKET

If you do a lot of riding, including touring for days at a time, versatility is the key to a good jacket. It must be livable on a 90-degree, humid Midwest summer's day, yet remain comfortable atop an 8,000-foot pass when it's 40 degrees and spitting snow. It must seal up like a bank vault to keep out the wind

---

Melting Point

As a petroleum product, nylon will melt if exposed to heat. Should your textile jacket slide off your bike's seat and onto its hot engine or exhaust pipe, it may soon be sporting a nasty melted spot. It can likewise deposit an unsightly, smoking blob of molten nylon on your pristine pipes. Should you get thrown from your bike and go road surfing, the heat of friction could likewise melt a section of a textile jacket.

---

and may offer controllable venting for hot days. For maximum versatility, the liner will zip or snap out for warm weather. Some liners are vest-style, but full-sleeve liners have the potential to be warmer. If you expect you may be removing the liner, be sure you have someplace to store it, such as in a tank bag, tail bag, or saddlebag. Whether it's leather or textile, here's a quick look at some desirable jacket features.

Staying warm on a motorcycle is all about sealing out the wind, so it's very important that any jacket have a good neck seal. If it doesn't, bring a scarf or a product like the Aerostich Wind Triangle (www.aerostich.com). It includes a layer of Gore-Tex sandwiched between two layers of nylon, with a soft backing. On the sleeves, look for adjustable cuffs, sealed by zippers or hook-and-loop fasteners, that are compact enough to fit inside long gauntlet gloves.

Air stealing up from the bottom of a jacket can be chilling, so many jackets have adjustable belts or drawstrings to seal them around the waist. For this reason, it's a real plus if a jacket and pants zip together. Also, should you go sliding down the road, a zipped-together jacket and pants can't separate and expose your skin to abrasion.

Pockets

Motorcycle jackets are known for their pockets, since riders need to carry many small items. Check that pockets are covered by storm flaps, as exposed

---

TIP

Layer clothing (a sweater over a shirt over a T-shirt) rather than wearing one heavy, bulky garment. You'll be warmer, and your gear will be more versatile. If the weather's going to be cold, wear a long-sleeved t-shirt and turtleneck. In an emergency, if you've got to keep riding and it's just too cold, layer newspapers down the front of your jacket.

Roadgear's Multi-Season Adaptive-Tec Vest and Jacket utilize Outlast "smart fabric" technology. It's designed to sense body temperature and adjust for comfort through a phase-change process, cooling when it's hot and warming when it's cool. The key is "Thermocules," microscopic containers encapsulating Phase Change Materials (PCM) that change from solid to slush to liquid, to store or give off heat as the temperature varies. *Roadgear*

This Tour Master jacket features shoulder and arm vents. In order for venting to be effective, the air needs to flow through, so back vents are also provided. *Tour Master*

Perforated jackets are ideal for warmer climates, as they provide excellent ventilation. Look for a windproof liner for use when the weather cools. This is the Roadgear Airtec Mesh Jacket. *Roadgear*

Cell Phones

You can't find the motel. Can't find gas. Your bike has broken down. You're separated from your group. You need to check your messages. Need I go on? Many motorcycle jackets now include a cell phone pocket, and companies like J&M and AutoCom offer equipment that allows for hands-free cell phone operation with a helmet headset.

In case of accident, paramedics will search an injured person's cell phone for identity and contact information. Create a file called "**ICE**" (In Case of Emergency) that includes the names and phone numbers of anyone who should be contacted, should you have a problem.

zippers will take in rain. Pockets are usually secured with zippers or hook-and-loop fasteners. (By the way, "hook-and-loop fastener" is a generic term for the peel-apart fastener that is commonly known by the trade name "Velcro." By saying "hook-and-loop fastener," we avoid receiving nasty letters from the lawyers at Velcro.)

For walking around on cold days, hand-warmer pockets are a plus. Most riders will carry their wallets in an inner pocket secured by a zipper or button. Other pockets are handy for carrying earplugs, spare change, keys, a wind scarf, shield cleaning solution and a rag, a candy bar (well wrapped), a tire gauge, or summer gloves. Pockets are both practical and a styling feature. Remember, if you keep your wallet in your jacket, don't leave the jacket on the back of your chair in the restaurant while you go wandering off.

Temperature Control

Controllable vents contribute greatly to a jacket's temperature versatility, so long as they're properly designed. When opened, vents must have a mesh backing to keep out insects, and they must remain open. Many jackets have zippered slit vents in the chest, but as soon as you reach forward for the grips on bikes with low handlebars, these vents just end up closed again. A few jackets also have mesh panels on the forearms. Back vents allow wind to flow through, but their zippers are difficult to reach while wearing the jacket.

When shopping, ask if you can step outside and try the jackets you're considering while sitting on your bike. You need to determine if the sleeves are long enough to seal your gloves when you reach for the grips, and if the cuffs can open wide enough to scoop some breeze up the arms in hot weather. Check that the front vents are easy to open while you're riding, and that they will remain open. Is it possible to open the rear vents (if any) without removing the jacket? If it's difficult, loop a leather tassel through the zipper pull to give you some added reach. Don't make it too big, or it'll just whip around when you get up to highway speeds.

Some companies offer fully perforated jackets through which the wind will flow constantly. These are fine for day rides in warm-weather climates, but if you stay out late or if the weather is changeable, they may not be the best solution. Look for such jackets to have a windproof, removable liner.

Care

If your shield gets dirty and needs to be cleaned several times a day, what will your jacket—which is passing through all the same airborne matter—look like after a season of riding? Wipe down smooth leather with a damp cloth, or clean it with saddle soap that has restorers built in. An alternative is to use a commercial leather cleaner. Test any cleaner or leather treatment product on an unexposed part of the garment first to be sure it does not remove the color. Once the item is clean, apply a commercial leather-care product.

I do not recommend suede leathers for motorcycle use, as bike jackets can become very dirty, and suede is difficult to clean. If the point of suede is to look good, it won't—especially if it gets drenched a few times. Leather garments should be treated periodically with cleaners and restorers.

Textile garments should be wiped down with a damp rag periodically to remove the most obvious bug carcasses. When gunk builds up, remove the liner and armor pads (if any) and toss the garment in the washing machine,

following the manufacturer's directions. If the liner is removable, check it for any special washing instructions. After cleaning, you may want to treat textile garments with a commercial waterproofing or protective spray.

Color

Harley riders seem to follow the words of Henry Ford by wearing every conceivable color of garment . . . so long as it's black. Attention purists: Bill Harley and the Davidsons were offering their machines in both black and Renault Gray in 1906! Color *is* traditional. Today, your bike can be had in a true multitude of colors, and so can many leather and non-leather jackets. Lighten up already!

One observation about colorful textile riding suits is that they may look

For warmer weather, consider something like the Roadgear XKJ perforated jacket and pants. They utilize wind-blocker and rain-resistant technology for when it's cool, and through leather surface perforations allow for serious cooling airflow with the liners out.

Textile jackets are often available in vibrant colors, as well as black. This Cortech jacket is fully featured and improves the visibility of the rider on the road. Unfortunately, bright colors show the bugs more readily. *Cortech*

TIP

The shiny paint on a motorcycle and the more saturated color of a textile jacket will rarely match. If you're shopping for colorful textile clothing, I suggest that you ride your motorcycle to the store and try the colors together. Often, you'll find that blue or blue/gray textile clothing will better complement a red motorcycle. Similarly, textile clothing with red, or red in combination with gray or black, will often better complement a blue bike. A helmet, because it also carries shiny paint, will often match or complement the bike. Many times we've done very satisfactory photo shoots in which the rider wore a red helmet on a red bike while wearing a blue textile jacket.

This armored Cortech gauntlet glove is not only stylish, but it also looks like it would come in handy in a bar fight! It features armor and insulation, and because it's long, it will seal jacket cuffs from the wind. *Cortech*

Traditionally, women have not had a great choice in motorcycle apparel. Now, however, many companies have awakened to the fact that not only do women like to ride, but they also want gear that fits. This suit is by Roadgear. *Roadgear*

great in the store, but once they become soiled it's difficult to get them as clean as new, and they'll always look grungy.

Which brings us back to the reason why most motorcycle riding gear is black. Unless your bike has such good wind protection that you rarely get bug splat on your gear, you may wish to stick with those traditional dark colors.

Reflectivity

Most motorcycle jackets are black or brown so they won't show the dirt, but textile jackets come in a variety of colors. If other motorists already can't see us very well under the best conditions, even with our headlights on, how much more invisible are we while wearing dark colors? Some leather jackets have color accents, and some textile jackets are quite colorful. Reflective striping will help other motorists see us in their headlights. Consider it a plus.

Armor and Foam

Take a tumble, and any protruding parts of your body (hands, elbows, forearms, shoulders, hips, feet, and knees) will probably get banged up. It's common for

motorcycle apparel to have a second layer of leather or textile material, along with some padding, sewn over these potential impact areas. Some just have comfort foam, the soft open-cell stuff that bottoms easily and is of minimal use in a get-off. Others will have much denser closed-cell protective foam, the best of which is sandwiched between layers of thin plastic and meets European Community (CE) standards. This CE-approved armor will absorb and disperse impac and is also an insulator. A layer of foam, especially across the back, will add warmth.

Old-style armor is simply a molded plastic shell that covers the area it's designed to protect, such as an elbow or knee. The problem with a simple plastic shell, or even a plastic shell with a layer of foam inside it, is that it transfers the energy of a blow directly to the body part it's protecting; absorption is minimal. Granted, the ensuing bruise is much less severe than what would have happened to an unprotected body part, but it still hurts. Modern armor designed to absorb impact energy is far superior and worth every penny. However, if it's a choice between old armor and no armor, well, the decision should be obvious. (Just to be sure: Take the armor.)

WOMEN'S APPAREL

Because a large percentage of motorcycle riders are male, most companies cut their motorcycle garments specifically for men, then hide behind the "unisex" designation for women. Let's see, if men and women are built the same, why am I more interested in a Dallas Cowboys Cheerleaders calendar than a Dallas Cowboys calendar? More companies are now offering motorcycle clothing cut specifically for women, but the buyer must be careful to verify this fact. I'm all in favor of rewarding performance, and in the realm of motorcycle clothing that means buying from

On the Mountain or In the Desert

Staying Warm

Staying warm means sealing out the wind, and the neck area is the most critical area to seal. Choose a jacket with particular attention to how well it seals the neck area. If you want extra warmth there, wear a dickey or turtleneck to hold in the warmth and a wind scarf to seal out the wind. A primary problem with some jackets is that while they seal well, they do not allow for the additional layers of clothing a rider may need in cold weather and thus don't allow for sufficient adjustment. If there's an adjustable tab at the neck, check that it is long enough to accommodate extra layers of cold-weather clothing.

For sealing the neck and head, balaclavas are great. They're those silk items, with an eyeport, that pull over your head. You often see them in war movies being worn by commandos sneaking ashore or through the forest.

Gauntlet gloves that fit over the jacket cuffs are a great way of preventing the wind from stealing up into the sleeves. For cold weather you'll need a lot of insulation on the outsides of the hands, but never in the palms because they're curled around the grips. Motorcycle-specific gloves are a plus here, as most all-purpose winter gloves have too much insulation on the palms to allow easy operation of the hand controls.

Staying Cool

Riding in the desert or in hot, humid weather makes additional demands on the rider. Becoming dehydrated or overheated will affect your ability to ride. Rule One in the heat is to drink plenty of liquids so your body's natural cooling mechanism of shedding heat through perspiration and evaporation is uninhibited. A bellyfull of cool liquid can also pull your temperature down when you start to overheat. Drink water and commercial thirst quenchers that replace the electrolytes your body loses. Do not drink alcohol—it will impair your ability to ride and is also a diuretic, which causes you to lose more fluid than you retain.

Drink liquids before you get out into the heat because by the time you're thirsty, you're already in danger. If you don't

like carrying those glass bottles that many commercial drinks come in, try plastic water bottles of the type bicyclists use. They are light, inexpensive, come in a variety of sizes and colors, and have an easy-open spout.

Learn from desert dwellers that it's cooler in the shade. People who live in desert countries don't go out shirtless wearing shorts, but they wear their shade in the form of loose-fitting, flowing clothing. Riding shirtless and in shorts exposes you to sunburn and serious road rash. A sunburn will bother you for the rest of the trip and make you feel too hot even in an air-conditioned room that night. You will also get dehydrated faster shirtless because sweat is your only protection from the heat. In hot weather, wear your helmet and loose-fitting garments. A cotton shop jumpsuit can keep you from sunburn and can be hosed down for a cooling effect.

In most situations, wear sturdy footwear and ventilated gloves. In extremely hot weather, when the heat coming in exceeds body temperature, I've found it's more comfortable to wear nonventilated clothing and to keep my helmet shield closed. Otherwise, the air stream is warming rather than cooling you.

Evaporation is the key to staying cool. Soak a bandana or other cloth and tie it around your neck. By being in the breeze and in close proximity to the arteries in your neck, it will cool you for awhile. When it begins to dry out, pull over and use the water bottle in your tank bag (a small luggage bag that straps to the gas tank or attaches with magnets) to soak it again. Or soak your hair and wear your helmet over it to control evaporation.

Another method that I've used and highly recommend is to soak a sweatshirt or other heavy riding shirt in water. You'll shiver when you put it on, and it will get your pants wet, but that won't last long. In the direct heat and airflow it will dry out relatively soon, so wear a nylon windbreaker over it and adjust the rate of evaporation with the zipper; it will keep you cool for hours. Some manufacturers offer cooling vests with pockets that accept sodden sponges.

companies that offer specific products for your needs.

THE BOTTOM HALF
Chaps

Invented by cowboys in the Southwest, *chaparreras* were made of leather and designed to keep legs from being cut to red ribbons by thorns and cactus needles. Today's chaps are similar. A pair of chaps is essentially a flat garment that fastens around your hips and the backs of your legs, fits loosely, and is simple to get into and out of. Versatility

The key to staying warm while riding is to seal the neck. These items by Roadgear not only seal, but they're warm, too. *Roadgear*

Wear a balaclava under your helmet on cold days. It folds to about the size of a handkerchief and can easily be stored in a jacket pocket.

is their reason for being, as many riders will wear chaps in the cool morning and then stow them when the day warms.

Chaps will keep off the wind, but they let the rain come around from behind. Their backless/crotchless design offers very little protection. In a get-off, they'll likely rotate on the body and may even come off. Finally, they

have sort of, well, a kinky look. But I'm not saying that's a bad thing . . . .

Pants Versus Overpants

Most riders tend to ride in denim jeans, or a similar fabric pant, and suffer the cold consequences. Though you can't beat them for comfort and universal acceptability in day-to-day activities, jeans aren't warm or protective on a motorcycle, nor will they keep you dry. But true motorcycle pants can be heavy and can become hot when the day warms up. One alternative is a protective overpant that you can wear all day if necessary over your jeans or remove and store when the weather warms.

In order to cover a rider's jeans without putting on the big squeeze, overpants are built a bit big and perhaps a little sloppy. It's the price we pay for that scosh more room. They're also not going to look as svelte or show the curves of your hindquarters to the best advantage to the opposite sex.

On the other hand, if you commute to an office job, or go anywhere else where you want to look your best, a jacket and overpants will protect your dress togs from bugs, dirt, and road grime. When you're giving that presentation on the 28th floor to the boys from

What Makes a Good Pair of Pants?

Congratulations on the purchase of your new motorcycle jacket. Unfortunately, it won't do you much good if your legs are left hanging out there with less protection—especially if your jacket is of the high-tech, non-leather, weatherproof persuasion. Many companies that make motorcycle jackets also offer matching pants, and sometimes overpants that fit right over your jeans. If you're getting an all-weather suit, don't forget to complement it with all-weather gloves and boots.

Much of what makes a good jacket applies to pants. Pockets are desirable, and most motorcycle pants will come with front and rear pockets. Bulky items (such as key chains) that are fine to carry in front pants pockets when you're walking around may get in the way when you're leaned forward on a motorcycle; they're best carried in a jacket pocket or tank bag. Pant legs should be long enough to seal over your boots.

Finance, no one has to prejudice his views by noticing the bug stains on your $1,000 suit.

When touring, the rationale behind overpants is that you put them on when the weather is cool or questionable and take them off when things warm up. If you didn't intend to remove them in fair weather, you may as well just go for full leather or textile pants. Therefore, it's a real convenience that overpants can go on and come off easily on the road without you having to remove your boots. The tradeoff is that the dirt on your boots can become deposited on the overpant liner and then rub off on your pants. To avoid that, either remove your boots when donning overpants or get the kind that are supplied with a lo-o-o-o-o-ng zipper up each leg.

A good overpant should allow access to keys and change in your pants pockets, though none will likely offer access to your rear wallet pocket. Well, that's why jackets have wallet pockets.

The two main varieties are textile overpants, which are often waterproof and sometimes armored, and leather overpants designed more with style and overall abrasion protection in mind.

Overpants

Overpants are motorcycle pants designed to be worn over other pants for the purposes of protection and comfort. Overpants take chaps that final step forward by offering full, wraparound protection.

Chaps are the original versatile garment. They're easy to get on, light but protective, and easy to remove and stow. These chaps are by Tour Master. *Tour Master*

Textile garments are often rainproof and insulated, but they're sometimes bulky and can become too warm. Roadgear's Xcaliber textile overpant works well when you need it, yet is easy to remove when you don't. *Roadgear*

Rain Suits Versus Terrariums

Some summers ago, my wife and I were blasting across Germany on one of their excellent autobahns, heading for the Netherlands, making some serious, high-speed miles on this hazy, overcast day. We donned our coated-nylon rain suits when the salmon-strangling rains came and were cozy and dry. However, when the welcome sun came out an hour later, the steam boiled off the pavement and our suits quickly became very hot and uncomfortable. We were stewing in our own juices; in their zeal to *keep* moisture out, the suit manufacturer had made no provisions to *let* moisture out. The rains came again, and the sun again, and each time we had to stop to change gear. We really regretted not buying rain suits made of breathable fabric, or at least with better ventilation.

Textile Overpants

These are often deluxe versions of rain suit bottoms and may offer insulation, pockets, armor, and additional features. Some are actually the bottoms of two-piece suits, so it's possible to purchase the jacket (sold separately) and have a coordinated outfit.

Keep in mind that textile pants and overpants, while wonderful in many ways, will likely make that dorky "whisk-whisk" sound when you walk.

The pockets and seams of some are sealed, but for those that are not it may be possible to spray them with a sealant (such as Scotchgard) and seam sealer to make them so. However, this may affect their breathability. Armor is a plus to protect knees and hips from impact.

Leather Overpants

It's cool, it's classy and comfortable, it looks like real motorcycle gear, and it won't melt on your exhaust pipes. Leather provides great abrasion resistance, won't flap as readily in the wind, and smells great.

FULL RIDING SUITS: ONE- OR TWO-PIECE?

A two-piece suit is one that has separate jacket and pants that may zip together to form a relatively tight seal. The advantage to the zip-together feature is that it will prevent the jacket from riding up and letting wind through, or worse—riding up should you go sliding down the pavement.

The major practical advantage of a two-piece suit is that, when you arrive at your destination and wish to walk around in the cool evening, you can wear the jacket and leave the bulky pants behind. And obviously, a two-piece suit is much easier to put on.

A one-piece is a full suit that does not separate, so it will obviously seal well. Racing suits are most often one-piece, as they cannot ride up or separate, exposing the rider to road rash. The disadvantages are that it's usually necessary to find a place to sit down in order to don a one-piece suit, and it's rather bulky for walking around town. Pull into a restaurant and you'll need to find a chair in order to slip out of your one-piece suit, while the others in your group just hang their jackets on the wall. If you left your keys in your pants pocket, it'll be tough to reach them while wearing a one-piece suit. It's simply not very versatile, which is why I favor the two-piece design.

When selecting a rain suit jacket, look for good neck and cuff closures, a long torso to extend over the pants in the riding position, sealed pockets, and bright colors with reflective material for visibility. *Tour Master*

Far Right:
Nylon rain suit pants often include suspenders to hold them up, stirrups to hold them down, and no front zipper, so there's no potential for water intrusion. Look for long leg zippers, too. *Tour Master*

RAIN SUITS

There are two philosophies among rain suit manufacturers. The usually less expensive way is to wrap the rider in an impermeable coated-nylon shell through which moisture cannot pass in either direction; some add venting. The usually more expensive way is to provide a breathable shell that fends off the rain but allows humidity and the body's natural moisture to escape.

Being dry is easy—just encase yourself in a body-sized baggie and seal up the openings where your appendages poke out. Staying dry, on the other hand, is tough. Dampness from the outside is bad enough on a rainy day, but when dampness from the inside permeates your clothing, you're stuck with that clammy, shivery feeling that just won't go away.

Like textile suits, nylon will also melt when it contacts a hot surface. For this reason, a few suits offer Nomex or other heat-stable fabric on the inner sides of the legs.

Sizing

Rain suits are sized to be worn over your riding gear. If you normally wear a size medium jacket, a medium riding or rain suit should fit over it.

One-Piece versus
Two-Piece—Mind Your Crotch

Two-piece rain suits outsell the one-piece by a handy margin, mostly for reasons of convenience and versatility. Once you get your legs in, it's more difficult to squirm your shoulders up into a one-piece suit, especially when your leather is already wet. A mesh liner on the rain suit helps here, and it also adds to comfort by providing a space for evaporation. Once it's on, however, a one-piece suit can potentially be drier because it has no split.

The potential problem with one-piece suits is that in order to make the main zipper long enough for easy entry, it usually dips down past the crotch. When you're seated on the bike, water may pool in the crotch and leak past the zipper if the suit is not properly folded, making it appear that you've had an embarrassing "accident." Arrange the suit so that it will not allow water to pool in the crotch.

The two-piece rain suit is usually easier to get into because the jacket opens fully. And with no zipper in the pants above the knees, your crotch stays well protected. A well-placed drawstring will keep the jacket tight around your waist.

Rainwear Tips

Plan ahead. Because your riding suit's pockets will be difficult to access once you're all bundled up in your rain suit, transfer keys, wallet, and change to a convenient pocket in your outer jacket or rain suit.

Wet weather is usually cooler, so I strongly recommend electrically heated clothing along with your rainwear. Electric gear plugs into a harness attached to your bike's battery—no sweat with a two-piece suit, but a challenge if your one-piece outfit doesn't have an opening for the plug to pass through.

Rainy weather is also dark weather. A brightly colored suit with reflective striping will make you more visible.

Rain suits block the wind very effectively. If you get cold, even on a dry day, donning your rain suit can keep you much warmer. Or if it has stopped raining but the road is still wet, wearing only the rain pants can protect your legs from filthy road spray.

Once the suit becomes wet, allow it to dry overnight before packing it away or you'll have mildew problems.

Hands and Feet

Many companies offer boots and gloves with breathable, rain-resistant membranes

With no split between top and bottom, a one-piece rain suit can potentially keep you drier. However, that long front zipper can be a problem if it allows water to pool in the crotch. *Tour Master*

TIP

A rain suit cannot protect you if you're not wearing it. The problem is, most riders delay putting on their suits till it's already raining in the (usually) silly belief that, somehow, they're going to be lucky this time. Most of the time you'll be climbing into a rain suit while parked beside the road, often in bad light and always in a hurry. For this reason, the legs *must* be wide enough for your boots to slide through easily. Of course, any dirt or mud on them will be transferred to the inside of the rain pants, then onto your pants.

The Boss biker-style boots by Wesco offer style, protection, and a sole that grips well while riding or walking.

These waterproof Roadgear TDF rain boots utilize the Outlast high-tech fabric, which is designed to keep your feet cool when it's hot and warm when it's cold for all-day comfort. *Roadgear*

TIP

Perhaps the best all-around solution no matter which type of riding gear you buy (whether leather, breathable textile, or waterproof textile) is to wear a rain suit over it. Not only will it keep you dry under any foreseeable circumstance, but it will also protect your riding gear from wetness and filthy road spray. Yes, it costs extra and we have to struggle to get into it, but it offers the surest means of keeping us dry and keeping our riding suits relatively clean. Still, personally, when the weather is chancy I wear a breathable textile suit and wash it when necessary.

---

made of Gore-Tex, Hipora, Reissa, or other such fabrics. Other companies offer nylon glove and boot covers, which are often slippery and are yet another layer to get into. My main criticism of most rain suits is that they need greater adjustability in the cuffs for cinching around gloves.

Rain Suit or Textile Suit?

Textile suits are essentially high-fashion, rain-repellent shells with insulation, venting, and armor, and some utilize a weatherproof, breathable membrane. Should you get a rain suit for $30 to $300 or a textile suit for $250 to $1,000?

Obvious benefits of a rain suit are price and that it goes over your existing riding gear. If you think leather is cool and prefer wearing it, a rain suit will be your choice—end of story. The biggest argument in favor of water-resistant textile suits is that if you're already wearing waterproof boots and gloves, you don't even need to stop to get dressed when the rain begins—just keep riding. And perhaps that's the greatest benefit of all.

The drawback to textile suits is that many of them wear their waterproofing on the inside, so the outer fabric layer will absorb water and become soaked. While the inner liner may not become physically wet, the rider is essentially wearing a wet bag and feels damp and chilly. If the suit does not dry out overnight (it rarely will if its shell is soaked), it's really unpleasant to have to slip back into it in the morning.

Some textile suits are made with a waterproof outer shell so they don't become wet, but if the day warms up the rider feels trapped in a mobile sauna. Either type of suit will also likely become filthy with road spray. The best compromise is to have a suit with a high-tech breathable membrane.

MOTORCYCLE UNDERWEAR— NEXT OF SKIN

Undergarments create a buffer zone between your skin and outer garments. They offer not only a soft touch, but also allow that all-important airflow so you stay dryer and cooler in hot weather and warmer in the cold. Whatever you wear when you ride, what's next to your skin is your first line of defense against the elements—and your first means of increasing your comfort level.

One of the big topics in sports and motorcycling underwear these days is the high-tech fabrics that keep you warm in cool weather and cooler in the heat. How's that? According to the manufacturers, these fabrics form another layer in cool weather to hold in the heat, and in warm weather they wick away moisture to help sweat evaporate and keep you cool. By wearing such fabrics you won't have to pack as many items of clothing, and that's a major consideration in touring.

For starters, be sure the underwear has no seams in the seating area and that any padding is properly placed so that it does not create bulky additional seams and uneven folds. Underwear fabrics must be thin enough to fit snugly under other garments and eliminate bulk. Some such fabrics offer odor-neutralizing properties so you won't smell like a goat when you arrive at your destination.

One example of a "smart fabric" is "Outlast," which is designed to sense body temperature and adjust for comfort through a phase-change process, cooling when it's hot and warming when it's cool. The key to the fabric is "Thermocules," microscopic containers that encapsulate Phase Change Materials (PCMs) that as the temperature varies, change from solid to slush to liquid, storing or giving off heat as the case may be. No, of course it doesn't leak—it's encapsulated! This phase change capability acts as a thermostat for the material—and the wearer. Neat!

Another area in which great strides have been made is in single-purpose motorcycling socks. Make sure they're machine washable and dry quickly without shrinking. Depending upon their purpose, they may be made of Coolmax polyester, which wicks away moisture for hot weather and includes channels for air circulation. Or they may be well insulated with wool or synthetics for cold weather. Socks may include arch support with padding around the shins and toes, with flattened seams around the toes for comfort. Silver anti-bacterial and anti-fungal filaments are added to polyester fibers so feet stay fresher longer. Cushioned foot beds on the heel and ball of the foot lessen shock, and strategically placed guards shield the shins at the front, cushion the tendons at the back, and protect the toe area from gear-shifting stress at the top.

ELECTRIC CLOTHING
Hooking Up
Wouldn't you love to pull the electric blanket off your bed and wear it on your motorcycle? That's essentially what

you can do with electric clothing, starting with an electric vest or jacket liner. The difference between the two is that the jacket liner has sleeves. I recommend a lightly insulated electric garment, as it will help hold in the heat without being too bulky.

Electric garments hook into your bike's battery via an easily installed

When riding in chancy weather, underwear can be as important as outerwear. The Rev'It Shield shirt and Defense pants are fully breathable, sweat-wicking base layers made of micro PE. They have been anatomically pre-shaped for a better fit and are designed to keep you cool in the summer by removing the moisture from the skin. They will also keep you warm in the winter by adding an additional layer of protection. *Rev'It*

Baby, It's Cold Outside

What's the coldest you've ever been on a motorcycle? In my 45-plus years of riding I can recall riding my Vespa scooter in Michigan during a windy December day in 1965, grimacing and shuddering in a light jacket. And touring to the South Rim of the Grand Canyon one March evening in 1979 with snow beside the road; I hadn't realized that the rim was at an altitude of more than 7,000 feet! And riding over a high pass in California during a snowstorm in 1983 with my wife on the back, the snow packing around the headlight and powdering my shoulders as little icicles formed off the fairing. If you don't have your own stories, you will someday.

Insulated clothing works to trap the heat your body creates, but only an electric garment can actually add heat. This is the Widder electric vest, which has optional heated sleeves and a thermostat.

wiring harness and produce heat by passing a current through a series of wires of a specific resistance sewn into the garment. Installing a hookup for an electric garment is simplicity itself. The battery hookup has an eye at the end of each wire. Expose the battery connections and remove the negative battery screw first, then the positive. Place the screw through the eye and replace the positive cable first. The line with the fuse goes to the positive post. To prevent losing radio, clock, and other settings, keep the battery cables in contact with the posts as you add the harness hookup; the harness stays permanently attached to the bike.

Be very careful not to allow any tools touching the positive post to touch other metal, as that will cause a spark and could damage your bike's electrical system. Route the garment's hookup wires carefully with zip-ties so they are not abraded by removing and

installing the seat. Note the amperage of the fuse used and carry spares.

Big Twin Harleys offer a maximum charging output of more than 480 watts for Softails and Dynas, while the touring models offer 650 watts. Sportsters generate more than 250 watts, and V-Rods more than 490. Except for the Sportsters, any of these bikes with a well-maintained battery and no obvious charging problems should easily be able to handle the 50- to 100-watt draw of one electric torso garment, or perhaps two.

Add electric gloves and pants, and the draw for a solo rider can exceed 160 watts. Too high a draw will likely blow the fuse on the garment's battery hookup and could potentially damage the bike's electrical system. However, the fuse should protect the system by blowing first.

For a two-up couple, I would not recommend wearing more than two electric torso garments, as much more in terms of heated gloves and pants could draw too much power from your bike. Running your electrical system dry dead ends your heat and your ride.

Because these garments hook directly to the battery, they will draw electricity even with the ignition turned off. This means that when you're fueling up and standing beside the bike, you should be able to stay warm; just don't stay hooked up for more than a few minutes with the engine off, as this will soon draw down the battery. When you're ready to ride again, turn off the electrical garments or unplug them before starting the bike, so as not to overload the battery.

It's highly unlikely an electric garment will hurt you, as the inline fuse should blow if there is a problem.

How to Wear Electric Garments

Torso garments generate a lot of heat, are often insulated, and are designed

TIP

To check if your bike can handle the added electrical draw, with the key off and garments unplugged, connect a voltmeter to the battery posts. It should give a reading of around 12.5 to 13 volts. Now start the engine, plug in a garment, and rev the bike to its usual rpm at highway speeds as you take a second reading. If this second reading is higher than the first, there should be no problem. Now plug in any additional garments, one by one. If at any time the reading goes lower than the original, indicating that the system is discharging, end the experiment immediately and unplug the garments. Using all these products could blow the fuse or damage the electrical system. You should be able to use any garments up to that point when the battery began to discharge. Seek your dealer's advice.

If you're running electrical garments while on the road and your lights begin to dim or your bike begins to misfire and run erratically, immediately unplug the garments but do not shut off the engine. If the problems were caused by too great an electrical draw discharging the battery, you'll need to keep the bike running awhile to recharge it. Turn it off too soon and it may not have enough electrical power to restart the engine. One ray of hope: if this happens and the battery won't turn the engine over fast enough, turn off all electrical components and wait about 20 minutes, then try again. Often, with a short "rest," the battery will generate just enough power to start the engine. When you arrive home, check the battery fluid level, replenish as necessary with distilled water, and charge the battery.

Gerbing's offers a number of electric jackets and full electric suits. The benefit of an electric jacket rather than a vest or liner is that there's nothing extra to carry and put on or take off as the temperature changes.

I have ridden with electric garments for more than 25 years and have found that they are indispensable in cold weather.

to be worn over clothing. Nylon is not comfy against the skin, so wear these garments over a T-shirt and heavy cotton shirt to even out and distribute the heat, with a sweater over them to hold in the heat. Get the optional thermostat because the day warms and cools, and electric garments can become uncomfortably hot if they're run full blast all the time.

The key to keeping warm is to wear windproof clothing and to seal the openings. A heated garment will not be as effective if the wind is coming in around your collar or up your sleeves. The garment should fit snugly. When

the torso is warm, the body circulates warmer blood to the extremities, which will also remain warmer. For this reason, a torso warmer is the basic garment, followed by gloves, because hand controls are so crucial to motorcycle operation. Heated pants or socks would be a distant third choice. While I love heated hand grips, heated gloves are the best solution to hand comfort because they cover and heat the entire hand.

I have ridden with electric garments for more than 25 years and have found that they are indispensable in cold weather. They can make the difference between a comfortable ride

Boot Covers

Sometimes a rain suit will come with nylon overboots that have a drawstring at the top. Unfortunately, nylon is slippery, and these overboots may not be satisfactory for walking around or supporting the bike unless they have some additional type of rubberized sole material. If you don't go for all-out rain-proof boots, try rubber overshoes or something like them.

Some companies, like Roadgear with its X Boots, take advantage of high-tech fabrics that sense body temperature and adjust for comfort. These utilize an Aerotex membrane that is waterproof, windproof, and breathable. Other features include taped seams and Dynatec reflective patches for increased nighttime visibility. *Roadgear*

Slip them off and take a good look at the sole. Does it seem to have enough grip?

leather, man-made fibers, or a combination of the two; here are some suggestions. In my experience there are generally two types of street boots: those that are very heavy and protective, and those that are very light and less protective. Racing boots are the exception, as they're both very light and protective, but often so very highly styled you'll not likely wear them on your Electra Glide.

Look for a shift pad atop the left boot so it won't wear through, plus stiff shin and toe guards, and some protection on the ankles, such as an extra layer of material or perhaps even a gel pad. Boots will be either side-opening or back-opening, and I've generally found the former to be easiest to enter. Look for a high-quality zipper with a flap that seals well, and the boots should be high enough that your pant legs will overlap them to keep out the breeze. It's important the boot grip your ankle snugly so your foot does not slop around inside when walking and lead to blisters.

It's a plus if boots incorporate breathable liners, made of Gore-Tex or similar material, that render them water

and a miserable one, and they are also very handy for eliminating that damp chill of rainy weather.

While torso garments go on quickly and easily, getting into vest/pant/glove combinations takes some time. Heated pants will go on over jeans, but some are not intended as outer garments.

BOOTS

Styles of boots include touring, biker, cold/wet-weather, roadrace, and others in between. They may be made of

What should you look for in a rain glove? The H2O-Tec from Roadgear features a nylon shell with a Hipora membrane liner that breathes, thanks to its micro-porous nature. For crash protection, the palm area is constructed of cowhide. *Roadgear*

Gloves Are Good, Gloves Are Great

To protect, a glove must stay on your hand if you go down. That's why some gloves incorporate a gauntlet and strap that wraps around the wrist and secures with a hook-and-loop fastener. Many gloves add protection with an additional layer of leather or other protective material on the palms, the backs, and along the fingers. Some use closed-cell foam; others use high-tech materials (such as hard carbon fiber forms) over the knuckles. Of course, most Harley riders tend to prefer gloves with more basic style.

TIP

Nylon rain mitts are sometimes part of a standard glove; they fold away out of sight till needed. Sometimes, these mitts are sold separately. These impervious mitts will keep you dry, but wet nylon will be slippery on the controls. Gloves with inner membranes may leave your hands encased in a cold, wet layer even if the liner itself remains dry. An alternative is extra-large, dish-washing gloves that will fit over your own gloves and will be less slippery on the controls. For footwear, the ever-popular Totes really can't be beat.

and wind resistant. Reflective material on the backs and sides provide added visibility, and look for nonslip rubber soles that hold the road (and the pegs) well. Slip them off and take a good look at the sole. This is what is going to save you from going over on that wet day when you come to a stop and put your foot down in an oil spot on the road. Does it seem to have enough grip?

GLOVES

There was a time when gloves were gloves. The gloves you wore in the winter to shovel snow were the ones you wore on your motorcycle, or to drive your car. They were just gloves.

Then bang, baseball players began wearing lightweight batting gloves. Sports car drivers wore ventilated gloves with leather palms. Bull riders wore gloves to help them grip the rope in rodeos. Today there are specialized gloves for snowboarding, skiing, kayaking. Heck, my kids even wear gloves to skateboard! Things were simpler when there were just gloves.

Simpler, but not better. Today, motorcycle gloves have become very specialized. Each attempts to address and balance several types of basic and specialized needs. The central purpose of every pair of gloves is to protect your hands from weather and bug hits, and from the road, should you go down. Along with that, they try to offer reasonable comfort, weather protection, and style.

Types of Gloves

Motorcycle street gloves generally fall into several categories, with some overlap. The well-dressed rider who travels a lot will need at least four styles: summer, three-season, winter, and rain.

Summer: To dispel heat, summer gloves are often perforated. The trick is for the holes to be large enough to shed heat, but small enough that they do not overly compromise protection or allow the rider to suffer sunburn. I do not recommend the fingerless variety or those with large open, unprotected areas because of their lack of protection from the sun and the road.

The central purpose of every pair of gloves is to protect your hands from weather and bug hits, and from the road, should you go down.

Cortech's Accelerator sport glove features a molded carbon fiber knuckle panel, a breathable, washable stretch leather palm, and gel patches on the thumb and palm. The perforated, top-grain, drum-dyed leather upper provides breathable durability.

Tour Master's Winter Elite glove features water-resistant goat skin and sheep skin leather, Thinsulate insulation, a waterproof and breathable barrier, as well as a precurved palm and fingers. *Tour Master*

Most Harley-Davidson riders like things simple, basic, and with heritage.

Three-Season: These are good, all-around gloves that offer dexterity, weather protection, and style. Because they're designed to be worn for long distances and for days at a time through a variety of weather conditions, they tend to offer a long gauntlet, some insulation, and basic protection features, such as added layers in the palms.

Winter: These are the most heavily insulated, but on the backs rather than the palms. Insulation on the palms is largely useless and will bunch up on the grips, which is one reason we no longer wear our old snow-shoveling gloves for riding. Wind-proof fabric will keep them warmer. Look for long gauntlets and high-tech insulation that's not bulky, as thick fingers can interfere with clutch, brake, or throttle operation.

Rain: As with outerwear, rain-proof gloves tend to offer either an impervious nylon shell that won't pass moisture in either direction and will become clammy, or a high-tech, breathable membrane that

will make them quite expensive. If you can afford it, I suggest going with the latter. These membranes can eventually wear out and tear, and their pores can clog, so to extend their life I suggest saving them for when it's actually raining.

Racing: The most protection for your dollar comes from racing gloves; they literally have armor on their armor. While keeping your hands intact is their main function, they're surprisingly comfortable. This makes sense: the last thing a racer needs is a distraction, and gloves that interfere with using the clutch, throttle, brake, and other controls aren't just distracting, they're dangerous. As with racing boots, they tend to be highly stylized. For that reason, we recommend the black version for Harley riding.

Sport: Only one step (if at all) removed from racing gloves, they are often highly styled, colorful, and heavily armored. Protection comes from closed-cell foam, carbon fiber, or other formed armor pieces, and from high-tech fabrics

Okay, most people don't like needles or the permanence of tattoos. If that's the case for you, try out a press-on tattoo!

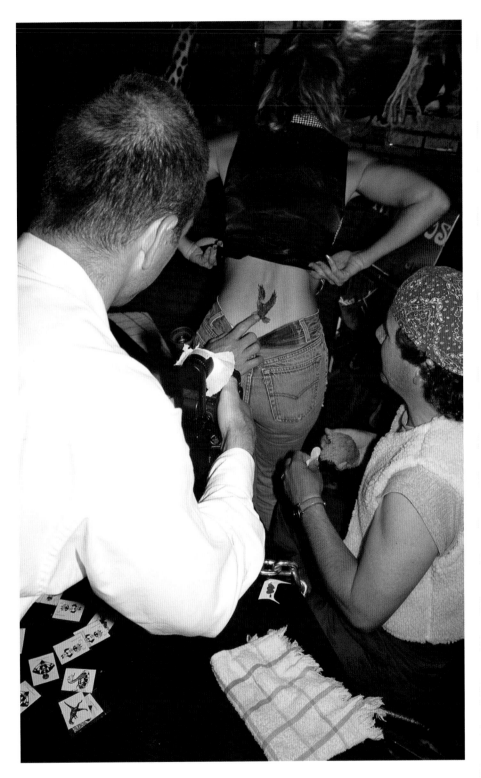

Fit

European gloves generally have a European fit, which to us Yanks usually means that they tend to run small for their listed size. I suggest that if you're trying on gloves made in Europe, go up one size from the standard American XS to XXL sizing. This is especially important when ordering gloves with hard carbon fiber or other protection, as it will not stretch as much as other gloves.

like Kevlar, Keprotec, and others. They focus on lightness, dexterity, and protection, rarely are insulated, and are often quite comfortable.

Traditional: Most Harley-Davidson riders like things simple, basic, and with heritage. That means their gloves are often made of plain, black cowhide or deerskin leather, without any of the fancy features or additional protection, other than perhaps an extra layer of leather, or a few rows of chrome studs, on the palm. Still, if you want that extra protection and style, consider one of the less flashy versions of sport or racing gloves.

HELMETS

Chapter 5

HERE WE WILL COVER:

- **Factors to Consider**
- **Helmet Types**
- **Safety Standards**

How far have helmets come in the last 40 years? I actually wore this thing with its minimal EPS foam layer in the mid-1960s. Today, bicycle helmets carry much thicker foam protection.

Over the years, helmets have become the politics and religion of motorcycling.

HEAD CASES

Over the years, helmets have become the politics and religion of motorcycling, the controversial subject one may not wish to mention when riding in polite company. They have been passionately defended on one side by those who credit them with saving lives, and passionately derided on the other by those who see them as a sinister intrusion on their freedom at best, and as a hazard at worst.

Whatever your position on helmets, you may wish to consider a statement by Harry Hurt, the researcher who studied motorcycle accidents back in the 1970s and whose "Hurt Report" has been a definitive source of information on motorcycle accidents for more than 25 years. Mr. Hurt once told me that if a rider did not wear a helmet, he was easy to kill. All you had to do was knock him off his bike at speed and have him hit his head. However, a helmeted rider had a much better chance of survival.

Frankly if big, strong guys such as football players, baseball batters, construction workers, and others accept the need to wear protective headgear, and they all deal with much lower forces than those involved in motorcycle accidents, well, there must be something to it. I am not trying to tell adults how to dress; you can decide that for yourself. However, I do want to present the facts and give you something to think about.

Let me tell you a story. Just after I completed my previous book, *Streetbikes: Everything You Need to Know*, I had the occasion to go riding in the dirt. Because I value my safety, I was wearing boots, gloves, leather pants, an armored jacket, and a full-face helmet. While I was riding downhill in second gear and turning to the left around a tree, the front tire suddenly began to slide. As a street rider my reaction was all wrong—I grabbed the front brake to stabilize the bike. The front wheel immediately caught, stood the bike up, and threw me off on the high side—in this case to the right.

As I was flying through the air head first, I knew two things: my riding day was over, and I was going to get hurt. I also fully expected to be knocked out. I landed hard on my head and right shoulder and lay there in a heap, fully conscious. In moments, other riders were carefully helping me into a sitting position and, with permission, carefully removing my helmet. The result of the get-off was a broken collarbone and many days of soreness. However, the only thing that did not hurt then or thereafter was my head, even though my helmet suffered a series of streaks and shallow gouges from the gravel where I'd landed. Had I not been wearing a helmet, I am certain I would have suffered serious head injuries. With it, I did not have so much as a headache. Several days later I had surgery and, with the help of a titanium plate and nine screws securing my collarbone, was riding a motorcycle again in five weeks.

NOISE CONTROL

A less noisy ride is a more relaxing ride, and helmets are much quieter today than they were some years ago. The manufacturers have come to under-stand that noise control (or quietness) is a selling point, and that wind noise is principally generated from two areas.

One is the front opening of an open-face helmet or the bottom opening under a full-face helmet; that's why the comfort liners of some full-face helmets now protrude quite a distance inward from the bottom edge of the

shell. You may have to push your head through it, as the fit is often quite snug along the bottom. Some full-face helmets even have a chin curtain in the front of the chinbar to seal them better. All this is in the interest of preventing the wind blast from noisily stealing up from below.

The second source of noise is protrusions from the helmet, which is why many manufacturers have done away with the side plates over the shield pivot area. They now utilize flat shields that place their pivoting mechanisms on the inside. Protruding vents can also generate noise, and helmet makers are doing all sorts of interesting things with shell shapes in the interest of styling, aerodynamics, and noise control.

PRICE

There was a time when you could look at a helmet on the shelf and easily tell the high-priced, full-face hat from the cheapo unit—it was in their shape, paint, and graphics, in the look of their shield, and in their venting. Today, helmets are better than ever. Graphics and comfort liners on even the least expensive name-brand helmets are of very good quality. Quality differences between high-dollar and inexpensive helmets are now mostly in the area of the fit and feel of the interior liner, the fit (but not necessarily the function) of the venting controls, and graphics and other fit-and-finish issues. My biggest complaint is that many helmets still do not have very good ventilation systems.

A major price factor is the helmet's place of manufacture. Most helmet production has moved overseas since the 1990s, and few, if any, helmets are still manufactured in the United States. Many of the less-expensive lids are now manufactured in Korea, Taiwan, and mainland China, while the high-priced spreads tend to come from Japan and Europe, where labor costs are higher.

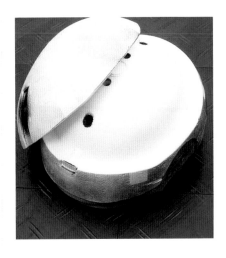

Here's a typical EPS foam liner from a contemporary helmet. It's more than an inch thick and features air channels for ventilation.

There was a time when you could look at a helmet on the shelf and easily tell the high-priced, full-face hat from the cheapo unit. Today, helmets are better than ever. A major price factor is the helmet's place of manufacture.

How Helmets Work

A helmet consists of an interior comfort liner, a layer of closed-cell expanded polystyrene (EPS) foam, and an outer shell. The shell is made of layers of plastic, fiberglass, or various composite fibers that are designed to spread the impact over a wide area, to resist penetration, and to prevent the EPS from shredding. The shell is also a major component in styling.

The EPS foam liner, which is about an inch thick and made to precise specifications, resides between the shell and comfort liner. It's a more high-tech version of the foam that's used in drink cups. The EPS foam is designed to crush at a controlled rate upon impact, absorbing and dispersing the energy that otherwise would have been fed directly into the rider's cranium.

Because the liner is designed to crush, it is very possible that even when an accident-involved helmet exhibits no outward sign of damage, the EPS inside may be crushed flat—used up. That's why it's important that any accident-involved helmet either be discarde or disassembled and inspected by an expert before it is worn again.

A helmet also requires a good retention system. Be certain your helmet is fully and snugly strapped on every time you ride, whether it utilizes the conventional D-rings or some buckle arrangement. Try this: Buckle your helmet securely, and then shake your head as if you were emphatically saying "NO!" If the helmet moves independently, it's too large and not the helmet for you. Try the next smaller size.

Now press your chin to your chest, grab the back of the helmet with your thumbs and try to slide it off forward. If it comes off, try another helmet. A half-head or "beanie" helmet will often fail this test, and in an accident will undergo much greater forces than those you just applied to it.

When a dealer has a wall of helmets this extensive, you know you're likely to find whatever you need. This is the selection at Ventura Harley-Davidson/Buell.

TYPES OF HELMETS

Full-Face Helmets

This type of helmet is also called a "full coverage" because it completely covers the head and provides only an eyeport for an opening. It unquestionably provides the most protection of any helmet style, as it fully covers the face. Its flip-up face shield provides full protection from rain, insects, and other flying debris, but not from penetration.

The full-face helmet generally weighs from about 3.4 to 4.0 pounds but is lighter than the modular-style helmet, on which the entire front flips open. Because it fully covers the head, a full-face helmet should have effective, controllable venting for comfort in warm weather and to prevent fogging of the shield.

Prices cover a wide range, from less than $100 to more than $500; the differences include shell construction, graphics, the quality of the interior liner, safety standards met, and ventilation. While some full-face helmets are available in colorful racy graphics, they're usually also available in solid colors for more conservative riders. Some full-face helmet manufacturers utilize high-tech, lightweight materials, such as carbon fiber and Kevlar, to strengthen the shell and reduce weight. The total weight saving will be about 10 to 15 percent.

Finally, for improved frontal protection, I suggest that any full-face helmet also have expanded polystyrene (EPS) foam in the chinbar. It's the same foam that helmet liners are made from.

Earplugs

The wind that comes rattling around a windshield or helmet can vibrate your head. Some helmets are noisier than others, and an aftermarket exhaust can be loud and tiring. Earplugs give you the best of both worlds—a more relaxing ride and much better concentration. They're also darn handy when sharing a room with a buddy who snores like an unmuffled Harley.

Foam earplugs are available in most bike, sport, and gun stores for about a dollar a pair, or free if you go to a bar with loud music. One size fits all, which has advantages and disadvantages. Another drawback is that they work better on higher frequencies than lower ones. Some might find this aggravating.

Custom-fit earplugs are also available—see an audiologist. They cost about a hundred times more than foam plugs but fit and work much better, too. Plus, you can get different filters for them. If you just want to use them for motorcycling, or jack-hammering or running a chainsaw, you can get completely closed filters. If you play in a rock-and-roll band or go to loud concerts or do something else where you want some auditory distinction, you can specify filters that reduce sound by 5 to 25 decibels.

The beauty of these filters is that they reduce sound pressure equally across the frequency spectrum. This is referred to as "flat" and is much more pleasing, acoustically speaking. All the intricacies of the sound wave are retained; just the amplitude is reduced. Despite their high initial cost, most riders feel they're not only worth it, but a bargain. Besides, if you ride every day and use a new set of foam plugs every, say, three days (they can get pretty foul), you'll come out ahead before the end of the first year with these washable earplugs. Unless you lose them.

Modular Helmets

A modular helmet is a full-face on which the front part, the faceplate (not just the face shield, but the whole front of the helmet), has been fitted with a pivoting mechanism so it can be flipped up with the push of a button or lever. I use the terms *modular* and *flip-up* interchangeably. The flip-up feature allows you to enjoy a coffee without removing your helmet, cool off on a really hot day, shout to your buddy "I need gas," or walk into a store without scaring the bejeebers out of some poor clerk.

Flip-up helmets have some drawbacks, one of which is the weight added by the pivot, latch, and release mechanisms. When I tested 15 full-face helmets for *Rider* magazine in the April 2005 issue, they ranged in weight from 3.40 to 3.96 pounds. The eight modular helmets I tested for the October 2005 issue ranged in weight from 3.64 to 4.14 pounds. In short, the average modular helmet weighed about the same as the heaviest full-face, and on average the modular was about 2 ounces heavier than the full-face.

Granted, a 2-ounce difference is not much, but a companion consideration is that in order for them to clear the face and eyeglasses, the faceplate portion of modular helmets must protrude farther forward than on their single-function, full-face counterparts. Most flip-up helmets also have noticeably larger shells than full-face hats, and thus offer slightly more wind resistance, which translates as weight and fatigue to your neck.

For maximum safety, I suggest you keep the faceplate on a modular helmet closed while riding. Because they're designed to open, there is the potential that under some foreseeable impact, the faceplate of a modular helmet could open and expose your face to injury. For this reason, inspect any modular helmet you may be considering to verify that it utilizes a metal-to-metal locking mechanism. Also look for expanded polystyrene (EPS) foam in the chinbar.

Open-Face Helmets

An open-face (also called a "three-quarter") helmet comes down over the ears and the back of the head but is open at the front, fully exposing the

Nearly every helmet made today carries controllable vents to keep them pleasant in warmer weather. The scoop vents on this Arai helmet tend to generate significant airflow, enough to tousle the hair at highway speeds.

Flip-up helmets have some drawbacks, one of which is the weight added by the pivot, latch, and release mechanisms.

There is no question that a full-face helmet offers the best head protection in terms of coverage, and it's a luxury on a cold or rainy day. A well-designed ventilation system prevents it from becoming too confining. *Bell Powersports*

On a modular helmet, such as this Nolan, the front piece pivots upward so the rider can easily talk or sip a drink without having to remove the helmet. Eyeglass wearers benefit, as they do not have to remove their specs with this helmet style. *Nolan*

face. It's lighter and cooler than a full-face, and the wearer will need eye protection in the form of a shield, goggles, or at the very least, shatterproof sunglasses. As with the full-face, venting is a plus. The obvious disadvantage to open and half helmets is that your face is exposed to potential contact with objects like insects, rocks, branches, and, of course, the road.

Half Helmets

Very popular with Harley riders, the half helmet covers only the top of the head, yet is fully legal in the United States, so long as it passes the DOT minimum standard for impact absorption. It's the lightest and least expensive type of helmet, but it also offers the least protection. Under impact or a tumbling fall, it's possible for these helmets to roll off the head, exposing the rider to severe or fatal injuries. You will need eye protection, and in cold or rainy

weather, they'll be the least comfortable. Some come with a neck curtain that provides warmth and is removable for warmer weather.

HELMET SAFETY STANDARDS

Any helmet legally sold for motorcycle use in the United States must pass the U.S. Department of Transportation (DOT) minimum standard. The DOT specifies that examples of these helmets must have been tested in two controlled drops onto a flat surface from a minimum height of 72 inches at a minimum fall speed of 19.7 feet/second, and two controlled drops onto a hemi-spherical surface from a minimum height of 54.5 inches at a minimum fall speed of 17.1 feet/second, and passed no more than 400 g's—400 times the force of gravity—to an instrumented headform inside. That 400-g number was chosen because it was considered to be the maximum amount of force the

A Clear View

Nothing is more bothersome than having to peer through a scatter of bug carcasses as you ride. Carry a wash cloth and a little spray bottle of cleaner for your windshield/helmet shield/goggles/sunglasses. Commercial shield cleaner is available in bike shops, or you can make your own shield cleaner by mixing a 50/50 mix of ammonia and water in a spray bottle.

Which Standard Should Be Standard?

What about the real world? As we ride along, we pass by many rigid items, such as rocks, trees, and curbs (or in Britain, "kerbs"). We also pass by other less-rigid objects, such as cars, shrubbery, and mailboxes. We go by them at varying speeds. While one standard may result in a helmet that withstands impacts with rigid objects very well, it may not do as well against less rigid items. Another standard may result in a helmet that handles a single hit very well but would not withstand a second hit on the same spot very well. The mind reels.

To get some clarification I called on Dave Thom, a helmet expert who was associated with Dr. Harry Hurt and the latter's famous accident study in 1981. Thom now works for a company called Collision and Injury Dynamics in El Segundo, California. One of the conclusions of the Hurt study was that, despite what we may expect, in 90 percent of motorcycle accidents, the impact delivered to the head was less than the 400 g's allowed in the DOT test. After more than a quarter-century of involvement in accident research and helmet safety, Thom told me, "Performance can only be measured by the situation.

However, we know from the Hurt report that 90 percent of the impacts are at, or below, DOT impact severity. Therefore, it makes sense to lean toward performance in the expected region—although you can't ignore the other 10 percent completely." For that reason, Thom believes that a helmet meeting only the DOT standard is perfectly adequate for most accident situations.

Some critics suggest that helmets that pass Snell necessarily have to be heavier than those that pass ECE or BSI. I also interviewed Steve Johnson, general manager of the Snell Memorial Foundation in Sacramento, California. Johnson told me, "It depends. Some less-expensive helmets tend to be heavier, as they may not use state-of-the-art materials. Most are not excessively heavy. Some lightweight helmets cannot perform to our requirements, and their lightness may reduce their protective capabilities. We don't want helmets to be heavier or hotter for the wearer." In my own research for my helmet tests in *Rider* magazine in 2005, I found that of the four lightest helmets in the test, two met the ECE standard and two met Snell. All, of course, met DOT.

human brain could withstand without suffering significant damage. With that figure as the maximum, it is very possible that specific helmets may have passed along much less energy.

In the interest of making more protective helmets, a number of other standards that allow even less energy transfer have been advanced. The best known to American riders is the Snell Memorial Foundation standard, and we're now seeing helmets sold here in the states that meet the BSI (British standard) and ECE (European Community) standard. All of these standards, including DOT, are accepted internationally by the governing bodies that regulate motorcycle racing. Still, no matter what other standard it may also meet, any helmet sold in the U.S. must meet the DOT minimum standard.

Today, there is a good deal of controversy surrounding the applicability of the various standards. I will not attempt to dissect these standards to choose a "best" one, as there are simply too many variables involved. For example, the DOT standard allows for 400 g's of energy to reach the headform, and the Snell standard allows for 300 g's; therefore, one might conclude that the Snell was the superior standard. However, it's not that simple. The DOT standard specifies a dwell time for how long the helmet may pass along the higher g forces, while the Snell standard has no dwell time provision.

To pass the DOT standard, a helmet with lots of cushion designed into its EPS foam will perform better. To pass Snell, a helmet with a stronger shell and stiffer foam will perform better. In fact, numerous helmet manufacturers have told me it is difficult to make a helmet that will meet both standards because DOT was designed for a minimal impact, while Snell was designed for a maximum hit.

Today, there is a good deal of controversy surrounding the applicability of the various standards.

An open-face helmet is a good compromise between a full-face and a half-helmet. It provides much greater head protection than a half-helmet and is unlikely to come off in an impact. It still provides the feeling of freedom so many riders crave.

A half-helmet offers the wind-in-the face feeling that is so widely associated with the freedom of motorcycling. It's also lighter and usually less expensive than other types of helmets but is obviously the least protective.

Some helmet protection standards require they be smacked against flat anvils, some call for hemispherical anvils, and others for "kerbstone" anvils. It's apples, oranges, and kumquats.

When one begins reading about the various standards and their testing procedures, things become even murkier. Testing methods differ. Drop heights and the number of drops differ, as do energy inputs allowed, where the helmets were struck, and what they were dropped against. Some helmet protection standards require they be smacked against flat anvils, some call for hemispherical anvils, and others for "kerbstone" anvils. It's apples, oranges, and kumquats.

For those who wish to see the specifics of the major standards as summarized by Snell, they appear on the organization's website. See www.smf.org/articles/mcomp2.html.

I asked Snell Memorial Foundation General Manager Steve Johnson if it was true that more expensive helmets tended to pass fewer g's to the headform during Snell testing. Johnson answered, "Some less-expensive helmets perform very well. We have a pass/fail standard, so I cannot tell you who performs better. All helmets that pass Snell perform very well; 300 g's is fairly low, given what is accepted to be the threshold of brain injury or death. Some helmets perform better in flat-surface tests than in hemispherical—that's why we stay away from grading them. A thick, soft helmet performs well on a flat surface. Because they have to withstand impacts from two opposite anvil types, a flat and a hemispherical, they have to be built somewhere in the middle."

Is there any truth to the idea that heavier helmets lead to greater neck injuries?

"We know that weight is a factor, but we have no conclusive data or scientifically collected physical evidence that this is occurring. Everyone's head is different, and everyone's neck is different, and every accident is different. We have seen a recommended maximum helmet weight of 1,800 grams (3.94 pounds) or less in one study, but we haven't seen any additional corroborating support for that data. It is logical that lighter is better, but we don't know how light that is."

Johnson is skeptical of lighter helmets if they come at the cost of lowering current impact standards. "The push in the industry for less demanding standards would facilitate lighter helmets being produced, and it is our belief that many of these helmets will offer significantly less impact protection than the current products available." He conceded, however, that "some very light helmets do pass Snell."

Dave Thom is a helmet expert who was associated with Dr. Harry Hurt and the latter's famous accident study in 1981. Thom has spent more than 25 years in accident research and helmet safety. He offered the following opinion of the various standards. "No study, including the Hurt study, has ever showed a benefit for helmets meeting any standard. . . . There are benefits to coverage, etc., but not based on what standard they meet. I personally am completely comfortable wearing a DOT-only helmet—or a DOT/ECE—and slightly less comfortable with a DOT/Snell helmet." As for his conclusion, Thom recommends, "Wear a full-face helmet with lots of styrofoam in the chinbar."

Regarding whether any standard is superior, I'll fall back upon a famous statement by a helmet manufacturer: "You tell me the impact you're going to have, and I'll build you a helmet that will protect you from it."

In conclusion, with the many variables of speed, what you may hit and at what angle, and how the various standards do or do not relate to the real world, I'll say this: Wear a good full-face helmet that passes at least DOT and has foam in the chinbar. Wear one you can afford, one that's comfortable, and, most importantly, one that you'll want to wear every time you ride. That's the best helmet for you.

OTHER CONSIDERATIONS

Most helmets have some form of controllable ventilation that allows airflow in warm weather. Often it is in the form of controls in the chinbar and above the eyeport that slide to open passages through the helmet's EPS foam; sometimes there is a controllable exhaust vent in the rear. Often this venting system is not very effective. Be certain the vents have positive closure and that they're easy to work while wearing gloves. Keep in mind that vents only work in airflow, so if you ride behind a big windshield or fairing, they will be less effective.

Some full-face helmets have a chin curtain (a flexible nylon sheeting spread across the underside of the chin area) designed to prevent the noisy (and possibly cold) wind blast from coming up from below. Some also have removable, washable liners in various sizes for easy cleaning and exact sizing.

While a particular helmet may be available in sizes XS, S, M, L, XL, and XXL, it may cover these various sizes with only two or three shell sizes. The rest of the sizing is done internally, by fitting different sizes of padding into those shells. If the helmet you like doesn't fit quite right, ask the salesperson if there are additional pads available for custom sizing.

The Snell/DOT sticker tells you that examples of this helmet have passed the standards set by the United States Department of Transportation (DOT) and the Snell Memorial Foundation. Other good standards I would trust with my head include the British Standards Institution (BSI) and the Ecnomic Commission for Europe (ECE) standards.

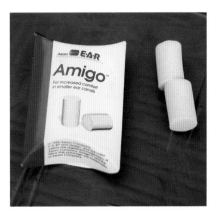

Wind noise and loud pipes can not only be fatiguing, they can also damage hearing. Foam earplugs are inexpensive and easy to wear, and one size fits all.

Keep the Lid On

While most helmets utilize conventional D-rings to secure the strap, some utilize seatbelt-style or other types of buckles or latches. These may be easier to latch and release (often with the push of a button), but their mechanism is bulkier and may be harder to fit into your helmet holder. Or the helmet may be easier to steal if the buckle unlatches with the push of a button.

Chapter 6

MOTORCYCLE TOURING
STRATEGIES FOR TRAVELING AND WHAT TO TAKE

HERE WE WILL COVER:

- **Touring Defined**

- **Touring Accessories**

- **What to Take Along**

When Wayne Willcuts and his buddies Earl and Norm all bought new Electra Glides in 1967, they picked them up in Milwaukee and took three weeks to ride around the country before returning to California. This was their campsite in North Carolina. *Wayne Willcuts*

WHAT IS TOURING?

My definition of touring is travel by motorcycle, and I define travel as being a trip involving at least one overnight stay. Go off on a weekend ride and, in my book, you're touring. Putting that overnight stipulation into the mix means you've got to pack some luggage and be ready for the vagaries of weather, and that's what separates a tour from an ambitious day trip. Add to this the possibility of touring for weeks or even months at a time, and you've got yourself something that's going to require some serious planning.

Just for the record, my most ambitious trip in terms of distance was across the United States from California to Virginia and back. I initially rode to Missouri, where I had a three-week project to complete, then my wife flew out and joined me. We continued on to Virginia for a friend's wedding, rode to Michigan to visit my family, and then went home via the direct route to California. I was on the road for about six weeks, traveling half the time.

A couple years later my wife and I spent six weeks in Europe on a motorcycle. We lived out of two saddlebags and a tank bag for the entire time and did a lot of laundry in hotel rooms. Starting in Germany, we journeyed all over the Alps until we reached Yugoslavia in the south, headed north to the Netherlands, then spent a few days in Berlin. It was the most enjoyable six weeks of our lives.

Finally, I've written three books on the subject of motorcycle touring, but they're all currently out of print. We'll have to make do with condensing some of that information into this chapter.

CAMPING BY MOTORCYCLE

Motorcycle camping has a lot in common with backpacking. In both activities the main concerns are weight and packing space. At least motorcyclists have the upper hand—we don't have to carry the weight on our backs!

Camping styles are quite personal, and you'll learn a lot more about camping or backpacking in books about those specific activities than you will here, but let's cover the basics of camping while motorcycling.

As you know, the problem is that carrying a passenger by motorcycle not only nearly doubles your luggage needs, but also takes up the valuable bit of cargo space on the rear portion of the seat. For that reason, riding two-up makes camping more difficult. I have done it, but found that it really puts a strain on your ability to pack and carry things. You'll still only need one tent if it's a two-person or larger, but what you have to carry in terms of sleeping bags, pads, and clothing will double.

Camp cooking requires a lot of packing space for cooking gear and food, so to compensate for the additional luggage needs of a passenger I have found it necessary to do away with any attempt to cook meals in camp. You may have found a way to cook in camp for two, but we eat in restaurants when packing double.

If you're riding solo, I suggest using the rear portion of the seat for a large nylon bag that will accommodate the tent, sleeping bag, pad, and camp chair. If the bag is not waterproof, line it with a sturdy waterproof liner bag. When packing double, those items will either have to fit in the TourPak trunk or on the luggage rack. The advantage of the trunk is that it's lockable and weather-tight, but it's also heavy and locates much of the weight behind the rear axle. For that reason, pack only lighter,

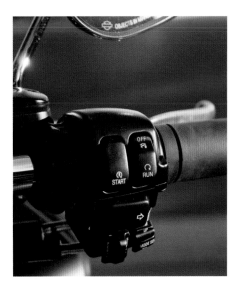

Below the standard switch gear is the electronic cruise control. These switches include "Resume," "Set," and up/down speed controls.

less dense items, such as sleeping bags and air mats, in the trunk.

CRUISE CONTROL

The cruise control is an electro-mechanical device built into some Harley models (such as the Electra Glides, Road Glides, and Road Kings) that allows the motorcycle to maintain whatever speed the rider chooses. It lets you relax on long stretches of road and move your right hand away from the throttle. After the cruise control is turned on, it can be set by pushing a button when the desired speed is reached. Additional controls, such as coast and accelerate, allow the rider to fine-tune the speed. The bike will maintain the set speed, regardless of hills or wind conditions. The cruise control can be overridden when the rider taps either brake, pulls in the clutch, or operates the throttle.

TOURING STRATEGIES
ORGANIZED TOURS

We all have our dream rides, and one of my dreams was to ride the Alps. However, such a trip was daunting in

Throttle Lock

Don't confuse a true cruise control with a throttle lock, which is often incorrectly referred to as the former. A throttle lock is a mechanical device that screws into the end of the throttle or up from below the throttle grip. It introduces sufficient drag to overcome the return spring, so the throttle will no longer rotate closed when the rider removes his hand from the grip.

The throttle lock is basically a poor man's cruise control, as it will maintain the throttle setting, but will not compensate for hills or headwinds, so speed will vary. Furthermore, it is essential that the rider dial in only enough friction to barely overcome the return spring. For safety, the rider must be able to overpower the throttle lock easily.

A throttle lock is a mechanical device that holds the throttle in one position. The rider must be able to override it easily to accelerate or slow down.

The Electra Glide is one very enjoyable and capable luxury tourer. *Scott Hirko*

Touring can take you places you've always wanted to go, like Monument Valley. *Eaglerider*

terms of shipping a bike over, dealing with several currencies and languages, and knowing where to stay and what to see. Thanks to organized motorcycle tours, I have not only ridden the Alps, but also Calabria in Southern Italy and the Isle of Man.

Tour companies can set you up with a bike, accommodations, an itinerary, and a group of like-minded souls with whom to ride. They carry your luggage in a chase van, so your bike is relatively unburdened during your ride.

Organized tours last from a few days to several weeks and are often the best way to explore an area that you probably would never have visited on your own. Then, once you've taken a tour or two, you're much better able to make arrangements for staying a little longer after the tour and returning on your own, if you wish. That is, unless you're too spoiled and just want to keep riding with tour groups. Most organized tours tend to provide locally sourced bikes, so you're likely to be riding a European bike in the Alps, though some companies do offer Harleys. On organized tours of the United States, Harleys are usually readily available.

On an organized tour, the day usually begins with the group meeting at breakfast. Members will be asked to

have their luggage outside their rooms after breakfast. The luggage-van driver will haul the bags to the next hotel by the most direct route while the riders go out to play. There is usually a recommended route, with an alternate route or two, about which the tour leader would have provided information the previous evening at the dinner meeting.

For the day, riders are welcome to go with the tour leader or simply ride on their own. As the tour progresses, riders usually gravitate to their own smaller groups. A day's ride in the Alps is only going to cover about 100 to 150 miles because of the slow, twisting nature of the roads, while a tour in the American West may cover 200 to 300 miles a day. Although breakfasts and most dinners will likely be included in the tour price, lunches are often on your own. The only rule for the day is be at the hotel in time for dinner or call the tour leader so he'll know where you are.

BIKE RENTALS

Several companies, including Eaglerider, Harley-Davidson, and others, rent motorcycles to the public. If you have questions about renting from H-D, check with your local dealer or the H-D website. While there are too many considerations to elaborate upon in this book, and policies change all the time, here are some basics. These companies will usually rent you a motorcycle for a specific time frame. You will usually have to be at least 21 years of age and show a valid motorcycle operator's license in order to rent, but some companies put the minimum age at 25. They would prefer that you have some years of riding experience.

If you're not familiar with Harley-Davidsons and wish to rent one, keep in mind that these are big, heavy machines and you may wish to sit on a few at your dealership to determine if you can handle the weight—particularly if you plan to carry a passenger and luggage. To be certain, rent a Harley for a few hours before committing to one on an organized tour far from home. As motorcycles go, Harley-Davidsons are not particularly difficult to ride and aren't intimidating at all, other than their size and weight.

You will likely pay about $100 to $200 per day for your Harley rental, depending upon model, condition, and which company you utilize, in addition to a hefty damage deposit that could be $2,000 to $3,000. Check with your credit card company beforehand to be certain you have enough balance left to cover this expense. When you sign the contract, be very sure what exactly constitutes damage. I have heard of renters being charged damage expenses for such things as stone chips to the paint, which most of us would consider to be part of normal wear and tear. The tour company may wish to sell you additional coverage, or add a surcharge if you are below their minimum age or have questionable riding credentials. The rental bikes will often have such amenities as a windshield or fairing, saddlebags, and backrests.

You may return the bike to the same location from which you rented it, or it may be possible to rent in (for example) San Francisco and drop the bike off a week later in Seattle, Las Vegas, or Denver. There may be an extra charge for doing so. There may also be restrictions regarding taking the bike on unpaved roads or out of the country. If you're renting in Europe, however, crossing national borders is usually quite easy.

If you do not have your own riding equipment, the rental company will usually rent you a helmet and other riding gear for an additional charge. Of course, showing up empty handed may be a red flag to the rental company that perhaps your riding experience is not as

---

TIP

There are tours of the Canadian Rockies, California, China, the Alps, Australia, Mexico, South America, and many other places. Tour companies are often quite flexible. If you wish to bring your own motorcycle, for example, you probably can. If you wish to rent one of their motorcycles to go your own route for a few weeks, you probably can.

Some people tend to look down their noses at such tours as being for those who aren't sufficiently adventuresome. But when faced with all the paperwork and challenges involved in taking a motorcycle to a foreign country, well, once I had taken an organized tour of the Alps and knew the drill, I was able to arrange for a motorcycle and go back there on my own with my wife several years later.

---

deep as they would like. You will be required to wear an approved helmet and other protective riding gear at all times, regardless of what local laws stipulate, and you will be asked to sign a contract and waiver that is approximately as long as this book. Insurance is usually included in the price of the rental, though optional coverage may be available at extra cost.

The rental agent will give you a full orientation when you pick up the bike that will explain all its features and needs. You will be asked to run a specific grade of gasoline in the bike and be shown how to check the oil level and tire pressure, but the bike should not require any actual maintenance during your ride. You will be given a toll-free number to call should you have any problems or questions.

LUGGAGE

Touring demands luggage capacity, and there are several types of luggage.

Hard Saddlebags: Hard luggage is usually made of fiberglass or hard plastic, and it offers the advantage of better protection, both in terms of keeping out the weather and in preventing theft; it is standard on Harley-Davidson touring models such as the Electra Glide, Road Glide, and

Part of the fun of touring is just stopping anywhere you wish along the ride to breathe the air and smell the flowers. *Buzz Buzzelli*

Tour companies can set you up with a bike, accommodations, an itinerary, and a group of like-minded souls with whom to ride.

A motorcycle allows you to travel places that may not be accessible to mere mortals who travel by four-wheeler. In any case, the touring rider will likely enjoy those places more. *Eaglerider*

Camping not only saves money, but opens the way to much more fulfilling adventures. Pack some fresh grub each day for the morning and evening meals.

Road King. Check with your Harley dealer for luggage availability for your bike. The aftermarket also offers hard luggage, some made of leather or with the appearance of leather.

Be sure to follow the loading recommendations provided by the manufacturer, and don't overload the bags. Be aware that hard bags may limit access to your bike's rear suspension adjusters and rear tire.

Hard saddlebags are usually lockable and generally weather-tight. They're usually color-matched to the bike and quite capacious. This makes them the best choice for hauling a lot of baggage and supplies. Disadvantages are the original purchase price and their weight. With simple hand tools you can remove them for when you're not touring.

A variant of hard bags are leather saddlebags or bags covered in leather or a comparable synthetic. Leather bags have great style and look classy, but require some care, just like a leather jacket. They are not usually lockable, but fasten with buckles. In recent years, Harley-Davidson has simplified the process of accessing some of its leather bags by hiding snap-fit nylon clasps behind the traditional buckles.

Soft: An alternative, or supplement, to hard luggage is soft luggage bags, usually made of Cordura nylon, pack cloth, or similar fabrics. Tank and tail (or "seat") bags can be used in conjunction with hard or soft saddlebags. Soft saddlebags are ideal for smaller bikes, like Sportsters, if you don't want to spring for the hard bags available in the Harley Parts & Accessories catalog. Stiffeners allow them to hold their shape even when empty, and they're usually available in black with a variety of trim colors, including red, blue, gray, and others. Some companies offer the entire bag

in those trim colors. While some riders may think it would be cool to have soft luggage in yellow, blue, or gray, those colors tend to show dirt more than black.

Installation is simple. Place the bags over the back portion of the seat, loop their front straps around the passenger footpegs and the rears around the turn signals, buckle and adjust them, and you're in business. In some cases, it's possible to remove the seat and place the bag straps over the rear fender to secure them and then bolt the seat back in place. Be very careful to keep them off the exhaust pipes, as hot pipes can melt the nylon. Several companies offer bag support brackets (such as H-D, Khrome Werks, and Drag Specialties) that will prevent the luggage from getting entangled in the rear wheel.

The advantages of soft luggage include its decorative style, lightness, and ease of installation. Reach your destination, unbuckle these bags, and carry them off. They're also significantly less expensive than hard saddlebags.

Disadvantages include the fact that others can just as easily remove them or steal from them if they're placed over the seat. Because the stitches leave holes in the fabric, a rain cover is necessary to protect their contents—you may also wish to use seam sealer on them or simply pack your belongings in heavy plastic bags before placing them inside. Tank bags and soft saddlebags that rest on painted surfaces can scuff those surfaces over time. Be certain to keep the painted surfaces clean and free of dust, and wax them frequently. Attach the bags tightly so they don't wiggle and rub the bike.

Expandable soft luggage has an expansion panel sewn into the body. This panel is folded away behind a zipper when the bag is lightly loaded.

If your bike is not equipped with saddlebags, and you tend to travel light, soft nylon bags such as these by Cortech are easy to install, lightweight, and relatively inexpensive. *Cortech*

These Slant Leather Saddlebags from Tour Master are more stylish than nylon. They hold a good deal and look more authentic on a Harley. *Tour Master*

TIP

If you expect to travel in rainy weather, buy the optional rain covers. They will not only keep the bags dry, but will also protect them from dirty road spray. Even with the covers, you may wish to pack the contents in sturdy plastic bags as added protection from the weather and to separate items.

When you need extra room, deploy the zipper and pull on the outer edge of the bag, allowing the panel (which usually adds about 3 or 4 inches) to come into play.

Tank Bags: A tank bag is usually a soft luggage bag (though some companies now offer hard-shell versions) that mounts to the bike's fuel tank by means of straps or magnets. They've never really caught on with Harley riders, and part of the reason could be that some bike models have a nacelle on the tank that would interfere with most tank bags. In any case, a tank bag is one of the most useful items you'll ever purchase for your motorcycle. A pad on the bottom protects the tank from being scuffed, and most come with a transparent map pouch on top. Because of the bag's location, you'll want to pack only soft items, as you could hit it with a very sensitive part of your anatomy in a frontal collision.

If you intend to utilize the map pouch, choose a bag with a pouch that's at least wide enough to display two folds of the map (about 8 inches), so you don't have to stop frequently to flip it over. Because maps can be hard to read while you're riding (and I do not recommend taking your eyes off the road), use a highlighter to mark your route so it's easy to find in a hurry. The safest way to utilize the map is to pull off the road and stop before you attempt to study it. And of course, never try to access the contents of the tank bag until you have pulled over to a safe area and stopped.

What's really great about magnetic tank bags is the ease of installation. Simply place it on your bike's steel fuel tank, and it should stick like glue. Many come with a quick-detach tether cord that can be looped over the handlebar and adjusted to hold the bag in place should the wind blast overcome the magnets. Because magnetic bags will pick up any stray metal upon which they're set, inspect the pad periodically. If you work in a metal machining shop, maybe you shouldn't use a magnetic tank bag.

Strap-on bags require one or more harnesses that may loop around the steering head, around a frame member, the rear of the tank under the seat, under the tank, or some combination.

The hard-sided Marsee magnetic tank bag is unique in that it holds its shape. Marsee even makes a Harley model with a tunnel in the bottom to accommodate the tank panel.

This barrel-shaped seat bag by Tour Master can hold a sleeping bag and lots of incidentals. If you're traveling two-up, mount it to the rack on your TourPak. *Tour Master*

A Jumbo Hauler by Roadgear provides additional luggage capacity, and it's available in a variety of colors. *Roadgear*

A set of saddlebags and stacking nylon sissybar bags will leave the rear portion of the seat open for a passenger, while enabling you to haul a great deal of luggage.

They require periodic adjusting and must be tightened securely, or their loose straps and pad could scuff the tank. When mounting such a harness around the steering neck, be certain it doesn't pinch any wires or cables, or interfere with the fork's ability to turn. When it's installed, turn the handlebar lock-to-lock in both directions to be certain the bag does not interfere with anything or contact the horn button.

Think of a tank bag as your bike's glove compartment. Carry in it items such as extra gloves, shield cleaning fluid and rags, a flashlight, maps, earplugs, first-aid kit, bungee cords, reading material, bottled water, snacks, etc.

Tail/Seat Bags: For the times you're not carrying a passenger, a tail bag that mounts to the rear portion of the seat can be very useful. Most are large enough to carry a full-face helmet or similarly sized object, and they often have additional pockets for smaller, more solid items you may not wish to carry in a tank bag, such as a tire repair kit or tools.

Seat bags mount with straps and buckles or shock cords, and they need to be attached firmly. While they won't likely scuff the seat, they can be disconcerting if they're wobbling around. On overnight or two-night trips when I've

wanted to travel light, I have often been able to fit my gear into just a tank bag and seat bag. As with any soft luggage, get the rain cover.

Duffels: In my early days of riding, back before high-quality hard and soft luggage was readily available, my standard luggage was an army-style duffel bag strapped to the back part of the seat, the luggage rack, or both. Though sturdy and capacious, the duffel was an ungainly bit of luggage, long and limp if not fully stuffed. Trying to dig something out of it on the road was difficult if I had failed to pack with an eye toward which items would likely be needed first. The canvas duffel is not waterproof, and therefore had to be covered or lined with plastic garbage bags.

Today, motorcycle-specific duffel bags are a huge improvement, with their strap mounting systems, rain covers or waterproof bodies, full-length zipper openings, and extra pockets. Just as a motorcycle is a tool for a job, so is any piece of luggage. What do you plan to carry in it? Does the bag need to be large enough to handle tent poles and a camp chair, or can it be something just a bit larger than a seat bag? Again, consider a rain cover. If the strap mounting system is too complex and time consuming, a pair of crossed bungee cords can be just as secure and less time consuming. If there is a handle on the bag, loop the bungee cord through the handle to keep the bag from sliding around or even off the seat. If you use bungee cords, keep a firm grip when securing and removing them. Many people have been struck in the face or eye with these cords, and they can do real damage.

Several companies now offer a wheeled airline-type bag for motorcycles that comes with a hook-and-loop wrap designed to fasten around a backrest or sissybar. They usually consist of a large main compartment with several smaller ones. When you reach your destination, lift the bag off the bike, set it on its wheels, deploy the retractable handle, and roll it away.

Day Packs: A day pack is much smaller than a backpack, has no frame, and does not protrude to the sides or above the head. It usually comes with a pair of padded shoulder straps and sometimes a waist strap. If you wish to use one, pack only soft objects and keep the weight reasonable. Holding yourself up on a motorcycle is hard enough. No need to add fifty more pounds to the equation.

Bungee Nets: For carrying a helmet or several loose objects on the back portion of the seat, a luggage net is a handy item. It is a loose-weave net made of several small shock cords that conform to the shape of the objects inside and attach under the seat or fender with a series of hooks. As with any piece of luggage, be certain it's firmly attached and that the items being carried cannot slip out through the gaps. It offers the option of slipping a jacket liner, chaps, or an entire jacket under it, as well as other items during your ride. You can also hook your gloves or sunglasses to it during gas stops so they won't slide off the seat. (Another good

place to rest your sunglasses is on the instruments, where you are sure to look as soon as you get back on the bike.)

PACKING BASICS

Mass Centralization: The next time you go grocery shopping, try this exercise. If you pick up a couple gallons of milk or six-packs of beer, place them in the front of the otherwise empty cart and go around a couple corners. Now place them at the rear of the cart and do the same. You'll find it's much easier to turn the cart when heavy objects are placed at the rear. The concept of mass centralization has to do with the fact that dense items located farther out from the center of mass will have more of an effect on stability than those packed in tight to the center; bikes turn more quickly if heavier components are kept in tight to the bike. For our purposes, it means to pack those denser, heavier items closer in to the bike, with lighter, less dense items to the outside. For example if you're traveling solo, the ideal location for your heaviest items would be either in the forward part of the saddlebags in toward the center of the bike or on the seat behind you—*not* in the trunk!

Luckily for Harley owners, the TourPak trunk is one of the best pieces

A cousin of the airline roller bag, Tour Master's Sissybar Roller Bag attaches to the sissybar. Off the bike, deploy the handle and roll it away.
Tour Master

> ### TIP
>
> A seat or duffel bag carried on the passenger portion of the seat can complicate rider mounting and dismounting, as you'll have to lift your leg over or around it. I suggest you deploy the sidestand as an extra prop whenever attempting this maneuver. It gets tougher with age . . . trust me.

> ### TIP
>
> It is imperative that tail, seat, and duffel bags be properly secured and checked frequently to make sure they don't come loose. A loose bag can slide off the side and be caught by the spinning rear wheel, which can jam it against the fender, lock the wheel, and throw the bike into a skid. It's not only possible but probable that this will cause you and your bike to go down, resulting in injury or even death.

The Harley-Davidson TourPak trunk is the finest piece of motorcycle luggage ever invented. It's sturdy and capacious, and it forms a comfortable backrest for the passenger. Because it opens from the side, the passenger does not have to dismount when the rider needs to access it.

of motorcycle luggage ever devised. It's large and roomy, and because it opens to the side, it's possible to access the contents without having to ask your passenger to dismount. Have you ever placed a heavy load in your TourPak and then noticed that your bike became harder to steer and wanted to run wide in turns? Look at your bike from the side, and note the location of the rear axle relative to the trunk. It's likely that the greater part of the trunk is located *behind* the axle. The weight placed in it will press down *behind* the rear axle and use it as a fulcrum point to lever the weight off the front wheel. That's why the bike wants to run wide in turns!

The solution is simple—centralize mass by placing heavy items forward in the saddlebags, between the axles, where they will have less effect on handling. Use the trunk for lighter, less dense items such as rain suits and sleeping bags.

THE TOURER'S PACKING LIST

My method of tour planning, which has worked for me for years, is to make a packing list on a legal pad for each trip; you may wish to keep your list on your computer. It is based on the list from an earlier trip that was similar. My categories include camping trips, motel trips, and trips to rallies or races. There are trips where I fly somewhere to pick up a bike and ride, and I even include lists from family vacations by plane or four-wheeler just to have a packing list for everything.

When it's time to plan the next trip, I pull out my most recent packing list from a similar trip and use it as a base on which to start the new list. I label each trip with its date and destination, and when the trip is over I add to the list anything I may have forgotten to bring. In this way the list always stays current, and important things are not forgotten.

Outer Wear
Helmet
Jacket
Boots
Riding pants
Hot-weather gloves
Cold-weather gloves
Sport gloves
Rain gloves
Rain suit
Rain boots

Inner Wear
Pants
Short-sleeved shirt
Long-sleeved shirt
Sweatshirt
Electric vest and
   thermostat
T-shirts
Underwear
Bathing suit
Hat
Shorts

Socks
Shoes

Bike Items
Earplugs
Shield cleaner and rag
First-aid kit
Jumper cables
Owner's manual
Multitool
Small toolkit
Tire gauge
Tire patch kit
Oil
Siphon hose
Map

Personal Items
Soap
Shampoo
Towel
Toothbrush and paste
Deodorant
Shaving equipment

Moisture lotion
Lip balm
Other personal
   hygiene items—ladies,
   you know what I'm
   talking about
Medications
Reading materials
Money
More money
Lots more money
Credit cards

Camping Items
Tent
Sleeping bag
Air mattress
Camp chair
Camera
Coffee cup
Flashlight
Water
Snacks

Make a List

Before every trip I make a list of what I'm going to take, bring all the items into the bedroom, and place them on the bed. As an item is brought in, I draw a single line \ beside it on the list. When it has actually been placed in the saddlebag liner or other luggage bag, I draw a second line / to complete the X. Once you can see everything laid out, you have a much better idea of how tightly you have to pack. It's also an effective way of packing in a motel room. When I'm ready to leave on my trip, I place the list in a file folder. When I return home from the trip, I pull out the list and add anything to it that I didn't take—but wish I had. Next time I travel, I make up my new list based on a previous list from a similar trip. If you really want to get obsessive about it, you can make separate lists for riding trips, fly-and-ride trips, camping trips, family car vacations, and the rest.

My film camera equipment consisted of two bodies and four lenses. When I used to carry it by motorcycle, I fitted the camera case with a large block of foam and cut out spaces for each component with an electric knife. In more than 25 years of floating in foam, my camera equipment never suffered a problem.

Here's a sample packing list for a motorcycle camping rally at which I would not cook in camp. Your list *will* vary!

WHAT GOES WHERE

Now that we've talked about a number of ways to carry luggage, here's a quick rundown of what sorts of items go where:

Jacket Pockets: Carry in them smaller items needed quickly, such as keys, change, earplugs, wallet, garage door remote, a small camera. Keep registration papers in your jacket, not on the bike. Should a thief steal your vehicle and be able to produce the registration papers, he may be able to convince a cop you loaned him the bike.

Fairing Pockets: If you have a Road Glide, use its fairing pockets to carry things that should be with the bike

A windshield, like this one from National Cycle, will help keep wind off the rider's torso. The wind deflectors will also route the wind past the rider's legs. *National Cycle*

The Road Glide fairing has hinged pockets that can hold a pair of gloves, snacks, or other incidentals.

Before each trip, write up a pack list based on that from a similar, previous trip. Here's an easy method for keeping track of your packing: As each item is located, mark it with a slash; when each is packed in the luggage, mark it with a backslash to form an X.

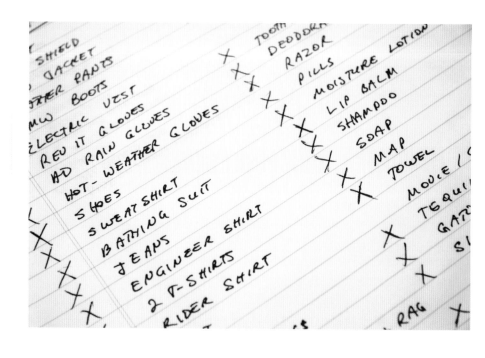

at all times. These include such items as a tire gauge, sunglasses, tire repair kit, multitool, duct tape, and electrical tape.

Day Pack: Light, soft, transitory items, including lunch, newspaper, spare sweater, computer discs.

Tank Bag: Larger, less bulky, soft items needed immediately such as maps, a flashlight, spare gloves, shield cleaner and rag, neck warmer, guidebook.

Small Seat Bag: Larger or bulkier items that would be oversized or inappropriate for a tank bag, such as tools, a helmet, heavy books, or manuals.

Duffel Bag on Seat: Use it for those big items that stick out to the sides, such as a tent, other camping gear, and a camp chair.

Saddlebags: Because they're low and tucked into the bike, this is the place for heavy, bulky items, such as tools and equipment. Of course, most of us carry clothing and toiletries here. In a pinch, light items such as sleeping bags can be strapped to the tops of the saddlebags if the proper anchors are added.

Trunk: Don't let the trunk's great capacity and big lid fool you; this is the

Essentials that you should carry on any tour include a toolkit, first-aid kit, tire repair kit, multi tool, and siphon hose. *Buzz Buzzelli*

Far Right:
The V-Rod isn't known for carrying a lot of luggage, but this accessory luggage rack from Harley-Davidson extends its luggage capacity greatly. It's simple to install and relatively inexpensive.

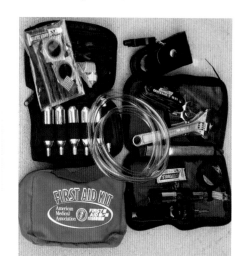

place only for light but bulky items such as sleeping bags, rain suits, and helmets. As explained earlier, heavy items in the trunk will cause the bike to turn more slowly by levering weight off the front wheel.

Luggage Rack: If your luggage rack does not carry a trunk, you can still use it for a seat bag or duffel bag. If it sits behind the rear axle, pack only light, bulky items, such as sleeping bags and rain suits.

Sissy Bar Bag: A whole lot more Harley riders carry sissy bar bags than tank bags, and it's a handy space for small luggage items.

Everything shown here—my tent, rain fly, sleeping bag, air mattress, and camp chair—fits into one large nylon bag that I carry on the rear portion of the seat.

A tire gauge is an indispensable part of your motorcycle gear. Check tire pressure daily on tour, as dropping tire pressure is an indication of a small puncture. *Roadgear*

Chapter 7

PERFORMANCE CONSIDERATIONS

GETTING MORE OF THE RIGHT KIND OF POWER FROM YOUR HARLEY

HERE WE WILL COVER:

- **Definition of Power**

- **Engine Performance Basics**

- **Suspension Performance Basics**

Riding a Harley is fun. Riding a Harley that makes more power than stock is more fun. Riding a Harley that hauls butt and shreds rear tires is the most fun of all. *Buzz Buzzelli*

Extracting torque and horsepower from your Harley is the subject of countless books, many of which go into the step-by-step, nuts-and-bolts procedures for doing so. One particularly good read is *How To Build a Harley-Davidson Torque Monster* from Motorbooks. My purpose here is to help you understand and define what you need, appreciate what is necessary to achieve it, then at the point when the wrenches come out, I'll sign off and hand you over to the experts in the field.

DEFINING PERFORMANCE

Performance is many things to many people. To some, it's just getting that little extra bit of power and sound quality from their Harleys to enhance the motorcycling experience. To many, it's being able to pull out and pass a car

while hearing that wonderful rumble as they do so, without having to shift down a gear. For dresser riders, it's being able to ride the Rockies or the Cascades or the Appalachians with a passenger and a full load of luggage, passing and climbing and pulling with confidence.

A few want to extract 100 or more horsepower from their engines so they can win the stoplight-to-stoplight derby. Or they want to go into the burnout pit or enter the dyno drag competition to impress their friends and others. That's cool, too, but really high-output machines create their own problems in terms of heat, noise, maintenance, reliability, and so forth. Not to mention rideability. My goal here is to consider how the average rider can get a more satisfying experience from his or her Harley and enjoy it more, without going to extremes. Your first task is to define what you want from your motorcycle in terms of performance.

Finally, I'll say a few words about the total package that includes not only enhanced engine power, but also the control features of enhanced suspension and braking that go with it. If your bike is going to produce significantly more power, and you're presumably going to ride it faster or harder, you'd better be able to control that machine with upgraded components.

WHAT IS POWER?

What do you really mean when you say you want your bike to make more "power"? Do you mean horsepower or torque? Or both? What are they?

Horsepower, according to my Webster's, is "1: the power that a horse exerts in pulling," and "2: a unit of power equal in the U.S. to 746 watts." Torque is "a turning or twisting force."

To understand the difference between the two, think in bicycle terms. Torque is that low-rpm pulling power when you're pedaling away from a stop. Your legs are pumping hard, your thigh muscles are working, and as you gain speed your legs are soon whirling so fast they're putting out lots of speed and rpm, but very little force. That's when you shift up a gear and start pushing again. For our purposes, think of torque as the low-end, pushing/twisting power and horsepower as the high-end, spinning power. Here are the dyno figures for a couple recent Harley models.

The first step in solving the performance equation is to define exactly what performance means to you. Do you want overall better response on the road, or do you plan to take your bike to the drag strip? For improved real-world performance, simply opening up and working with what's already there in your engine should yield very satisfactory results.

Model	Peak Horsepower	Peak Torque
V-Rod (1,130cc)	105.6 @ 8,200 rpm	71.9 @ 6,500 rpm
Heritage Softail Classic Twin Cam 96 (1,584cc)	62.3 @ 5,200 rpm	79.1 @ 3,000 rpm

Joe Minton, who writes technical articles for *American Rider* magazine, runs a Dyna on a dyno to measure horsepower and torque output. By making such runs before and after installing performance products, accurate information is obtained about the effectiveness and usefulness of these products. *Buzz Buzzelli*

This motor has been disassembled in preparation for the installation of an H-D Screamin' Eagle performance kit. It will consist of larger pistons, cylinders, cams, and more.

Why are these figures so different? How is it that the V-Rod, with considerably less displacement, makes considerably more horsepower than the Softail Classic? Why does the Big Twin make more torque and do so considerably lower in the rpm range? And wait a minute, isn't displacement supposed to be a major factor in horsepower? Yes, but also keep in mind that an engine is an air pump, and the faster you can get it to spin, the more air it can move and the more power it can generate. In order for the V-Rod to produce greater power from less displacement it has to spin much faster—and likewise has to generate its peak torque at a much higher rpm. All this has to do with the liquid-cooled V-Rod's four valves per cylinder, dual overhead cams, cam timing, fuel injection, exhaust tuning—basically, its overall breathing.

The result of these factors is that the V-Rod has very different power characteristics from the Big Twin. Traditional Big Twin Harleys are all about that lovely rumble as you pull away from a stop at low rpm and shift lazily. The V-Rod engine feels much more like a sportbike's, with smooth, high-revving power. Different engine characteristics result in different power characteristics. Many riders who love their traditional Big Twin Harleys do not care for the power characteristics of the V-Rod . . . even though it makes considerably more horsepower. And that's okay, because H-D developed the V-Rod to attract a different kind of buyer, which it has done.

ENGINE PERFORMANCE BASICS

An internal-combustion engine is basically an air pump, and the faster you spin it, the more air it processes within a given amount of time. Because the amount of power it produces is governed by the amount of fuel it burns, which depends on the amount of air it can breathe, more air can mean more power. Turn the engine over twice as fast (twice as many revolutions per minute), and it will flow twice as much air per minute—within limits. And with this increased airflow it will inhale more fuel and hence will develop more power.

How fast you spin the engine is also a main determinant of how much power it will produce. You must understand, though, that spinning the engine considerably harder and faster than stock will change its characteristics dramatically. Remember our dyno figures on the V-Rod and Big Twin.

Compression is also an important power determinant. The more air the engine compresses into the combustion chamber with each stroke, the more fuel it can burn in each air/fuel charge. Ignite more fuel, produce more power. There are six different types of compression, though, so be sure you're addressing the proper one. Mechanical compression, for example, is the one most people are familiar with. But it's really only a benchmark; corrected compression is the one you want to deal with in the real world. And changing compression ratios can be much more involved than simply bolting on a few parts.

Have a Plan

Consult a professional mechanic before starting your project to learn which products work well in concert with others. Here's a true story of how things can get complicated. A friend wanted to increase the power of his Harley-Davidson FLH dresser, so he installed larger displacement cylinders and larger pistons with high-compression heads. Because of the higher compression, he now had to install a larger starter motor to turn over the engine. Because the starter was physically larger, it interfered with the dipstick, which had to be extended. Because of the higher compression, the studs that hold the cylinders down began to rip out of the cases; my friend was told that he needed to install expensive aftermarket engine cases. What he thought would be a simple installation that would give him quick, trouble-free power turned into an expensive, frustrating, long-term project. To avoid costly surprises, research your intended modifications carefully. Talk to experts who sell or install the parts you're considering about any additional costs or modifications that might be likely or prudent.

One method of gaining performance, especially when building a bike from the ground up, is to purchase a complete aftermarket engine. This engine by STD Development makes considerably more power than a stock Harley.

Airflow volume is a determining factor in power. You can bolt on a certain amount of flow (and power) just by opening up what's there, but to add power beyond that point will require serious (and expensive) engine modifications.

This leads us to our second basic premise, that displacement is king. As the saying goes, "There's no substitute for cubic inches." Or, as the other saying goes, "There's no replacement for displacement." If you increase an engine's displacement, you increase the amount of air it pumps at a given rpm. For example, if you increase an 80-inch engine by 10 percent to 88 cubic inches, the bigger engine would theoretically pump 10 percent more air and produce 10 percent more power.

One of the main reasons that stock Harley engines today don't make nearly as much power as optimal for their displacement is, of course, that H-D has designed them that way. After all, probably no motorcycle company in the world understands its customers better, and The Motor Company knows that most of its buyers are interested in enjoying motoring down the road at reasonable speeds, and may not even want high performance. Harley ads are all about enjoying the motorcycling experience and the open road, not speed. The way the great majority of Harley owners use their bikes calls for torque, not high rpm.

Another factor is that riders who buy Harleys want a certain look and style, and that includes small mufflers. This is an important Harley styling feature. However, small mufflers cannot flow a lot of air and meet EPA noise standards at the same time, so out of necessity, the engines cannot make a lot of power.

By keeping power reasonable, stresses (and warranty claims) are reduced. Also, doing so means that demand remains high for Harley's Screamin' Eagle aftermarket performance parts, and Harley dealers are kept plenty busy installing them. Keep in mind that if you buy a new or used Harley from your dealer and want certain factory or Harley accessories installed, if you have them installed by your dealer *before* delivery they will be fully covered by the same warranty as the bike. However if you buy and install them after delivery, these parts will only be covered by the standard 90-day parts warranty.

An engine cutaway (such as this one of an Evo) can show you a lot about how an engine works. *Buzz Buzzelli*

Parts on the bench await assembly into a new, higher-performance engine. Every stock Harley motor wants this. You want it. Why are you sitting there? Go!

One way to increase low-end performance is with a stroker motor. As the name implies, a stroker increases displacement by replacing the crankshaft with a longer-stroke model, plus matching rods and pistons. Strokers are known for cranking out a lot more torque than a stocker. Here's JIMS Twin Cam Stroker Kit. *JIMS Machining*

By not running the engines hard, it's easier for them to meet noise and emissions restrictions imposed upon vehicles by the U.S. Environmental Protection Agency, Department of Transportation, and others. Also, the state of California has imposed even tighter emissions restrictions on vehicles sold there than the federal government has in the other 49 states. Making significant changes to a motorcycle engine will likely cause it to exceed these legal restrictions, though Screamin' Eagle parts usually keep the engines within the law despite adding more power. This whole subject is a gray area. Please note that the EPA has cracked down recently on motorcycle dealers, and I was told by a Harley dealer that if parts do not meet EPA specifications they are allowed to sell them, but not install them.

Since motorcycling began, riders have modified their engines for more power and better quality sound. This is distinctly an "American hot rod" thing. However, be aware that making modifications that increase emissions is not technically legal, and there are those who would argue it's not socially responsible, either. Because

the possibility exists that you could have a change of heart, sell the bike, or be legally required to convert the bike back to stock, I suggest that you hold onto your stock parts if you make modifications.

WORKING WITH WHAT'S THERE

Part of having a plan is to appreciate the dividing line that exists in the Harley-Davidson performance market, and on which side of that line you wish to be. On one side of the line is working with what's there, utilizing the stock carburetor or injectors, pistons, and cylinders, but tweaking them a bit by adding a set of aftermarket pipes and dropping in a set of cams. At the low end, the cheapest and best power gain for the dollar is to go with a set of slip-on mufflers and a high-flow air cleaner, along with carburetor jet changes or remapping the fuel injection. The cost will be about $1,000 in parts and labor, and you'll gain perhaps 10 horsepower.

The next step is to replace the cams with those that offer different valve opening times and possibly even higher lift. This can be a bolt-in operation and does not require removing the heads. You remove the rocker boxes, rocker arms, and the cam covers, and you replace the cams. The pushrods must be replaced in order, front or rear oriented, as must other parts. Be sure to use a service manual. It's about a three-hour process on an Evo or Sportster, or four hours for a Twin Cam.

These few thousand dollars in parts and a mechanic's time can take a stock Harley Big Twin from about 65 to 85 horsepower. To go beyond this line, to add serious muscle, the Law of Diminishing Returns kicks in. It means "getting into the engine" by replacing stock cylinders, pistons, and other parts with aftermarket items. You're adding substantial power with all the attendant

Look at all those parts and tools scattered around. Could you put everything back together? If not, find a trustworthy technician at your local Harley dealership or independent shop.

problems and getting the bike up to 100 horsepower or more, but now that extra power is costing serious money. Because the engine is making so much power now, it may be necessary to use stronger aftermarket engine cases and an aftermarket transmission. For the purposes of this book, I'd like to stay on the conservative side of the line of simply releasing the power that's there.

THE FIVE BASICS OF HARLEY PERFORMANCE

The Five Basics to releasing the power in your stock engine include a freer-flowing intake system, carburetor/fuel-injection changes, a camshaft upgrade, ignition module, and an aftermarket exhaust system. These changes, with their significant gains of 20 horsepower or more, can usually be achieved (depending on the parts you buy and how much work you do yourself) for around $3,000 to $5,000. Ah yes, which brings us to a Sixth Basic: "There's no substitute for cubic dollars." Keep in mind that performance takes money.

Stock 80-cubic-inch Evolution Big Twin Harleys made about 58 horsepower, and 88-inch Twin Cams (introduced in 1999) delivered about 65 horses. The 96-inch motor, introduced

for 2007, makes about the same horsepower but offers an increase in torque. Add an aftermarket exhaust, less-restrictive air cleaner, an ignition module that allows the engine to rev higher than the factory-set 5,500-rpm limit, and a reasonable cam and the Evo can be putting out a safe, sane, and enjoyable 70 to 75 horsepower without any drawbacks, potential problems, or undue stress on the engine—so long as the rider doesn't abuse it. A Twin Cam can deliver about 80 to 85 horsepower, with a corresponding increase in torque.

Intake System

The process begins with increasing airflow through the intake system. Though the stock Harley-Davidson air filter is a pretty good unit, installing a less-restrictive filter will allow for a slight increase in flow and power. However, do some research and be certain that the filter element is not *too* open. If it's so open that all it filters from your system is stray sparrows, it's going to allow in a lot of engine-destroying crud, such as what's in that dust cloud you're about to ride through. You will also notice increased intake roar when it's installed. It's a good rule of thumb to use a pleated filter, such as one by K&N.

A high-flow air filter by K&N will allow an engine to breathe more easily on the intake side.

One of the most common performance upgrades, especially for older bikes, is the installation of a Mikuni or an S&S carburetor. They tend to be easily adaptable and tunable, and they provide a real performance advantage over stock. *Buzz Buzzelli*

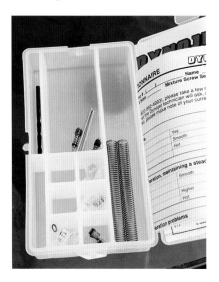

If the labor and expense of installing a new carburetor is unappealing, consider changing the jetting on your existing carb. It's often necessary when changing the exhaust system. Here's a typical dealer jet kit.

Carburetor and Fuel Injection

Stock Harley-Davidson carburetors are very good, starting with the CV units that began to appear in the early 1990s. They flow well and are easy to tune. Today, if you wish to increase usable torque rather than high-end horsepower, you can do so very satisfactorily by re-jetting the stock carburetor or fitting an aftermarket unit. A Mikuni carburetor costs about $500, takes about two to three hours to install and calibrate, and will provide about a 5 horsepower increase.

While an aftermarket exhaust will often provide a slight power gain, it is important to be aware that an internal-combustion engine is a system and that installing aftermarket pipes alone may not deliver the sought-after power. In fact, it may negatively affect power. I have seen dyno charts that indicate some aftermarket pipes actually produce less power than the stock units; drag-style pipes seem to be the worst offenders. While drag pipes are effective for increasing top-end power, they tend to run poorly in the midrange (2,000 to 4,000 rpm), where most Harley riders spend the great majority of their time.

If you do install an aftermarket exhaust system and want your bike to make more power, at the very least expect that the carburetor jets will need to be changed. Or, if your bike has fuel injection (as all Harleys do, starting with the 2007 model year), you'll need to alter its air/fuel mixture map. Dealers have a diagnostic tool called Digital Technician/Race Tuner, and independent and other shops have Direct Link, which allows them to access the electronic control module (ECM) and obtain information from it, check the parameters of the sensors, and remap the air/fuel mixture and ignition timing parameters.

Skilled technicians can work with the existing ECM, or you could get a piggyback electronic fuel-injection (EFI) module such as a Dynojet Power Commander. A piggyback module plugs into the system between the stock EFI box and the injectors, and alters the signal the electronic control module (ECM) sends out. It comes with an array of preprogrammed maps that cover a range of engine/exhaust combinations, or you can use your PC to create your own map. I have heard mixed reviews of various brands, and models change, so ask your mechanic for input.

Ignition Module

A Harley's stock ignition system is designed to work with all the restrictions imposed upon it by the government. It's also designed to prevent engine damage and thus protect your investment—while limiting warranty claims for the manufacturer.

The module does this by limiting engine revs and by sensing detonation should the owner use lower-grade fuel or ride on hot days while hauling heavy loads. If the engine is opened up, it can utilize a more aggressive advance curve. An aftermarket module can be set to retard the spark and provide more push at low rpm, but the tradeoff is some loss in economy. Some modules are adjustable and have various advance curves. They're priced from $200 to $500 and will take one to three hours to install and set up.

Camshafts

Is more always better? If I like a half-pound burger with onion, will I feel

What's in that black box? An ignition module controls the ignition advance curve and limits engine revolutions to prevent over-rev damage. When you hop up an engine, an aftermarket ignition module (that's a stocker in the photo) will help unleash more power.

even better after choking down two of them? If two beers make me feel good, will slamming 10 of them make me feel five times as good? If I love my wife, will taking on a girlfriend improve my life because I feel I have more love to give? Whoa, those are some classic "watch out!" scenarios.

There are likewise some watch-out scenarios in Harley performance, some mistaken beliefs that can cost you a lot in terms of money and power. For example, a common mistake is to install a cam with too much valve overlap and duration or too much lift. Remember, it's all about flow, and too many riders are seduced by the lumpy "rump, rump, rump" idle of those drag bikes. Don't make the mistake of equating cam timing and duration numbers with the kind of power you seek. Excessive timing narrows the powerband, which is often the opposite of what you want to achieve.

Rather than adding a big cam, you will be further ahead by flowing and porting the heads. With a milder, short-duration cam, the cylinders fill more quickly and thus the engine will produce its peak power at a lower rpm. Install a cam with longer duration, and the power will come at higher rpm,

which can result in some power/torque loss at lower rpm where you may really want it. Again, Harley engines are not high-rpm engines, and they deliver their most usable performance in the form of torque rather than horsepower.

Exhaust Systems

The simplest and most direct way to add power is with an aftermarket exhaust system. They're also popular for reasons of enhanced sound quality and styling. Market research conducted in 2004 showed that 44.6 percent of the more than 6,000 new-bike buyers of all brands surveyed had purchased an aftermarket exhaust system within their first six months of ownership.

Stock exhaust systems are designed to develop a broad range of power for an "Everyman" rider within the sound and emissions limitations of the U.S. Department of Transportation and the Environmental Protection Agency. Why do so many riders tend to change them so frequently? One reason, of course, is to personalize their bikes. Many riders regard their motorcycles as a personal statement, and no one wants that statement to proclaim, "I'm ordinary!" We prefer to be perceived as a person with taste, stature, and power. A

Camshafts are the "bumpsticks" that open the valves and allow them to close. By installing cams with more lift (to open the valves further) or with more duration (to open the valves sooner and close them later), it's possible to realize a substantial performance increase from the engine. For general riding around, select cams designed to provide more usable midrange rather than maximum high-end power.

Here's a common sight: a stock Harley exhaust system lying on the work bench because an aftermarket system is being installed. The stock system is heavy, restrictive, and not all that attractive. An aftermarket system can allow your bike to maximize its existing power, and it usually sounds better than stock. But don't throw away your stock system—just in case.

Another piece of the performance puzzle is to increase engine displacement. You can do this by removing the stock pistons and cylinders and replacing them with larger components. *Buzz Buzzelli*

properly designed exhaust system installed as part of a complete engine breathability package can indeed add significant power to a motorcycle, and also that "mellow" sound we all crave.

Because chrome tends to discolor and "blue" when it is heated and cooled, stock Harley exhaust systems have an inner wall that routes the exhaust gases and an outer heat shield that hides that unsightly blue inner wall and presents an attractive, clean, chromed cover for the stock pipes. Stock systems are also well baffled, and in order to have sufficient volume to deal with and dissipate the sound energy, they necessarily have to be bulky, and usually look so, though H-D does its best to extract optimal power while still retaining a stylish system.

A properly designed aftermarket exhaust system will usually be lighter than stock, it will allow the bike to develop more horsepower (usually higher in the rev range), and it will put out a more mellow sound (okay, it's louder) than stock. It may not now allow the engine to meet emissions regulations, however. If you find a system that's labeled for off-road or competition use only, it's the manufacturer's way of telling you the pipe is not street legal, so don't

use it there. Of course, this does not deter many riders who see having a rebellious nature as part of the deal.

The stock equipment on production Harleys is very good, but of course stifled by the needs to meet the government restrictions. The determining factors in exhaust flow are pipe length, diameter, and resonance. H-D engineers, for example, know which header pipes work best in terms of dimension, so in most cases a set of slip-on mufflers (a muffler system that slips onto the stock exhaust headers) will enhance performance substantially, without the added expense of changing the header pipes.

It's important that you not confuse a louder exhaust system with a more powerful one. Dyno tests have proven that there is no direct, proportional relationship between sound level and power. True, racing bikes will always be louder than stock, but that doesn't necessarily mean that a louder engine is a more powerful engine. In fact, some quieter aftermarket mufflers actually make more power, especially in the midrange, than some louder ones.

A louder pipe may give the impression that the engine is more powerful, but that may well be just the psychological effect of the increased sound. It might not deliver on the dyno. Generally, a louder exhaust system will indeed deliver more top-end horsepower, but at the expense of low- and mid-range power. What's good for drag racing is generally a detriment for practical street use.

BACK TO BASICS

Remember that part about defining power in terms of what you really will use? Let's go back to basics. Torque is the pushing power that occurs lower in the rpm range (as in our bicycle analogy), and horsepower occurs at higher rpm. For most riders, it makes little sense to increase engine performance from 4,000

Do Loud Pipes Save Lives, or Do They Just Make People Mad?

It is illegal for a motor vehicle to put out more sound or pollutants than stock, but lax enforcement (except at certain bike events) seems to be the rule. As long as the exhaust system is not obnoxiously loud, or if they are not receiving regular complaints, law-enforcement officers tend to look (listen?) the other way. Still, even those of us who love motorcycles cringe when a bike is so loud that it hurts our ears. If you love motorcycles but are annoyed by the noise levels some produce, how will people who don't like motorcycles respond? These citizens vote, too, and complaints always seem to move government officials more than promises to keep things under control in the future. Towns that make wonderful motorcycle gathering spots can become annoyed when nobody can carry on a conversation and the china rattles in the cabinets every time a bike blasts by. Annoy enough people and the best gatherings will disappear like the many legendary auto race tracks that noise complaints have chased onto history's pages. If you come upon a fellow rider whose bike is obnoxiously loud even for your pro-bike ears, you may wish to say something—in a polite manner, of course. If we don't take care of our own now, eventually someone else will "take care" of us in the future.

How does a shock absorber damp spring energy? In this cutaway illustration, picture the top chamber of the shock containing hydraulic fluid and the rod and piston being forced upward into it by a bump. Small holes called orifices are arranged around the outside of the piston. These orifices allow the fluid to travel between the upper and lower chambers in a controlled manner. As the hydraulic fluid is pressurized by the piston, it is forced back out these orifices into the lower chamber. The resistance to this fluid movement is what damps the energy, partly by coverting it to heat. *Progressive Suspension*

to 6,000 rpm when the great majority of your riding occurs between 2,000 to 4,000 rpm, especially when doing so negatively affects torque. This means going with displacement and compression, rather than opening the engine too wide with huge pipes, giant carburetor, and wild cams.

GOING BEYOND WHAT'S THERE

Higher compression means packing the charge more densely into the cylinders, so it lights off with a bigger bang and produces a harder push on the pistons. "Milling the head" means using a milling machine to grind off material from the cylinder head where it mates with the cylinder block so the head sits slightly lower, bringing the top of the combustion chamber closer to the piston and thereby raising compression. Thinner head gaskets achieve the same purpose, but not as drastically. Milled heads and stock cylinders can, with other appropriate changes, get you to about 85 rear-wheel horsepower with an Evolution engine, and perhaps 95 with a Twin Cam.

The step beyond this is to raise compression farther with high-compression pistons, which of course means getting into the engine and we all know that means "expensive." The simplest way to increase displacement is to bore the cylinders you have and install larger pistons. As long as you're buying pistons, get the higher-compression variety. Resist the temptation to raise compression beyond about 10.0:1, as at this point fuel quality becomes an issue and detonation can become a frustrating and expensive problem. With a high-compression engine, installing a compression release will aid in starting.

If you don't mind spending cubic dollars for cubic inches, buy larger aftermarket cylinders and pistons. Torque tends to increase proportionally with displacement, so if you were to increase displacement by 8 percent you would likely get about 8 percent more torque—and that's the most usable type of power to get.

Another way to increase torque and displacement is to "stroke" the engine,

A louder pipe may give the impression that the engine is more powerful, but that may well be just the psychological effect of the increased sound.

Most stock Harley-Davidson shock absorbers offer spring preload adjustment, but not damping adjustment.

> **TIP**
>
> The fork's rake and the bike's steering will be affected by ride-height adjustments to a slight degree. Racers will adjust spring preload at both ends to change rake and cause their bikes to steer more or less quickly for different tracks. Whenever preloading the springs or adjusting the damping on dual shocks or on the fork, be certain that both shocks or fork legs are given the exact same settings; otherwise, the suspension will be out of balance.

which means increasing the distance the pistons travel up and down in the cylinders. This is achieved by adding a stroker crankshaft and changing the connecting rods to suit.

OTHER ENGINE MODIFICATIONS

The biggest immediate power gains come from changing both the intake and exhaust systems. Modifying the ignition system enhances these changes. As you open the motor to start changing cams, valves, pistons, and cylinders, however, you begin to reach the point of diminishing returns in terms of dollars. Cams are a way of refining how the power is delivered, but you have to choose between low- and top-end power. Porting and polishing the heads can optimize flow for more power at higher engine speeds; it does not help below about 4,000 rpm.

Internal modifications involve complex issues. I suggest you do a lot of research and, unless you're a talented mechanic or willing to bear the cost (in time and money) of a lot of trial and error, have the work done by a professional. And enjoy that new power.

SUSPENSION UPGRADES

How do you know your bike needs an upgraded suspension system? When it has no adjustments, but you wish it did so you could tune out the wallowing in turns and bumps, the way the bike feels like a pogo stick, the way the front end dives under braking or how, when you ride it over a series of bumps, it feels like it's constantly bouncing and does not settle down until the bumps are long past. If you wish for more comfort and control and are going to buy aftermarket suspension components, choose ones that at least offer rebound damping and spring preload adjustment. Compression damping adjustment is also desirable. There are even systems available now that have high- and low-speed damping

adjustment capabilities, for both rebound and compression.

ADJUSTING YOUR BIKE'S SUSPENSION SYSTEM

Everything about riding, from how well a bike handles the bumps to how comfortable it is carrying a load and a passenger, is largely influenced by the quality of its suspension system and how well it's set up. In the days before swinging-arm frames and telescopic forks, motorcycles were like overgrown bicycles, in that they had rigid frames and, at best, a sprung fork.

Whenever the subject of suspension systems arises, most riders relate it to ride comfort. While comfort is a major reason for suspending a motorcycle, the far more important reasons are for traction and control. Think of an old balloon-tire bicycle being ridden down a bumpy street. The only suspension action is from tire flex and frame flex. As the bike bounces over bumps, its tires are sometimes not in contact with the pavement; at those times it is incapable of braking, accelerating, or turning. The suspension system helps to keep the tires in contact with the pavement, so you can control the motorcycle.

Most stock Harley-Davidsons are delivered with dependable suspension systems that work well enough for most situations. The only Harley models I recall that offered spring preload and damping adjusters on the fork included the 1996–1998 Sportster Sport, the Sportster 1200R, and the Dyna Convertible. The other, more permanent means of "tuning" a fork is by changing the quantity and viscosity of fork oil and by changing the fork springs. Shock absorber springs can also be changed. One source of information on fork and shock springs is www.progressivesuspension.com.

If you add high-end suspension components, here's how to adjust them intelligently.

Types of Springs

Straight-rate (or constant-rate) springs have coils that are the same size and distance apart all through the spring's length. They therefore compress at the same rate across their range of movement. If 100 pounds of force is required to compress the spring 1 inch, then another 100 pounds will compress it a second inch—and so on until the spring becomes coil bound.

A progressive-rate spring is wound in such a way that the coils have a different rate from one end to the other, and they becomes stiffer as the spring compresses. The coils on these springs are closer together at one end than they are at the other. While only 50 pounds of force may be needed to compress a progressively wound spring its first inch, perhaps 80 pounds will be required to compress it a second inch and 130 pounds its third inch . . . and so forth.

Finally, a dual-rate spring uses two springs (or occasionally three) with different rates stacked atop each other. The spring with the lightest rate will begin to compress first, then the heavier-rate spring will begin to compress. These springs offer a softer ride under most circumstances, but resist bottoming as the suspension compresses further.

What's the difference between a straight-rate and a progressive-rate spring? A specific- or linear-rate spring (on the left) has all of its coils spaced equidistant. A constant amount of force is required to compress the spring throughout its travel. A progressive-rate spring (on the right) has lighter-rate coils, which are spaced further apart, that will compress first. Less force will be required initially to compress the spring, so it will yield a "softer" ride at the beginning of the suspension travel. When the lighter-rate portion of the spring has been compressed, greater force will be required to compress the heavier coils, which are spaced much closer together. At this point, the ride will become more firm. *Progressive Suspension*

Spring Preload

The length a spring assumes when not confined is called its "free length." Place that spring in a motorcycle fork, or around a shock absorber, and it will be confined and compressed somewhat. When the bike is sitting on its wheels, the spring will now be compressed slightly by the weight of the machine. This is called "static sag." Place the rider(s) and luggage aboard, and the spring is now loaded even more. This is "dynamic sag." But how much more or less should we adjust the "preload" of a spring for riding? Dial in enough to prevent bottoming over normal bumps, but not so much as to prevent a smooth ride.

There are precise steps involved in setting up a motorcycle's suspension for racing, but for our needs the primary purposes in pre-compressing (or preloading) the springs will be to gain cornering clearance when the bike is leaned over and to raise it higher in response to higher loads. What is adequate spring preload for a solo rider under normal circumstances may become inadequate when luggage and/or a passenger are added. If parts of your bike drag too easily in turns, increasing spring preload should raise the ride height and help the situation. Most Harleys have a preload adjuster on the shock absorber springs. It's usually a ramped collar that can be turned with a special tool from the toolkit, sometimes consisting of a drift inserted through a circular hole in the shock cover. Consult your owner's manual for the exact procedure in adjusting the suspension on your bike.

Most bikes do not have fork spring preload adjusters, but if they do it will usually be a large nut at the top of each fork tube that can be screwed into the tube to increase preload, or out to lessen it. Adjusting preload in the fork will not only affect ride height slightly, but also fork compression under braking.

Increasing spring preload will increase the bike's ride height, which will raise seat height a corresponding amount. It will not, however, change spring rate unless the bike has progressive or dual-rate springs. In those situations, preloading will use up more of

TIP

If the suspension feels like it's too restricted and not working much at all, back off the compression damping settings. It's a common mistake to dial in too much compression damping, which prevents the suspension from compressing and working. If, however, it compresses too readily and wallows, that means it does not have sufficient compression damping.

If the bike feels like it's pogoing after a bump, it needs more rebound damping. If you find the suspension bottoming out after a succession of bumps, there's too much rebound damping.

Air Suspension

You will sometimes notice a Schrader (air) valve atop each fork cap, at the end of a handgrip on some Harley models or on a bracket near the shock absorbers. An air suspension system utilizes air pressure as a spring and often backs it up with an actual spring in case the system leaks. The problem with an air suspension system is that, as the air chamber is compressed, the pressure inside (and spring rate) increase dramatically. This is always a problem when air is kept in a confined area, such as a fork. Harley-Davidson got around this problem on some touring models by actually pressurizing the safety bars (some call them "crash bars") or the handlebars. Some touring models had an actual reservoir to increase air volume and even out the pressure rise. Please note that the Schrader air valve atop the fork cap was discontinued in the late 1990s, as was the one on the engine guard. By 2002, the front air suspension system was eliminated from touring models.

Air pressure has such a dramatic effect on an enclosed container in that a little goes a long way. Don't ever use a service station air hose on an air suspension system, as it can deliver such high pressure so quickly that it'll likely blow out the seals. Instead, obtain a little hand-operated pump (Progressive Suspension offers a selection of them at www.progressivesuspension.com). Air suspension systems typically hold such a small air volume that even checking the pressure can change the setting. I recommend a pump with a gauge mounted to it for precise readings. These are also available as a Harley-Davidson accessory.

Progressive Suspension's 418 shock features a chromed spring and polished body. Rebound damping can be adjusted by rotating the white control wheel near the top. *Progressive Suspension*

the lighter part of the spring rate and leave the firmer part of the spring to deal with the load.

Damping

Imagine a motorcycle with only springs for suspension at each end. Once a spring is compressed and released—or extended and released—it wants to oscillate, moving up and down until all the energy has been disbursed. We've all seen this with a "bobblehead" doll or an object suspended from a spring; it moves up and down or back and forth repeatedly. Part of our confusion in understanding suspension behavior is our terminology. In the United States, we call dampers *shock absorbers* (the Brits call them *dampers*). The problem with our system is that it's actually the spring that absorbs the shock. The "shock absorber" then dampens the spring's movement so that it becomes

still again immediately afterward, rather than continuing to oscillate. Modern motorcycle suspensions have internal damping systems that are designed to control the ride by damping out the energy as the system compresses and rebounds. Some are velocity sensitive, and will respond more aggressively to larger bumps at higher speeds.

These automatically damped systems work fine under most circumstances, but often those circumstances change. You will need more damping when you carry a passenger and luggage, or when you ride faster on a bumpy road. Also, as a suspension system ages, its damping characteristics begin to deteriorate. Under these circumstances, it is desirable to have the ability to fine-tune the system.

Damping Adjustment

Only a few Harley models have had fully adjustable suspension systems, but they're widely available through the aftermarket. Here's how to adjust one for street riding.

First, be mindful that what works for Rider A may not work for Rider B. It's very common for riders on the same racing team, who are similar in size and riding identical bikes, to set their bikes up quite differently for the same track. Some riders like a relatively plush suspension and will push on through despite the suspension's movement. Others want a stiff ride and don't want the bike moving around on them a lot. We're not going racing, of course, but still some street riders like a more plush ride while others prefer it taut. It's a personal thing, so keep in mind that another rider's suspension settings are not necessarily going to work ideally for you.

To get an idea of the limits of your bike's suspension system, set the preload according to the owner's manual and place all the damping settings on their minimal/lightest settings. Then take it to the type of road you expect to ride, and ride it through for several miles at your usual pace as you feel the suspension working; note at what points it begins to slop around or move too much for your tastes.

When you reach the end of the section, place all damping settings at their stiffest/maximum, and then ride it through again. Feel how differently it works. This will give you an idea of the range of adjustment.

For your third trip down the same road, place all adjusters at what you believe would be their ideal settings, which should deliver a nice compromise of ride comfort (plushness) with control. When further fine-tuning the adjustments, try to change settings one at a time; otherwise, you might not be able to discern which adjustment did what. Ultimately, you want suspension that feels well controlled without being harsh, yet comfortable without feeling sloppy.

LOWERING A MOTORCYCLE

Do you ever watch Supercross or those X-Games contests, where riders launch over triple jumps or do those seemingly impossible stunts while flying 30 feet off the ground on their dirt bikes? If so, you're probably wondering how guys *do* jumps like that and how their bikes take the abuse.

It helps that they ride very light bikes with state-of-the-art forks and shock absorbers that may offer 12 inches or more of suspension travel. Every inch of it is needed to disperse the huge amount of energy generated by landing one of those bad boys from 20 or 30 feet in the air off a triple jump. With only 3.5 to 5.0 inches of suspension travel, a street bike could not possibly disperse enough of the energy of such a major jump to prevent its suspension from bottoming; the bike and rider would then absorb the excess. Ouch!

One of the reasons Harleys are so popular is their low seat height. A low seat allows the rider to get both feet on the ground for a secure feel, and it also looks cool, but it offers less suspension travel to absorb the bumps. Still, if low is cool, lower is cooler, right? Here's how to lower your bike properly.

Lowering the Fork

Lowering kits come with specific instructions, but here are the basics. To lower the front of the bike, use a lift or stand to support the motorcycle with the front tire off the ground. There are three ways to lower a front suspension.

The easiest is to loosen the bolts pinching the triple clamps around the fork tubes and slide the fork tubes a bit higher. Then tighten the bolts to their proper torque values and ride on. Of course, you need to make sure you slide each fork leg the exact same distance. Not only is this the easiest and least expensive method (it is an adjustment and no parts are required), but it also retains all of the fork travel. It will change steering geometry slightly and tighten steering. Just be certain you don't slide the tubes up so far that the lower triple clamp can contact and damage the front fender when the fork compresses.

The second method is to install shorter fork springs, which are available from various suspension companies. To install them, support the front of your bike with the front wheel off the

In this Fork Lowering Kit the fork springs are shorter than stock. The white spacers can be cut to length to fine-tune the ride. A shorter spacer lowers the bike and makes the ride softer, while a longer spacer raises it and makes for a more firm ride. *Progressive Suspension*

> ## TIP
> Before removing the shocks, you'll need to support the bike with the rear wheel off the ground by means of a lift or stand placed under the frame. Remember that the swingarm will drop when you pull that second shock bolt. It helps to have a friend support the swingarm as you work the bolts free, then set it down gently.

Progressive Suspension's rear Airtail AIS kit for the Softail features the Inertia Active System (IAS) with dual air chambers. These permit the rider to adjust ride height independent of suspension firmness, which means that a lower ride height will not compromise ride quality. With the available on-board compressor, on-the-fly tuning is possible. *Progressive Suspension*

Harley-Davidson offers both Type B and E fork fluid for its machines. Check your owner's manual for information on which type is recommended for your bike.

TIP

To keep the bike riding level, raise or lower both the front and rear equally. Failure to do so will change the steering geometry and affect steering and handling.

Do not combine shorter shocks with a rear lowering kit.

Don't overtighten shock mounts. Remember, the shock needs to describe an arc as it compresses and extends. Use the proper washers and sleeves to prevent binding.

Finally, lowering a bike can gain you style points, but also can have serious consequences. Plan your moves before you do them.

---

ground. Unscrew the fork caps and extract the existing fork springs. If they're not easy to reach, bend a stiff wire (like a coat hanger) into a hook shape and use that to extract the springs. Slide the aftermarket springs inside and check the fork oil to make sure it's at the level prescribed in your owner's manual; you may have to add or remove a little.

The third and most involved way is to install a spacer under the damping rod in each fork leg. This effectively shortens the rod's stroke. A typical lowering kit will slice 1.0 to 1.5 inches off fork travel. Lowering a suspension unit more than 2.0 inches will seriously impact ride quality and ground clearance, and I don't recommend it.

You may have to disassemble the fork slider to remove the damping rod. Be sure to have a supply of the correct viscosity fork oil, as you'll have to drain the fork before you disassemble it. Because the fork controls your steering, ride, and braking, if you're not sure what you're doing, take it to a pro.

Lowering the Rear End

The least expensive method of lowering a bike's rear end is to install a lowering kit—hardware that relocates the bottom shock mounts farther rearward so the tire travels farther up into the fender. This allows the shocks to retain their full travel, but it does change the leverage parameters, so ride quality might suffer slightly. Softails, whose shocks are mounted horizontally under the frame, have their own types of lowering kits available.

The other method is to replace the stock shock absorbers with shorter units. Of course, buying new shocks is much more expensive than buying a lowering kit, and they offer less stroke to handle bumps. Still, because they are premium products, ride quality may actually improve even though their stroke is shorter. Progressive Suspension and other suspension companies offer adjustable air shocks, which allow you to choose any height within a specified range.

THE DOWNSIDES OF GOING DOWN

If you've ridden with guys who have lowered bikes, you've probably seen and heard them scraping their footboards and pipes while going around turns, and possibly you have even seen them dragging their frames or engine components while going up inclines into driveways. Lowering the suspended portion of the bike drops the frame and everything attached to it, reducing ground and cornering clearance. However much the bike drags with just the rider aboard, it's going to drag that much more while carrying a passenger and luggage.

If your stock suspension kept the tires a few inches from the insides of the

---

When Sparks Fly

While dragging footboards in turns may seem like cool, innocent fun, there is a serious side. Get too hot into a turn at 60 miles per hour, start dragging your footboards and exhaust system, and what are your options? Braking will further compress the suspension, further limiting cornering clearance, and the bike will want to run even wider in the turn. Leaning it harder over onto its unyielding hard parts can lever the tires off the pavement, sending rider and passenger sliding to the outside of the turn—possibly into a rock wall or oncoming traffic. This is serious, life-threatening stuff!

fenders and you lower the bike significantly, the tires may now rub the fenders on moderate bumps. Lowering can also lead to clearance problems with the swingarm, drive belt or chain, and brake calipers. A rear tire that contacts the inside of the fender can cause all sorts of problems, ranging from noise to wear on tires and fenders to ripping out taillight wiring to possible loss of control. If the front tire contacts the inside of the fender, it can also lead to steering and braking problems.

Then there's the comfort issue. When you subtract wheel travel, you subtract the suspension's ability to deal with bumps. Replace a 5-inch-travel shock with one having 4 inches of travel, and you've subtracted 20 percent (all else being equal) of that shock's ability to deal with bumps. The shorter shock will need a stiffer spring to make up the difference.

The only way a shorter shock can be as comfortable is for it to be of much higher quality than the shock it replaced, or you will simply have to slow down. If you carry a passenger, and your passenger is already telling you the ride feels stiff

or bumpy, perhaps you don't want to lower the bike.

BRAKES

Brake Pads

Harleys come with very serviceable brake pads, but the aftermarket offers all sorts of pads with specific characteristics, such as a greater coefficient of friction at certain temperatures, and they'll usually claim to be easy on brake rotors. Replacing pads is easy, but because it's such a critical safety item, I suggest you either have the dealer perform this operation or obtain a shop manual and follow the instructions listed there.

Braided-Steel Brake Lines

In addition to their obvious custom looks, braided-steel brake lines also have a functional purpose. Under hard usage, rubber brake lines can swell slightly. Some of the force applied to the lever or pedal that was meant to be utilized by the brake caliper will instead be dissipated in causing the brake hoses to swell. This results in a mushy feel at the lever or pedal and an increase in the amount

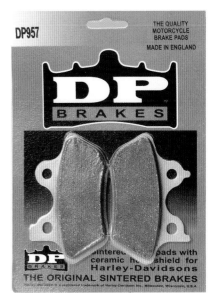

High-quality brake pads will deliver a high coefficient of friction for more effective stopping, wet or dry, while being kind to your brake rotors.
DP Brakes

The brake caliper contains pistons that, when actuated, squeeze the pads against the brake disc rotor resulting in the friction that slows the bike. Brakes can be made more effective by changing to high-performance pads, calipers, and rotors. Note the recommended fluid change intervals, and change the pads when they're worn.

Braided-steel casing offers additional support to the rubber brake lines, making them less prone to swelling and delivering more hydraulic force to the caliper. Plus, they're available in a variety of colors.

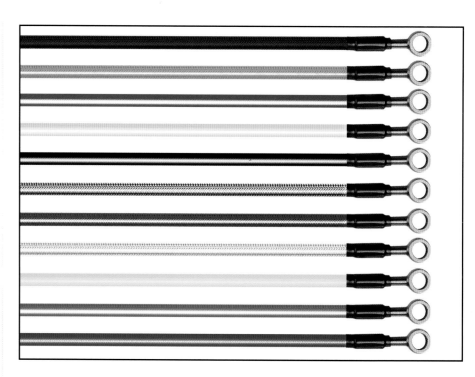

What type of brake fluid should you use in your bike? The information listed on the master cylinder cover will tell you.

of force needed to apply the brakes. A braided-steel housing around the rubber brake line prevents it from swelling, so more of the braking force is utilized, making lever and pedal operation much firmer.

Braided-steel brake lines come in standard, -2, and -3 sizes. As the minus sign indicates, the latter two sizes are smaller diameters than standard. Smaller diameter means faster displacement of brake fluid when pressure is applied to the lever, due to the venturi effect. (Picture a nurse clearing air from a syringe. The liquid moves slowly through the wider syringe body, but as soon as it's forced into the needle's narrow confines, it moves much faster, covering the length of the needle almost instantly and shooting out the end.) This means that you don't need to pull the lever as hard to get really strong

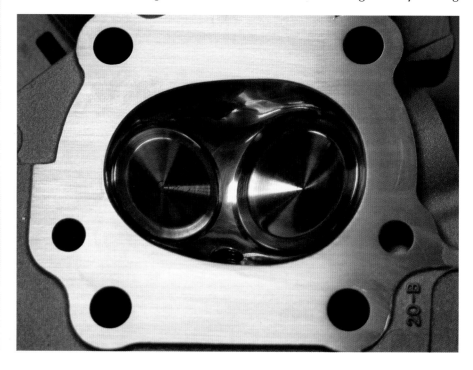

A "ported" or "flowed" cylinder head (such as this one by Jerry Branch), has had material removed from the ports and combustion chamber in order to improve flow characteristics. The head should be tested on a flow bench prior to porting and afterwards to quantify the improvement in airflow.
Buzz Buzzelli

The primary drive chain connects the engine with the transmission. The clutch (right) offers an infinitely variable connection between the two for starting from a stop and for disconnecting them while shifting gears.

If you want to upgrade to a heavy-duty six-speed transmission, consider JIMS 8085. It's made to take the abuse of a seriously breathed-on engine. *JIMS Machining*

stopping power, and it's much easier to modulate that stopping power. Gone are the days when you needed all four fingers clamping on the brake lever for a decent stop—now two fingers should do just fine. The only problem with these smaller-diameter lines is that not all of them have been approved by the DOT for street use.

In addition to a variety of sizes, braided-steel brake lines are also available in a variety of colors. It used to be that if you wanted to customize your bike by adding colored brake lines you had to use Kevlar. However, Kevlar expands ever so slightly under pressure and can crack if made to expand and contract too many times. So, although Kevlar brake lines are available, they're no longer widely distributed. Luckily, the folks who make braided-steel lines took up the challenge, and you can now get them with colored plastic sheaths. So, not only do they look good, they won't scratch painted and chromed surfaces.

Brake Line Installation Tips

Installation requires bleeding the brake system, so have a brake-bleeder kit and brake fluid from a sealed container handy. Always use the correct type of brake fluid for your bike; common types are DOT 4, DOT 5, and DOT 5.1. They have *very* different characteristics and should *never* be mixed. If you're not sure which your bike requires, read the info on the master cylinder cover.

The reason the container must be sealed is that brake fluid is hygroscopic, which means it absorbs water—including moisture in the air. Brake fluid can become extremely hot, and when it does the moisture in it can boil, which is not good for delivering braking force to the caliper. Also, moisture promotes internal rust in the system.

Chapter 8

MAINTENANCE
UNDERSTANDING WHY IT'S NECESSARY

HERE WE WILL COVER:
• **Maintenance Basics**
• **Understanding Oil**
• **Understanding Tires**

Who plays better ball, the pro that does it for a living or the guys in the Saturday softball beer league? Who can fix your bike better, the guy who does it for a living or the tinkerer who once changed his oil in less than two hours? Here's a technician giving a fork a serious inspection at Ventura Harley-Davidson/Buell.

Everyone knows that regular oil changes are a good thing, but do you know what's in the oil you put back in your bike? Do you know how to care for your bike's battery? When tires wear out, do you know how to shop for new ones that better suit your bike's needs? Do you know what tools to bring along on your ride?

When a bike is brand-new, all its parts are in near-perfect condition, but they haven't been worn in yet. For example, piston rings have to wear in against the cylinder walls, scuffing the microscopic high points from each mating surface. The same thing happens with gear surfaces, valves, and virtually all moving parts of an engine as well as chassis parts. During the first few hundred miles of operation, these parts wearing in together shed tiny bits of metal that you want to remove from the

engine promptly so they don't damage bearing surfaces. It's therefore critical that all internal-combustion engines be given an oil and filter change early in their lives.

Once engines are "broken in" (the tiny irregularities between parts shaved and flaked off), the rate at which they wear decreases greatly—though it continues. Despite excellent modern lubricants, some friction still exists, and it, plus stresses from metal fatigue and heating and cooling cycles, will cause the spatial relationships of your engine's mating surfaces to change. Moving parts must be brought back into adjustment so they work precisely with each other again. Cables stretch, spark plugs wear out, lubricants become contaminated and break down, chains and belts stretch and gradually go out of adjustment. Because all modern air-cooled Harleys have hydraulic valve lifters, valve adjustments are not part of the maintenance schedule. V-Rods, however, require an adjustment every 10,000 miles.

THE BASICS OF MAINTENANCE

When it comes to maintaining your Harley-Davidson motorcycle, most riders simply take it over to the dealership on a regular basis. Others, who like to interact more with their machines, will pull out the wrenches and work on their own bikes. Each particular Harley model family has its own similar but specific maintenance routine. You'll find the particulars pinpointed in a shop service manual, and the intervals are in your owner's handbook.

Here's an overview of the basics of Harley maintenance. On a new Harley, all fluids should be changed at the 1,000-mile mark. Cables and the drive belt should also be adjusted. If there are any other issues, bring them up with the dealer at this time. It's more expensive, but to safeguard your warranty, it's best to have the dealer perform maintenance service during the two-year warranty period. Keep in mind that the dealer gets

updates from the factory about specific issues that are not available to you. If you do your own maintenance, should your bike have a problem relative to these issues, the dealer may have reason to void your warranty on those specific items.

Until recently, Harleys have required a minor service every 2,500 miles, and a major one every 5,000 miles. For later models, oil changes have been extended to 5,000 miles for bikes using synthetic oil. Also, cables should be adjusted, and certain inspections should be performed, such as on brake pads. Every 5,000 miles perform these same tasks, and also change the primary and transmission fluids, the spark plugs, lube the cables and pivot points, and tighten the spokes on wire wheels. Adjust the drive belt, primary chain, and clutch, check all critical fasteners for torque, and check all electrical components. Steering head bearings should be greased through the Zerk fitting every 5,000 miles.

On Evolution models, the fork oil should be changed and the steering-head and swingarm bearings should be lubed at 10,000 miles. Depending upon the model and year, the consumer can usually perform these operations, but

A great way to carry tools on your bike is with a product such as Roadgear's Sport Touring Tool Pouch. It holds a good selection, keeps them tight so they won't rattle around, and is available in a variety of colors. *Roadgear*

On a new Harley, all fluids should be changed at the 1,000-mile mark. Cables and the drive belt should also be adjusted.

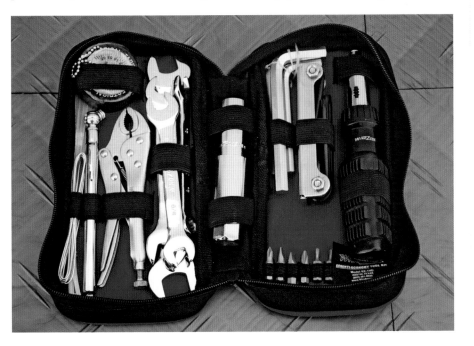

What tools should you take along? This Wind Zone Essential Tool Kit pre-selects them for you.

Tools

Except for some touring models, Harleys don't come with a toolkit. That means it's up to you to buy or assemble one to take on the road. Don't skimp by buying cheap items. I have seen substandard tools round the edges of bolts, round themselves on Phillips-head screws, and occasionally break. A better-quality tool can make the difference between getting on your way in a few minutes or spending some hours or even a night somewhere you would rather not be.

The toolkit should allow you to remove or tighten any bolts on the motorcycle that are likely to need attention, change a fuse, adjust drive belt tension, and deal with any standard road emergency, such as plugging a tubeless tire. The Motor Company offers toolkits for specific models that are priced in the $100 range. An aftermarket kit from a company such as Cruz Tools ranges from about $40 to $160.

I asked a couple long-term Harley mechanics what they would recommend in a take-along toolkit for a rider going on tour for a couple weeks. Here's what they recommended:

Phillips and flat-head screwdriver

A set of Allen wrenches and Torx wrenches

Standard and needle-nose pliers

7/16, 1/2 and 9/16-inch wrenches for most Harleys, and metric wrenches for the V-Rod

5/8-inch sparkplug wrench, though certain models use the 13/16-inch

10mm wrench for access to battery cables

12mm wrench for clutch adjustment; if you have aftermarket cables, check them for size

Spare headlight bulb

Wire, electrical tape, duct tape

Rag

Wire cutters

Once you have assembled your tool set, obtain a tool roll and keep it in a saddlebag or special tool bag that may attach to a sissy bar or down on the frame. Include a rag; it'll come in handy.

Also consider some other handy carry-alongs:

Multitool: Like a Swiss Army knife, a multitool includes several knife blades, small screwdriver blades, little pliers, can opener, bottle opener, scissors, and other little tools. Some come with a belt pouch.

Tire gauge: Check your tire pressure daily when touring, or weekly otherwise.

Tire changing tools: If your bike has tube tires, you'll need tire irons to pry the tire off the wheel so you can patch the tube. If you ride a dresser and a saddlebag has to come off to gain access to the rear tire, be sure you have the proper tools to remove it. Finally, because Harleys do not have a centerstand, you'll need to find a means to prop the bike upright with the proper wheel off the ground in order to work on it. Or lay the bike on its side. Nah, better just call the dealer.

Tire plugging and patching kit: The kit should consist of both plugs and glue for tubeless tires, and patches and glue for tube-type. Why carry both? While your bike may be equipped with one type of tire, your buddy's bike may have the other. Some utilize CO_2 cartridges for re-inflating the tire, while others offer a hose that plugs into a cylinder and inflates the tire as you crank over the engine.

Axle tools: You'll need to remove the axle if the wheel has to come off the bike to change a tire. Or . . . maybe you should just call a dealer.

Flashlight: No explanation needed.

Zip-ties: For routing wires and cable and keeping things out of the way.

Duct and electrical tape: The all-purpose items. If you don't want to carry an entire roll of each, wrap a few feet of tape around a wrench or other tools.

Siphon hose: About 5 or 6 feet of the clear stuff.

Sewing kit: I grab those little kits from hotels, as they come in handy for stitching up snagged sleeves, torn trousers, gimped gloves, ripped rain suits, etc.

A Swiss Army knife is handy for a lot of things, but a multi-tool is better suited for heavy-duty mechanical usage. Check out the pliers on this Harley tool by Gerber.

Running out of gas is no fun, so pack a siphon kit. Stick the short hose in the donor bike's fuel supply and the long end in the recipient bike's tank, and squeeze the bulb.

they require some mechanical aptitude and skill. Late FL touring models have cartridge forks whose servicing should be left to the dealer. On 1999 and earlier models, wheel bearings should be repacked. Starting with the 2000 models, wheel bearings are sealed.

On Twin Cams, the fork oil does not need to be changed until 20,000 miles. Adjust and lube the steering-head bearings at 10,000 miles—except for Springer models, whose steering-head bearings should be lubed and adjusted every 2,500 miles. Disassemble and inspect Springer steering-head bearings every 20,000 miles; other models should be disassembled and inspected at 30,000 miles.

You may wish to perform engine oil changes yourself, in which case you'll need an oil filter wrench and measuring cup for the oil. If you keep specific maintenance records along with all related receipts, your dealer may honor any claims you have during the standard warranty period. If you also hop up the engine, however, it becomes a gray area and your warranty may not be honored.

You've got to have a tire patch kit along! This one, by Progressive Suspension, provides a holder for the CO2 cartridges and a short hose for the Schrader valve. The tool is to enlarge the puncture hole in a tubeless tire so the plug can be inserted. Tube patches and rubber cement are tucked in the pockets.

Sometimes it's tough to read a digital tire gauge while taking a pressure reading. That's why Roadgear came up with its Talking Tire Gauge. It calls out the tire pressure in half-PSI increments. *Roadgear*

Adjusting an air suspension system can be tricky, as you're dealing with a very small volume of air. Sometimes just taking a pressure reading can drop pressure by several PSI. For those tricky adjustments, Progressive Suspension offers its Gauge-Mounted Pump, which allows you to read the pressure as you pump.

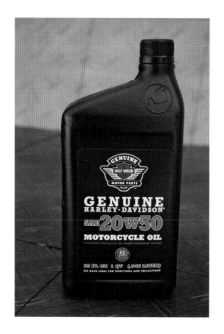

What brand and viscosity of motor oil is best for your Harley? Consider using genuine H-D oil in your bike. Why? Think about it—choosing the wrong oil can lead to increased warranty claims and dissatisfied customers, which will cost The Motor Company a bundle. They've done a lot of research to be sure that their oil fills the bill.

If you like interacting with your bike and doing your own oil changes, the gallon container of Harley-Davidson motorcycle oil will have a place of honor in your garage.

Oil Is Oil, Except When It's Really Good Oil

What if you run your Harley on inexpensive automotive engine oil rather than that recommended for it by The Motor Company? If you ride in a low-stress, steady-state manner, keep your bike tuned and change oil frequently, it will probably suffer no damage. But if you run the bike hard, travel two-up, haul a heavy load or a trailer, or ride in hot, dusty conditions while generating a lot of power and heat, you may notice some accelerated valvetrain wear causing more mechanical noise short-term, and in extreme cases eventual breakdown. Stop-and-go traffic also contributes to the lubricant breakdown.

If you intend to keep the bike for a number of years and many thousands of miles, it will likely survive in much better shape if you use high-quality, specialty motorcycle lubricants.

OILS AND LUBRICANTS

Your Harley (especially if you've modified the engine) likely produces more power per displacement than your car. Unless you ride a V-Rod, your Harley has an air-cooled engine that does not cool as efficiently as a water-cooled motor and is more subject to the vagaries of weather. Add a passenger and luggage to your bike, and its power-to-weight ratio becomes much less favorable than if you add the same amount of weight to your car. Most riders tend to use more of their bike's power and rev it to redline more often than they do their cars. The point is that bikes place different demands on motor oil and therefore need a lubricant formulated specifically for motorcycle use.

Oil's purpose is to coat the hard parts of the engine and lubricate them, preventing them from rubbing together. It also carries heat away from hot spots. Let's see how it works.

Additive Packages: What's in Oil

Here's a quick compendium of what's added to high-grade, four-stroke motorcycle engine oil.

Antiwear Agents: To protect the camshafts from the lifters, motorcycle oils carry zinc (an antiwear and antioxi-

dant) in greater concentrations. Plain-bearing engines need phosphorus, an important antiwear ingredient.

Antifoam Agents: High revs can churn oil into a froth. Silicone-based antifoam agents reduce surface tension so bubbles won't form. Bubbles are full of air, and air does not lubricate. Foam is also not amenable to pumping, so the engine's oiling system can't distribute lubricant effectively once it froths.

Antiacids: Acids are formed when condensed moisture reacts with combustion contaminants. They'll eat your engine alive from the inside out.

Detergents and Dispersants: If allowed to circulate, the bits of metal that flake off bearings, piston rings, clutch surfaces, etc., would eventually interfere with moving parts and clog oil lines. Detergents and dispersants help dissolve sludge and keep particles in suspension so they can be trapped by the filter.

Multi-Viscosity Oils

Many of today's quality oils have multiple viscosities. For example, in cold weather a 10W–40 (the "W" means the oil meets viscosity specifications for low temperatures and is therefore suitable for Winter use) flows like a 10-weight at 0 degrees Fahrenheit, then thickens to a 40-weight at 212 degrees Fahrenheit. This viscosity shift is caused by chains of polymers that, like microscopic noodles, shrink when cold for easy starting, and then thicken at operating temperature to cling better. Use lighter weight oils for cool weather, and higher weight for the heat.

Synthetic and Petroleum Oils

Synthetic oils are those that have been synthesized, or formed from other components. They're made from either poly alpha olefins (PAO), which are petroleum based, or from esters, such as mineral oils, vegetable oils, or other natural sources. Both types are formulated in laboratories, on a molecular level, from base stocks, a process that causes synthetics to be more heat stable. When an engine is used hard in hot weather, a low-quality, petroleum-based oil may overheat and begin turning to sludge.

Petroleum oils begin to break down chemically and lose lubricating qualities at temperatures above 220 degrees, but synthetics maintain their qualities beyond 300 degrees Fahrenheit. Many new motorcycles have their fuel injection or carburetion set extremely lean to meet emissions standards, which causes them to run hotter, and sometimes they will reach operating temperatures that cause petroleum-based lubricants to break down.

When to Change Oil

Oil is worn out when it has used up a significant portion of its additive package and viscosity or become contaminated or broken down from excessive heat. Oil-change intervals specified by manufacturers are recommendations, but how a specific bike is used determines when its oil should be changed.

A person who rides a liquid-cooled bike solo on the highway at legal speeds, and runs a high-quality synthetic oil, may actually be able to extend oil drain intervals beyond factory recommendations. At the other end is the rider who runs petroleum-based automotive oils in a high-powered, air-cooled bike, two-up in hot weather, at high speeds pulling a trailer—when he's not commuting through stop-and-go traffic. He had better drain and replace oil more frequently than recommended. Throw in a clogged air or oil filter, stuck choke,

Checking your engine oil must be done regularly, as failing to do so can lead to engine damage and costly repairs.

Periodically check the operation of your brake light—with both the lever and the pedal.

The interesting thing about Harley Syn3 lubricant is that it can be used in engines, transmissions, and primary cases. It's no longer necessary to have several different lubricants for these needs.

Oil Is Oil, Part II

Oils range from low-end, inexpensive, pure petroleum products adequate for most uses to high-end, expensive synthetics with full additive packages able to handle racing stresses. In between are many etroleum/synthetic blends that keep costs down while increasing the performance value of the oil.

or an engine in need of tuning, and engine life may be shortened.

The bike manufacturer provides a warranty with each new bike, and its oil-change recommendations reflect what it believes to be a safe interval that will protect the bike under most conceivable conditions and minimize claims. Some riders have told me, "My bike manufacturer recommends that I change my motor oil and filter every 2,500 miles. Just to be safe, I change the oil every 1,250 miles. I figure I'm extending my bike's engine life." While this could be true to some minor extent, it would likely only apply if the rider were using his bike in an unusually aggressive manner. Otherwise, it's probably unnecessary.

Over the course of 50,000 miles, this policy will cause the rider to pay for

an additional 20 oil changes and dump 60 quarts of waste oil unnecessarily. When I started riding 45 years ago, I was told that changing oil more often was "cheap insurance." Now, with better oils, filters, and motorcycles, I'm not sure if that statement is still valid. It is unlikely that doubling up on oil changes will extend engine life to any significant degree.

Mix It Up

What happens if your bike runs low on oil when you're traveling, but you can't find the particular synthetic brand or blend you're running? Is it okay to mix a petroleum-based oil with a synthetic oil, so long as they're the same viscosity?

Yes. The two oils should be fully compatible in a chemical sense, but you're downgrading the overall quality of the synthetic by mixing it. Of course, you understand that this would be an emergency situation. While the proper amount of mixed oils is much preferable to not enough oil, it's best to carry a spare quart of the good stuff if your bike tends to use it.

Gear Oil

On Harleys, the transmission is separate from the engine, and each component has a separate oil reservoir. Give each lubricant the sniff test and you'll note that engine oils tend to have a sweeter vegetable aroma, while motorcycle hypoid gear oils have the nasty smell of sulfur, an extreme-pressure additive that lays down a barrier to prevent metal-to-metal contact during the pushing/dragging action of the gears. However, Harley-Davidson has developed its Syn3 20W50 motor oil, which can also be used in the transmission and primary cases. This is handy for when you take long trips, as you won't have to pack two or three different lubricants.

TIRES

Just as a motorcycle is a tool for a job, so is a tire. Its job should reflect that of the motorcycle. Tires are as specifically designed as the bikes that carry them. Here are some basics about motorcycle tires to help you understand them so you can make informed choices when the time comes.

Every tire must balance several factors, including mileage (tread life), adhesion (grip), and ride/handling characteristics. In a perfect world, every tire would provide the perfect ride for every bike, would stick like a pit bull on a mailman's pants, and would wear like granite. But this isn't a perfect world.

At one end of the motorcycle tire spectrum are purebred racing tires, wide radial slicks with ultra grip and handling. However, they're not usable on the street because they need track speeds to reach operating temperature, and they lack tread grooves to channel away rain. They'll be toast after a single race.

At the other end of the spectrum are bias-ply touring tires that will carry two full-sized people and their belongings for in excess of 10,000 miles at highway speeds. While they wear well and carry a good deal of weight, they may not offer as comfortable a ride, and if you tried to push them in a track environment they'd turn gummy and slippery.

Radial Versus Bias-Ply Tires

In simplified terms, a motorcycle tire consists of the carcass and plies, the rubber compound and the tread pattern. The carcass is made up of layers of flexible belts, called plies, which tend to be arranged in either of two ways. When the plies run directly across the tire from edge to edge (bead to bead), 90 degrees to the direction of rotation, the tire is a true radial-ply. This construction will result in a very compliant, flexible sidewall that allows the tire to grip well and provides a comfortable ride, but it offers less relative load-carrying capability.

Now cut those plies at an angle (on a bias) of maybe 20 or 30 degrees and run them bead to bead. As several layers overlap, the tire becomes stiffer; this contributes to a higher load rating but diminishes ride comfort. Those overlapping plies also rub against each other, generating heat, and they insulate the tire like a blanket. Bias-ply tires tend to run hotter than radials, and heat is the enemy of tires as it softens the rubber and causes it to wear at an accelerated pace.

Radial tires usually offer superior comfort and grip to a bias-ply, but the latter will usually offer greater load-carrying capacity. Here's the profile of a Dunlop radial front tire. *Dunlop Tire*

Another potential problem is that, at high speeds, centrifugal force can cause the tire to expand slightly (its diameter can grow as much as 3 percent), leading to clearance problems and accelerated wear. When a tire expands because of high speeds, its rubber becomes less dense at the very time the rate of flex and the resultant heat are placing more demands on it. To limit tire flex and growth, some manufacturers add a circumferential belt just below the tread surface.

Because a radial sidewall doesn't offer as much load-carrying capacity, the tire manufacturers make them short, or low in profile. When designed for sportbikes, radial tires tend to be relatively

A tire is a complex piece of high-tech equipment consisting of alternating layers of plies and much more, as this Dunlop cutaway illustration shows. The arrangement of those plies determines if the tire is a radial or bias-ply. *Dunlop Tire*

This "cut-slick" Dunlop radial rear tire puts a lot of rubber on the road. The ratio of solid rubber to channels (or "sipes") is the tire's "land/sea" ratio. More land makes for a better grip (consider a racing slick), but sipes are necessary in the real world to channel away water, such as on this Dunlop Elite 3 radial. *Dunlop Tire*

The Mix

Making a tire is like making a cake. The manufacturer pours the ingredients into a mold, cooks them, and pops out a new tire. "Compounding" is the science of mixing the materials that give the tire its characteristics. It could result in a "soft" tire that wears like a pencil eraser but sticks like a federal indictment. Or it could create a "hard" tire that wears like a locomotive wheel on a steel rail—but slides about as easily, too.

wide in search of ultimate grip. By comparison, bias-ply tires tend to have high-profile sidewalls and are narrower.

Because of their different designs, if a bike came standard with bias-ply tires it is not advisable to switch to true 90-degree radials. The latter could tangle with the swingarm and fenders and may not fit. And even if they did fit, a low-profile radial in place of a bias-ply would lower the bike's ride height to such an extent that ground and cornering clearance would be affected, and parts would drag easily in turns.

If you fit a tire with a different diameter, it will affect speedometer readings.

Note that some tire manufacturers offer compromise radials with a slight bias cut and higher sidewalls with internal stiffeners that allow them to be used on a wide variety of motorcycles. For fitment information, see your dealer. Again, because radials and bias-ply tires are

designed to flex in opposite directions, do not mix them on the same motorcycle.

Tread and Grip

The most visible part of the tire is the tread pattern, that series of squiggles and lines that gives the tire its style and characteristics. The proper term for these grooves is "sipes," which are channels designed to break the surface tension and push water away so the tire doesn't hydroplane in the rain. Racing slicks, as we all know, have no sipes because maximum surface area equals maximum grip on a dry track. The problem with slicks is that without sipes, they aren't worth spit on sandy or wet surfaces.

Because they are open areas, sipes are weak points that allow street tires to be designed with a bit of "give" or squirm near their edges. When the rider is going hard and leaning way over, this bit of controlled squirm sends a message that it's time to slow down. A disadvantage of some racing tires is that they will provide maximum grip—right up to the point at which they slide away entirely.

While cutting-edge motorcycle tire design through the 1990s focused mostly on sportbikes (which spawned the radial revolution) and touring bikes (with high load-carrying capacity and good wear characteristics), manufacturers finally began to offer new tires for more mainstream models, too.

Consider the two-up touring couple on their FLH. Their bike will spend hours rolling at the speed limit or above, loaded at or near capacity. They need a tire with a deep tread and great load-carrying capacity. They don't plan to go haring around in the corners, and as a result are willing to trade some sporting grip for longer tread life, higher load capacity, and wet-weather grip. Because their bike won't exceed 130 miles per hour (nor would they dream of attempting to do so), its tires require only an H speed rating.

A Sportster, Dyna, or Softail needs a tire that is somewhere in between. Its job is to handle a bike that may weigh from 500 to maybe 700 pounds and will often be ridden solo but sometimes will be taken on tour with a passenger. When the road starts winding, Harley's typically low cornering clearance will limit the bike's lean angle, so maximum cornering performance grip isn't an issue, but maximum braking ability always is for any bike. Again, if you're like most Harley riders, you're willing to sacrifice some cornering capabilities for longer tread life.

Styling is important to a Harley rider; you expect the tires to look as exciting as your bike. You may even have mounted a big, meaty rear tire, much wider than stock, that suggests horsepower, heroes, and hooliganism. The message is that your bike is modified and needs a flexed bicep of a tire to handle the power. As a result, you'll tend to run bias-ply tires that are designed more for wear than ultimate grip, with a medium to high load rating and an H speed rating. For traditional bikes, white sidewalls are a plus.

Load Range

This refers to the weight a tire can support at its maximum inflation pressure. Here are some examples of code numbers listed on motorcycle tires, and the corresponding amount of weight they can handle: 57H (230 kilograms, or 506 pounds; H speed rating), 62H (265 kilograms, or 583 pounds), or 68H (315 kilograms, or 693 pounds).

Inflation Pressures

How do you know what air pressures to run in your tires? Start with the listing in the owner's manual or on a sticker on the bike, which gives a suggested pressure range for solo and two-up. Also, the tire will have a maximum inflation pressure imprinted on the sidewall, but it is

Where the Rubber Meets the Road

The ratio of rubber to sipes on tires is referred to as the "land/sea ratio," the sipes or grooves being the sea portion and the tread blocks, protruding like islands, the land component. Until the 1980s, motorcycle tires tended to have a lot of sea, as the tread bristled upward from the carcass. With lots of sea, the tread begins to squirm under heavy cornering loads because each tread-block "island" is unsupported around its perimeter. From racing development, tire designers came to realize in the 1980s that a superior tire design utilized the solidity of the slick's solid block of rubber, with sipes cut into it. This came to be known as the "cut slick" design, and it has become common.

only for maximum speeds and loads and will not deliver a comfortable ride in most situations. Tires compensate for weight by adding pressure, but keep in mind that as you add pressure beyond optimal, the tire will suffer in ride compliance, handling, life, and possibly even grip. Both over- and underinflated tires will wear faster than those that are properly inflated.

Tube Versus Tubeless

A rubberized material along the inner surface of cast wheels helps create the seal that allows motorcycles to run tubeless tires. Wire-spoke wheels cannot use this material, as it would gum up the spokes and interfere with the process of replacing them. Therefore, if you have wire-spoke wheels, you'll likely have to run tubes. A few wire wheels on foreign bikes are sealed and designed to run with tubeless tires, but if your Harley has wire wheels, it carries tubes inside its tires.

The problem with tubes is that, if punctured, the tube will usually deflate in seconds. A tubeless tire will often capture a nail and hold it for a time, gradually seeping air, but allow the rider to limp to a dealer for repair or replacement. My advice is that if you have a choice between cast wheels with tubeless tires or wire wheels with tubes, and style isn't your prime consideration, go

Styling is important to a Harley rider; you expect the tires to look as exciting as your bike.

As of this writing, rear tires of up to a 250 aspect ratio are now available on stock bikes. However, wide rear tires with aspect ratios of 300, 330, and even 350 series are hugely popular with custom bike builders. *Avon Tyres*

Go, Speed Rater

The common speed ratings for auto and motorcycle tires are S, H, V, and Z, which translate to:

S: For sustained speeds up to 112 miles per hour

H: For sustained speeds up to 130 miles per hour

V: For sustained speeds up to 149 miles per hour

Z: For sustained speeds in excess of 149 miles per hour

H-rated tires tend to have the greatest load capacity. As the speed rating increases beyond that point, load capacity decreases.

with the cast wheels and tubeless tires. They may not look as trick, but one flat will convince you there's more to riding than style. You can do a quick flat fix on a tubeless tire at the side of the road, but with a tube-type your trip is most likely done until you can have a dealer pick up your bike and take it to the shop for repair. If your Harley has tubeless tires, pack a tire repair kit. If it has inner tubes, pack a mobile phone and a prayer book.

Sizes and Speed Ratings

A tire will fit on your bike only if it is the proper size. Here's a quick course in how to read metric tire sizing, which is by far the most common today. A 2007 Harley Softail Classic carries a 150/80B16 71H rear tire. This means that it measures 150 millimeters at its widest point when mounted on a rim and properly inflated. The 80 refers to its aspect ratio, which means it is 80 percent as tall as it is wide. An "R" or a "B" in the next space refers to a radial or a belted tire. The 16 refers to rim diameter in inches, and the 71 is its load rating, while the H is its speed rating.

In Europe, the sustained high speeds possible on the autobahns and autostradas can shred tires quickly. In response, the tire industry established speed ratings for automotive and motorcycle tires to alert consumers that properly inflated examples of these tires have been successfully tested at certain sustained speeds at certain loads. These tires now carry their speed ratings on their sidewalls as part of their sizing information. For example, on our 140/90H-16 tire, the "H" refers to the speed rating.

How to Plug a Tubeless Tire

Because motorcycles are so hard on their tires, which are so critical to your safety, repairing a tire or tube should be considered only as a last resort. It's a temporary emergency repair to get you home or last only until you can replace the tube or tire. And if the hole is in the sidewall, don't even consider patching it; call for help.

Should you get a nail in the tread area of your tire, how it will be patched depends on whether it is a tube-type or tubeless tire. In either case it usually is fixable if you have a proper repair kit.

If your bike has tubeless tires, you do not need to remove the tire from the wheel. Locate the nail, remove it with pliers, and insert the probe in the hole to roughen and enlarge it. Soak a tire plug with the appropriate rubber cement, and place it in the clip of the probe. Insert the plug in the hole and remove the probe, which should leave the plug securely in the hole. Inflate the tire with a pump or those CO_2 cartridges so popular in emergency repair kits.

Once the tire is inflated to the proper pressure, check the plug for leaks by soaking it in liquid or squirting some water on it and checking for bubbles (in a pinch, spit will do). If all is snug, cut away any excess plug material, wait a few minutes for the glue to set, and ride away. Again, remember that the tire is far from 100 percent competent; limit your speed to about 50 miles per hour as you limp home to replace the tire.

How to Patch a Tube

To gain access to the tube, place the motorcycle on a stand that lifts the wheel off the ground. Remove the wheel from the bike, and lay it on the floor horizontally with rags underneath to prevent the wheel from being scuffed. Remove all air from the tube by depressing or unscrewing and removing the valve core from the Schrader valve. Break the bead (separate the tire from the wheel). This can sometimes be done by standing on the tire; be sure to place rags on the floor so the wheel is not scuffed, and *don't bend your brake disc.* Locate the leak; it may be necessary to partially re-inflate the tire to determine this. Use tire irons *carefully* to lever one wall of the tire off the wheel, exposing the tube, then locate the hole. You must be certain not to pinch the tube between the tire iron and the wheel while doing this, as this can cause additional leaks.

With the tube exposed, use the roughening tool from the patch kit to scuff an area around the hole that is somewhat larger than the patch. Apply the glue according to the directions in the patch kit. When the glue starts to become slightly tacky, apply the patch. Roll a round object such as a bottle over the patch to be sure it lies flat and adheres well.

When the glue has set, inflate the tube slightly and listen for any leaks. Apply liquid to the patch and watch for bubbles. If all is well, deflate the tube and insert it into the tire. Carefully use the tire irons to lever the tire back onto the wheel. Re-inflate the tire and listen for leaks. To set the bead, you will need to use a high-pressure hose, such as you find at a service station. Those CO_2 cartridges do not offer enough pressure. Wet the tire bead so that it will more easily slide into place. Reinstall the wheel. A patch is a temporary, emergency measure. Replace the tube at the first opportunity.

BATTERIES

The Basics of Battery Care

If you have a savings account, you already have some understanding of your bike's battery. When utilizing the battery to start your bike, you're making a withdrawal from its electrical savings account. When running at normal rpm, you are making a deposit and building it back up. Let either your bank account or your battery become overdrawn, however, and the results can be problematic.

A lead/acid battery requires only a little monthly maintenance. Charge it any time the starter sounds weak, the lights appear dim, or the battery hasn't been used for two weeks or more. At least every month, follow the steps outlined below.

Check the electrolyte level on a conventional lead-acid battery: (If you have a maintenance-free sealed battery, you can skip this part.) Set the battery on a level surface and visually check that the electrolyte level is between the maximum and minimum lines. If any cells fall below the minimum level, the lead plates can be exposed to air, leading to sulfation and permanent damage.

To replenish electrolyte levels, remove the filler plugs on the cells that are low (first extinguish all flames). Add

The Writing on the Wall

The information listed on the side of a tire makes for some interesting reading. Here is some of the information presented:

Country of manufacture: Where the tire was made.

DOT compliance symbol: Tire complies with U.S. Department of Transportation requirements.

Directional arrow: Mount the tire so that it rotates in this direction.

Tube or tubeless designation: A tubeless tire can carry a tube if necessary.

Maximum pressure: This is the greatest amount of air pressure the tire should carry—it is *not* the recommended pressure.

For tire inflation information, check your owner's manual. Here's some tire information in a Sportster owner's manual.

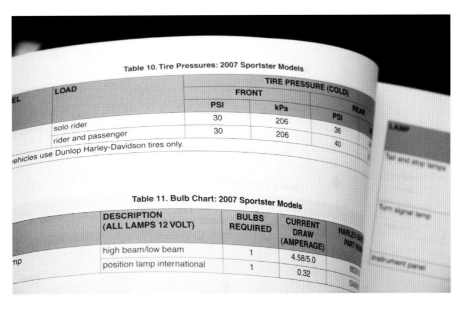

Table 10. Tire Pressures: 2007 Sportster Models

	LOAD	TIRE PRESSURE (COLD)			
		FRONT		REAR	
EL		PSI	kPa	PSI	
	solo rider	30	206	36	
	rider and passenger	30	206	40	

vehicles use Dunlop Harley-Davidson tires only.

Table 11. Bulb Chart: 2007 Sportster Models

	DESCRIPTION (ALL LAMPS 12 VOLT)	BULBS REQUIRED	CURRENT DRAW (AMPERAGE)	HARLEY PART
np	high beam/low beam	1	4.58/5.0	
	position lamp international	1	0.32	

Deltran's Battery Tender is widely regarded as the best friend your battery can have. It fully charges the battery and then changes to provide a "float" charge that maintains the battery at peak charge over long periods. Shown is the 2-Bank Battery Tender that can handle two batteries simultaneously. *Deltran*

Huh?

What's that? Warm weather is harder on a battery than cold? Then why do I usually only have starting problems on cold mornings?

Don't confuse starting problems with battery problems. The reason internal-combustion engines have starting problems in the cold is because fuel does not atomize as well and because oil thickens, which causes more resistance to turning the engine over. Also, if the bike has been parked a few weeks the more volatile and combustible elements of the fuel will be the first to evaporate. What's left is a weaker blend of fuel that makes starting harder.

distilled water to bring all cells to near the maximum level. Do not overfill, as this can cause leakage. Battery acid is corrosive, so take care not to spill. As an added precaution wear eye protection, rubber gloves, and old clothes.

Keep the top of the battery clean: It's best to remove the battery from the bike for this step. Clean the terminals, and any electrolyte that may have spilled onto the battery or bike when refilling cells, with a solution of baking soda and water. Leave the filler plugs in place so that no dirt enters the battery. Rinse with water and dry.

Check the cables, clamps, and case for damage: The most common cause of a sudden battery "failure" is a loose connection. Make certain the connectors on cables and clamps are snugged down, and that the protective cap covers the positive terminal (+) when you're done.

Be very careful that the tool you use to tighten the positive cable fitting does not contact any metal, as a spark will result and could cause a fire. Keep your hand fully around the tool to prevent this, or wrap electrical tape fully around the wrench to prevent it from making metal-to-metal contact.

Clean the terminals and connectors if necessary: It's best to remove the battery cables before cleaning the terminals. If the terminals are corroded, clean them with a wire brush. For final cleaning, use fine sandpaper or emery cloth. Once the battery cables are disconnected from the motorcycle, you will lose any clock, radio, or other settings.

Check the state of charge: A battery that's not in use will lose 0.5 to 1.0 percent of its charge per day, higher during warm weather and less in cool. With a voltmeter hooked to the terminals, a fully charged battery should read

12.6 volts (or 12.8 volts for a sealed battery as it has a different electrolyte, which offers a slightly higher terminal voltage). If the battery is below this voltage, it needs a charge.

I recommend using a trickle charger (such as a Deltran Battery Tender) that charges at a rate of 1.5 amps and switches to a float mode once the battery is fully charged. Less expensive chargers do not have sensors to limit overcharging, which could cause the battery to overheat and the fluid medium to evaporate. Some chargers come with connectors that can be permanently installed on the battery terminals to simplify access.

Check for excessive sediment or sulfation on the plates: This gunk on the plates can lead to early failure. If you see much of it, replace the battery soon, before it fails and lets you down. Skip this step on sealed batteries.

Check that the vent tube is open and free of kinks: Batteries build up pressure, and a hose blocked by a kink can potentially explode.

Winter Battery Storage

If you live in a cold-weather area where your bike is put away for the winter, remove the battery from the bike, perform the steps listed above, and fully charge it. Store it in a cool, dry area away from kids and pets. Mark on your calendar every three to four weeks to charge the battery, or simply place it on a smart charger that goes to a float charge once the battery is fully charged.

Although it has nothing to do with batteries, drain the fuel before storing your bike for the winter, including from the carburetors/injectors. If this is impractical, add a fuel stabilizer. Follow this religiously, and in the spring it should only be necessary to place the battery back in your bike and start it up.

PRE-RIDE INSPECTION

Your owner's manual comes with a pre-ride checklist. Use it as the basis for your riding. However, humans tend to be creatures of habit, and we may begin to neglect this important task. Consult your bike's owner's manual for its specifics, but here's a sample of what to check on your bike before every ride.

Tires: If you don't have a manual, the recommended tire pressures should be listed on your bike. These are cold tire pressures and should be taken before the bike is ridden (when the tires are still cold). As air is heated, its pressure increases, so once the bike is ridden its tires will gain about 2 to 3 psi or more, depending upon ambient temperature, altitude, and how hard the bike has been ridden.

Check tires periodically for cuts, damage, and tread depth.

Engine oil: Note whether your model specifies that this check be performed with a cold or warm engine. Also, on some models the check is to be performed with the bike on the sidestand, and on others the bike should be upright. Pull and wipe the dipstick, then insert and pull the dipstick again. The oil level should be between the lines on the dipstick.

Fuel supply: Whenever you fill the tank, zero the tripmeter so it can record the number of miles on that tankful of gas. A glance at the miles utilized will give you a rough idea of how far you can ride until you need fuel again. Occasionally check the condition of fuel lines. If you see cracks, replace them.

Coolant level: If you have a liquid-cooled V-Rod, eyeball the coolant level before each ride. Note that coolant hoses should be replaced periodically.

Clutch: Check for adjustment. If it's a hydraulically actuated clutch, check the fluid level in the reservoir and the condition of hoses. If it's cable actuated, check for play and lubricate when necessary.

Brakes: Check for operation, and check hydraulic reservoirs for fluid level and for condition of hoses. If hydraulic brakes feel spongy, have your dealer bleed the system and replenish the fluid. While he's at it, have him check pads and shoes for wear. Brake fluid should be replaced about once a year.

Throttle, clutch, and brake control cables: Check for smooth operation and lubricate when necessary.

Lights: Check for headlight operation on both high and low beams; check brake light (as actuated by both the brake lever and brake pedal) and turn signal operation.

Final drive: Check the slack on the drive belt or chain final drive, and adjust if necessary. If it's a drive chain, be sure it's properly lubricated.

The experienced home mechanic can maintain a Harley with just a basic set of tools. Until your warranty expires, however, you may better safeguard your investment by taking your bike to the dealership.

Brake fluids of different types (DOT 3, DOT 4, DOT 5, etc.) have vastly different properties and should not be mixed. The notation on the top of your bike's master cylinder will tell which type to use.

SIDECARS, TRIKES, AND TRAILERS

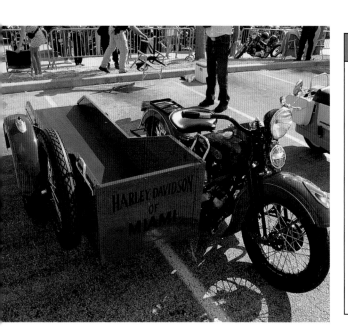

HERE WE WILL COVER:
• Sidecars and Trikes
• Towing a Trailer with Your Bike
• Trailering Your Bike

This antique Harley of Miami sidecar rig is a great attention getter, even at Daytona!

A Sidecar Named Desire

Sidecars have a different feel from riding a bare motorcycle because they don't lean. Instead, the rider has to push and pull on the handlebar to turn them, and shifting his or her weight helps. With the sidecar mounted on the right side, turning left is very solid and stable with that "outrigger" wheel. However, on right turns, the weight of the hack wants to push the motorcycle wide. In an extreme situation, the sidecar wheel can actually come off the pavement and threaten to overturn the rig.

We all enjoy riding motorcycles and being on two wheels, but sometimes three or four wheels can make a lot of sense. Here's how it's possible to have a lot of fun on a Harley with more than two wheels.

SIDECARS

Sidecars can provide practicality, hauling capacity, and style points. They became popular in the early days of motorcycling, during the teens and '20s and again in Europe after World War II when times were tough and people needed mobility at a bargain price. Once things improved to the point where most everyone could afford an automobile, sidecars lost much of their practical appeal.

Today, they're coming back into fashion because they evoke some of that nostalgia and because they really are cool. You can put mom on the back and the kids in the hack. Some folks stick the family dog in the sidecar, goggles on and nose to the wind. Hacks haul your camping gear and more. And as the motorcycling population ages, well, it becomes harder to swing a leg over and hold up that big bike. A sidecar offers more stability and dignity when one wants to slow down.

And did I mention that sidecars garner a lot of attention everywhere they go? No matter if it's carrying dogs, kids, or lumber, pull up somewhere with a sidehack, and people are going to talk to you.

An excellent source of information is Doug Bingham, who owns Side Strider Inc., a sidecar shop in the Southern California area. Check out his

website at www.sidestrider.com, or call (818) 780-5542.

If you decide to ride a bike with a sidecar, take it easy until you figure out the handling. You don't lean to turn this setup, so it takes some getting used to. Keep your speeds low until you get the hang of it.

TRIKES

Another way to keep riding a big bike as you age is with a trike, short for tricycle. A trike is a three-wheeled vehicle that may have started as a standard motorcycle, or it may have been purpose-built as a trike. Several companies offer trike conversion kits that turn a standard dresser into a three-wheeler with the appropriate bodywork and differential to turn the rear wheels. Because those wheels go where the saddlebags were, most trike conversions provide a trunk between them.

In late 2006, Harley-Davidson announced it had signed an agreement with South Dakota's Lehman Trikes to develop a range of Harley-branded three-wheeled vehicles based on its motorcycles. The trikes are now sold through Harley dealers. Lehman has also been building three-wheeled conversions of Honda and Suzuki motorcycles, among others, for many years.

On an historical note, Harley-Davidson offered its three-wheeled Servicar with a 45-cubic-inch flathead (!) engine until 1974. The Servicar had a large box on the back between the wheels and was used by small businesses for deliveries.

Trikes have many advantages for riders of all ages. They don't need to be supported by the rider at stops, but still take a little getting used to, as they don't lean. Like sidecars, trikes are steered by pushing and pulling on the handlebar, which is a bit more work than simply leaning. And of course, with that extra wheel and differential, trikes are heavier than motorcycles and will use more fuel.

TRAILERS

There are two types of trailers: those that are used to haul motorcycles, and those that are hauled *by* motorcycles. Let's begin with the latter.

TRAILERS YOU TOW BEHIND YOUR HARLEY

I was heading for a rally a few years ago when I came upon some other ralliers at a rest stop. It was a group of five bikes, two pulling cargo trailers, and my first reaction was a smirking "Wouldn't you really rather have a Buick?"

If you decide to ride a bike with a sidecar, take it easy until you figure out the handling.

This blue flathead dragon trike with skull is a playful ride.

If you're traveling solo, be certain you can set up your new camper trailer alone.

What wiped that smirk off my face was when the group arrived at the rally that afternoon, and started unpacking their magic boxes: tents, cots, mattresses, coolers, grilles, luggage, lawn chairs, sports equipment . . . as I was cramming my limited collection of stuff into a little dome tent.

The second wave rolled in a little later with their camper trailers, and here came more of the above equipment. They all had a good time that afternoon, playing catch and throwing Frisbees, then spent the evening sitting around a fire in lawn chairs, with tinkling ice from their coolers in their drinks and soft music playing in the background. I squatted in the dirt with a couple cans of warm beer.

When it rained that night I was mucking about trying to keep my gear dry and my air mattress afloat, while those guys were snoring away on cots or had real beds up off the ground. In the morning they could dress standing up while I was flat on my back struggling into damp jeans on a wet floor. And as I was stumbling off bleary-eyed to wait in the rally chow line, they were passing around orange juice, bagels, and coffee and sizzling up a mess of bacon and eggs.

Hauling a trailer behind a motorcycle isn't for everyone, but it sure as heck could have been for me that weekend. Trailers towed by motorcycles come in two flavors, cargo and camping. The former tend to be relatively inexpensive and will haul a lot, while the latter provide that coveted bed up off the ground with a major amount of cargo space underneath.

Cargo trailers: Cargo trailers are basically big, enclosed boxes on wheels that will haul all manner of items, and generally carry from about 9 cubic feet on up to more than 20. The lid usually opens like a clam shell, and they offer options that include lid racks, coolers, larger wheels, light bars and bumpers, custom colors, and more. They'll carry a tent, but if you're camping it can be a much larger tent, and you'll wind up sleeping up off the ground if you pack a cot or two.

Camping Trailers: These are larger and fold out into full tents. On smaller versions the top lifts up to form a roof, while some larger ones have a fold-out, stand-up vestibule that can be used for dressing and sitting. The area under the mattress is storage space for your gear.

If you're traveling solo, be certain you can set up your new camper trailer alone. Could you do it in a high wind? How long does it take to erect? Do a dry run before taking your new camper trailer on the road.

Motorcycle Size

Trailers vary greatly in size and weight, but for most I would recommend utilizing a motorcycle of at least 750cc. That would include all Harley-Davidson models manufactured in the last many years, but an 883 Sportster with only 40 horsepower at the rear wheel may struggle a bit. Big Twins and Sportster 1200s generally have the required power, tire, and frame dimensions necessary to handle the extra weight. As a rule of thumb, a loaded trailer should weigh no more than half as much as the motorcycle towing it. Exceeding this can cause a "wag the dog" scenario, in which the trailer begins swaying side to side, making your bike difficult to control. If you experience this, slow down promptly, as pushed to extremes this sway can cause a crash.

Both trailers and motorcycles have gross vehicle weight rating (GVWR) plates, usually displayed inside the trailer in a prominent place and on the motorcycle's steering stem. The figure lists the maximum allowable weight of vehicle *and* load, including luggage and rider(s). Exceeding this figure can affect the bike's handling. When hauling a trailer, remember to add the tongue weight to the total weight figure on the motorcycle.

Hitches

Motorcycle trailer hitch brackets usually attach to the top shock mounts, and to the passenger footpeg mounts. Since Sportster passenger pegs mount to the swingarm, this may not be the ideal situation for mounting a trailer as it becomes unsprung weight. When you talk with the trailer manufacturers, ask which brand of hitch they recommend for your motorcycle. Installing the hitch will also involve tapping into your motorcycle's wiring to incorporate the trailer's lighting system.

Hitch installation is usually forthright. Most hitch arms bolt to the upper shock mounts and follow along the inside of the rear fender and support the ball just behind the fender. Some will bolt to both the upper shock mounts and the passenger peg mounts, which triangulates the mounting and is generally stronger.

Trailers tend to come with either ball-type or swivel hitches. While you may have your own opinions about which is better, I've turned up no research indicating one to be superior to the other in all circumstances.

Safety Chains

I've heard several stories about state troopers who test the security of a trailer's safety chains by stepping up onto them. They regard chains as a serious safety issue and so should you.

> ## The Fun Factor
>
> Once you've assimilated all this information and have your trailer, be sure to have fun. And as you're sitting there in your lawn chair with your drink and your music and your friends, don't forget those of us who are sleeping on the ground and who are less fortunate. Be sure to rub it in every chance you get.

In 2006, Harley-Davidson announced that it had partnered with Lehman Trikes of Westlock, Alberta, Canada. Lehman will create three-wheelers based on its models at a second plant in Spearfish, South Dakota, which will be sold through Harley dealerships. This black and red Lehman trike is based on a Harley, but was converted prior to the partnership.

Trikes can be colorful and fun. This one was entered in a rally light show and was quite impressive.

The purpose of safety chains is to keep the trailer attached to the tow vehicle should the hitch separate. Keeping things attached is the responsibility of the tow vehicle driver, and should things detach, he's the guy who should be at risk—not the family in the van approaching from the other direction.

When you attach safety chains, allow them sufficient slack so they don't bind when you turn the bike sharply at parking-lot speeds. Also, should the trailer tongue become detached from the hitch while still attached with safety chains, the worst possible scenario would be for the tongue to drop down, dig into the surface, and flip the trailer. This is why you want to cross the safety chains under the tongue like a cradle, so the tongue will drop onto it.

Tongue Weight

No, I'm not talking about your mother-in-law's influence on your marriage, but whether the dog wags the tail or the tail wags the dog. Much of this will depend on the amount of tongue weight the tow vehicle carries. Tongue weight is important both when you're towing a trailer with your bike and when you're towing your bike in a larger trailer.

Tongue weight refers to the amount of downforce exerted by the trailer tongue on the hitch when it's being pulled. Loading too much weight behind the trailer axle will result in too little, or even negative, tongue weight. This will pull upward on the back of the tow vehicle and can induce the trailer to sway and for the two vehicles together to wander and porpoise. On the other hand, excessive tongue weight (too much weight ahead of the trailer axle) could, depending upon hitch dynamics, overly weight the rear of the tow vehicle, lightening the front end and causing wander and understeer. This latter situation is also tough on the suspension and rear tire. Trailer experts tell us to load the trailer so that tongue weight equals 10 percent of the total weight of the trailer and contents.

Calculating Tongue Weight

Here's how to figure tongue weight on a large enclosed trailer used to haul your motorcycle and gear behind a four-wheeler. The same concept works with smaller cargo and camping trailers hauled by motorcycles.

Let's say that your enclosed trailer carries a statement that it weighs 800 pounds empty, your motorcycle weighs 750 pounds, and you're carrying an additional 50 pounds of luggage in the trailer. The combined weight of the trailer and contents is 1,600 pounds, and 10 percent of that would be 160 pounds.

To measure tongue weight for a cargo or camping trailer you're going to pull behind your Harley, load the trailer as you would for the trip, then place a bathroom scale at the same height as the hitch on your bike. You can do this with milk crates, blocks of wood, bricks and concrete blocks, jacks and jackstands, anything you can find that'll do the job. Place the end of the trailer tongue on the scale. If tongue weight does not equal 10 percent of total weight, shift luggage in the trailer or reposition the hitch on the motorcycle until it does.

Get it right. Too much tongue weight places too much weight on the rear of the tow vehicle, which unweights its front wheels, leading to braking and steering problems. Too little tongue weight, on the other hand, means that hard braking may allow the trailer to push upward on the rear of the tow vehicle, unweight the back end, and cause the vehicle and trailer to jackknife. This can lead to serious injury or death.

Wheel Size

Trailers designed for motorcycle use tend to be equipped with 8-, 10-, or 12-inch-diameter wheels. All else being equal, a larger wheel tends to provide a higher and smoother ride; also, larger tires tend to step over holes that smaller wheels can drop into. An 8-inch wheel will rotate at a higher rpm at any given speed than a larger-diameter wheel, so tire wear could be more of a factor. With today's high-quality wheel bearings, rotational speeds should not pose a problem.

Electrical

The trailer manufacturer will provide the wiring and plug necessary to tie your trailer's lights into your bike's electrical system. As for providing the other end of the plug on your bike, it's usually a very simple deal to splice this colored wire into that colored wire. If you don't understand how it's done, take the bike, wiring harness, and wiring diagram to a dealer or service shop.

Weather

When the weather turns nasty, you know what to do—slow down. Crosswinds can be a real handful with a tall trailer. On the other hand, some riders suggest a trailer helps to stabilize their bike in crosswinds.

Fuel Mileage

When you're hauling a trailer, its additional weight, wind resistance, and rolling resistance will reduce your bike's fuel economy. Expect to use about 20 to 25 percent more fuel, and plan your stops accordingly. High speeds, headwinds, and mountain roads can increase fuel use even more.

Maintenance

Trailers are low-maintenance—but not no-maintenance—vehicles. Check wheel bearings periodically according

Sway

Ever see a towed vehicle sway from side to side? The amount of sway has to do with many factors, including the relation of axle width to length. A narrow-axle trailer with a short tongue will tend to wander side to side behind the tow vehicle, while a trailer with a longer tongue and wide axle will tend to pull straighter. A general rule of thumb is that the distance from the hitch ball to the axle should be about 1.5 times the length of the trailer axle.

If sleeping on the ground gets old, a small camping trailer might make sense. This Kompact Kamp unit is relatively light and easy to tow, carries a good amount of luggage, and folds out into a comfortable home on the road. Kompact Kamp

Tire Inflation

Be sure those little trailer tires are properly inflated to the pressure recommended in the owner's manual. Because a trailer will put additional weight and stress on your motorcycle's rear tire, correct inflation pressure is critical here, too. Consult your bike's owner's manual for a range of proper inflation, and inflate the rear tire accordingly. Keep a close eye on tire tread depth, as pulling a trailer will accelerate tire wear, especially on the rear.

Provided you have the parking space at home, an enclosed trailer can also come in handy for other hauling jobs—like moving the kids off to college.

to the instructions in your owner's manual. And keep the hitch ball or swivel lubricated.

TRAILERS FOR HAULING MOTORCYCLES

Riders who trailer their bikes to events take a lot of heat from the stalwarts who ride, but hauling your bike doesn't necessarily mean you're less of a rider—or less of a…you know, less of a guy. Instead, it may mean very different things indeed.

Here are 10 good reasons why riders—real riders—will sometimes trailer their bikes instead of riding them.

1. There are 4-foot snowdrifts in your backyard when you leave for Daytona. Or, it's going to be around 100 degrees on the way to Sturgis.

2. You're hauling your show bike and want it to be pristine when you get there.

3. You want to go with your buddies, and you'll have more fun partyin' in the truck for three days than grinding out the miles.

4. Why put all those miles on a couple of $25,000 customs when you can put them on a beat-up old pickup instead?

5. You can carry a whole lot more tools, luggage, camping equipment, and riding gear.

6. You can load up at the swap meets and from the vendors.

7. When you park at the event, it's possible to sit on top of a larger enclosed trailer for a better view of the festivities.

8. There's less chance of a bike getting stolen from a locked, enclosed trailer. Don't forget to lock your hitch, too.

9. You aren't getting any younger. When you ride hundreds of miles for several days straight, your back hurts and your butt hurts. Things get stiff that shouldn't get stiff, and things that should—well, let's not go there.

10. Finally, if the bike breaks down—okay, let's not go there, either.

TRAILERS ON WHICH YOU TOW YOUR HARLEY
Open Trailers
The two basic types of bike-hauling trailers are open and enclosed. Open trailers, flat and rail type, are much less expensive but they also expose the bikes and equipment to weather, theft, and rock damage. It's easier to tie your bikes down on an open trailer, as you can walk all around it and don't have to duck and bend much. Pull into a gas station or restaurant with your bike in full view, and people will often come up to admire it. Finally, when your trip is over, smaller open trailers may be

Rider Experience

Practice towing your trailer in a low-traffic area if you're new to trailering or have a new trailer. The first rule is never, ever to forget that your trailer is back there. You're going to have to adjust to three tire tracks when it comes to potholes and such, along with more leisurely acceleration and greater braking distances. You'll need much more distance to pass, as your vehicle is now considerably longer and heavier than it was previously. Always make sure that you can see the corners of your trailer in your mirrors; add flags or proximity indicators if you can't.

Slow down. Allow more time to get there, and don't try to keep up with others who have more experience or ability—or who aren't hauling a trailer. High speeds have a much more pronounced effect on a vehicle towing a trailer, which exerts its own forces, than on one without.

Enclosed trailers for hauling motorcycles come in all sizes. Haulmark's Low-Hauler can handle two bikes with lots of luggage. Plus, it allows you to buy all sorts of stuff from the rally vendors! *Haulmark*

stored upright against a wall, and some even fold.

To save potential damage, select an open trailer with a full floor (rather than open rails), full skirting up front and solid fenders. The floor allows the trailer to hold boxes of equipment in addition to bikes, especially when side skirting is added.

Enclosed Trailers

Enclosed trailers offer all the obvious advantages of full protection from the weather and from thieves. Provided you have the parking space at home, an enclosed trailer can also come in handy for other hauling jobs—like moving the kids off to college. Negatives include the initial cost, weight, and attendant fuel costs, and storing the thing. You may wish to consider renting a trailer at first to see if it's what you want.

Unless it's a purpose-built motorcycle trailer, you will likely have to install tie-down points in the floor or walls. An enclosed trailer will need a drop-down ramp door in the back and a side door that allows access to the front of the bikes without your having to fight your way in from the back. Be certain it's tall enough to clear the windshield of your dresser and wide enough to accommodate two bikes—if that's what you plan to haul. Be sure there's also room to store the usual boxes and luggage.

TRAILER TRENDS

One of the major trends in trailers now is convertibility, or multipurpose usage. Some companies offer open trailers that can be adapted to haul motorcycles, watercraft, snowmobiles, lawn equipment, or whatever. And of course, enclosed trailers can haul darn near anything.

Storage

It's a pain having that trailer taking up parking space in your driveway. That's why open folding trailers have become popular. And again, renting a trailer solves the storage problem.

Aerodynamics

Since gasoline prices never seem to go down, trailer manufacturers are beginning to pay more attention to aerodynamics. Instead of the typical boxy shape, enclosed trailers are now sporting V-noses and aerodynamic rounded edges.

LIVING QUARTERS

If you've ever tried to get a room in Daytona for Bike Week, or Sturgis, or Myrtle Beach, you know all about limited availability and exorbitant rates. A large enclosed trailer with compact living quarters, parked in a campground, can save you a lot of money. Some such trailers have a drop-down ramp in the back, and a small

When Trailers Need Brakes

Brakes are required by law on trailers with a load capacity of more than 3,000 pounds. Also, it's a good idea to have independent brakes if the loaded weight of the trailer exceeds 40 percent of the weight of the tow vehicle. An enclosed trailer set up to haul four motorcycles will likely have, and need, brakes.

Since gasoline prices never seem to go down, trailer manufacturers are beginning to pay more attention to aerodynamics.

The Legalities

By federal law, safety chains are required on every trailer, and are designed to keep the trailer connected to the tow vehicle should the hitch fail. Ask the manufacturer to specify that its safety chains meet or exceed the gross rating of the trailer.

Above all, a trailer must be safe! Be certain it meets or exceeds all applicable laws regarding such things as DOT lighting, safety chains, brakes, and tire tread depth. Other requirements vary by state. Hey, don't forget to check that tire pressure!

area into which you can ride a couple bikes. Even so, be sure to reserve your space early.

BRAKES

The majority of trailer brakes are electric, which are usually less expensive, but they require a brake actuator. This black box allows the trailer's brakes to be applied independent of the tow vehicle's brakes. They're a plus in heavy traffic and in the wet. If a trailer begins to sway at speed, a touch on the trailer brakes will usually settle it down.

Should the trailer break away, it will disengage a plug from the tow vehicle that signals the trailer braking system to activate immediately. This system runs on its own battery power, so be sure to maintain this battery in a charged capacity.

Surge brakes are more expensive, noisier in operation, but fully independent of the tow vehicle. They have their own hydraulic system, which actuates by inertia. When the surge brakes sense the inertial change caused by the tow vehicle braking, they apply automatically.

Uni-servo surge brakes tend to actuate when the tow vehicle backs up.

Free-backing surge brakes automatically lock out the brake shoes when the vehicle backs up, but they're more expensive. Surge brakes are also designed to apply automatically should the trailer separate from the tow vehicle.

TOWING TIPS

Towing laws vary by state. Visit your state Department of Motor Vehicles (DMV) for a booklet on your state's laws. For information on proper tongue weight, see the above section on towing a trailer.

Be certain that the mirrors on the tow vehicle protrude far enough to show what's behind. Read the tow vehicle's owner's manual for towing recommendations. Likewise, read and understand the trailer's manual. Be sure the trailer is properly wired and all lights work. Always use matching hitch and ball sizes. Be certain the hitch is properly locked to the ball.

When it comes to loading the bike on the trailer, it's much easier to ride a bike up a full-width, drop-down ramp than to try to push one up a narrow, one-wheel ramp. On most enclosed (and some open) trailers, the rear end hinges down to form a full-width ramp. If you must push a bike up a one-wheel ramp, have one person push from behind as the other steadies the bike from the side and controls the front brake lever. I don't recommend riding up such ramps as, if you were to stall the bike, you've got nowhere to step and could take a nasty fall.

Ratchet-type tie-downs are easier to use when working alone, and provide a more positive grip. Some riders swear by the cam-buckle variety, as they're easier to release. Rather than putting the metal strap hook around the handlebar, use soft straps as there's less potential for damage. Be certain that the front wheel is firmly seated in a wheel chock. If you're concerned that

Cross the trailer's safety chains under the tongue to prevent it from falling onto the pavement should it accidentally detach from the tow vehicle.

Getting Tied Down

Use at least two pairs of tie-downs, one pair off the handlebar and the other off the rear end. A third pair, anchored on the middle of the bike, will provide additional stability. If the trailer does not provide adequate floor anchors for the tie-downs, install them. Tie the bikes down so as to load (but not bottom) their suspension. They'll need some suspension travel to absorb bumps. If the forks and shock(s) are compressed too far just from the tie-downs, you could blow one or more rather-expensive-to-replace seals.

compressing the fork fully may damage fork seals, see if it's possible to attach the straps to the fork sliders. Tie to the handlebar, not the grips, as grips can loosen and rotate. Be certain the handlebar clamps are tight.

Tie the motorcycle down at both ends. In the rear, loop the straps around a luggage rack, frame member, or even over the seat (pad it with a towel), then attach the hook to the strap loop.

For security, lock the bikes to the trailer with case-hardened chains. And use a hitch lock—always.

Do not drive with the trailer in the fast lane of a multilane freeway, as vehicles towing trailers may only occupy the first two lanes. Allow more stopping and maneuvering distance. Follow a maintenance schedule for wheel bearings and other items and keep the trailer's tires properly inflated.

Steel trailers are heavier, but stronger. Enclosed trailers with aluminum skins will ding easily.

Aluminum walls should be protected on the inside with paneling. A half-inch-thick plywood floor may be adequate for handling a single machine or a few dirt bikes, but 3/4-inch plywood is recommended as a minimum if you're carrying more than one Harley.

Hitches are rated by the weight they can carry, so be certain to buy an appropriate hitch for the weight of your trailer, bike(s), and luggage. The 2-inch ball has become the standard. Receiver hitches generally have higher ratings than bumper hitches, and the smaller Class 2 is adequate for most two-bike trailers.

For safety's sake, be certain the hitch is positioned so the trailer is level when it's towed. A retractable wheel on the hitch is a desirable feature, especially on heavy enclosed trailers. It makes it easy to move the trailer around when it's disconnected from the tow vehicle.

A retractable wheel on the hitch is a desirable feature, especially on heavy enclosed trailers. It makes it easy to move the trailer around when it's disconnected from the tow vehicle.

Chapter 10

LET'S RIDE
RIDING TIPS, TRICKS, AND INFO

HERE WE WILL COVER:

- **Riding Tips**

- **Road Strategies**

- **Commuting**

- **Rallies and Other Events**

Think of yourself on a Harley with a group of friends, riding across the desert near sunset with the wind in your faces. Eaglerider will rent you some bikes to make it possible if you don't want to handle the logistics yourself. Eaglerider

With a street-legal motorcycle, the world is your oyster.

WHERE TO RIDE

With a street-legal motorcycle, the world is your oyster. You can ride it on virtually any public road, anywhere. As for deciding where to go, here are a few suggestions.

The motorcycle magazines often carry stories about destinations and roads. *Rider* magazine (for which I have worked since 1990, www.rider-magazine.com) not only carries frequent tour features, but also covers favorite rides, rallies, and clubs. And *American Rider* magazine www.americanrider.com), which is specifically for riders of American-built motorcycles, also carries road tests, product tests, and travel articles. I have also written for *American Rider* since its inception in the 1990s. Of course, there are many other fine magazines out there to satisfy your two-wheeled V-twin lust.

Staying a couple days with friends allows you to have a nice time visiting, get some rest (maybe), sleep in a bed (or on a couch), do the laundry, get a home-cooked meal (sometimes), and see the local sights.

Also consider events. These include the national events such as Daytona, Sturgis, Laconia, the Laughlin River Run, and smaller local and club events. I suggest you join a club that caters to your interests. The Harley Owners Group (HOG) is for Harley riders and is a great way to meet new friends and take part in rides. See your Harley dealer for details, or call 1-800-CLUB-HOG.

Finally, consider all the local events in your area. Your nearby Harley-Davidson dealer probably has a HOG chapter that plans regular rides and other activities. You can find events in the free monthly publication *Thunder Press* (www.thunderpress.net); it has three regional editions for the West, Northeast, and Southeast. It is probably available at your dealer. There may also be other free local or regional motorcycle publications in your area, too.

RIDING TIPS

Ride your own ride: Ted and Mary go to a rally and meet Jim and Alice, who are locals. They hit it off, and Jim and Alice offer to show them the local sights. Jim likes to impress people with his riding skill and he knows the roads well, so he takes off hard, leaving Ted struggling to stay up. The result is usually only a strained early friendship, but sometimes it can be tragic.

Before the ride, make it clear, "We just want to cruise and enjoy the sights." If they ride faster than you want to go, hang back. Don't feel obligated to ride with the pack. Ride your own ride. If Jim sincerely wants you to ride with him, he'll notice you're no longer in his mirrors and slow down. If he doesn't, well, maybe it wasn't meant to be.

RIDING THE LINE

Improvin' your Cruisin' by Knowing about Turns

Has this ever happened to you? You're cruising an unfamiliar winding road, poking along, when you realize that you've really got to put on some miles to get where you're going by dark.

So you step up the pace and soon are lunging out of corners, winding the bike up a bit, shifting, then braking hard for the next corner. But now you're taking the turns in a series of lurches, grinding your floorboards on the pavement, sawing at the handlebar, working hard, and feeling totally out of synch. Then you notice a glitter in your mirrors—a headlight. Soon a rider rolls up behind you. You brake, grind through the next turn, and as you're exiting it you hear a low rumble and he's beside you, looking cool and in control. He nods at you mid-corner, then blasts away and in two corners is gone. *And he's riding the same model Harley **you** are!* Obviously the man is taking chances and is a reckless fool; doesn't he understand he can't ride that kind of bike that way?

Why is one rider able to go through a series of turns smoothly, quickly, and safely with little effort or trouble, while another rides hard yet is slow, awkward, and on the edge of control? It's probably because the smooth rider understands the lines in a turn, and the other does not.

Do You Need to Read This?

You need to read this section if the above has ever happened to you, or if you've ever thought the following:

1) I want to feel smooth and competent in the turns, but don't.

2) I can't seem to understand where to position myself in the lane.

3) I'm not sure how to "read" a turn.

4) I scare myself.

5) I often brake too hard—or too little.

Maps

I love maps! If I have some time with nothing to do and need to go somewhere, my first consideration is to spread out some maps and make plans. I prefer maps with national and state parks marked in green, and I plan my rides around these.

Set out a map and mark the locations of several friends around the country you'd like to see, several national parks, and several roads you've heard about and always wanted to ride. Check the events calendar of clubs of which you're a member or would like to join, and mark the locations. There's your general area to be covered and your general time frame. Call your friends, set some dates, port and polish your credit card, and get your bike tuned. You're in business!

An annual rite of spring is to attend Bike Week in Daytona Beach, Florida, in early March. It's actually more than a week, and it is said that you can find anything you want there.

Daytona's Main Street is wall-to-wall bikes, bars, shops, and fun during Bike Week. There's also Biketoberfest in fall, which is a smaller version of Bike Week.

If you live in the north and it's too cold to ride in March, Daytona gives you the opportunity to get your bike out for the first ride of spring. *Buzz Buzzelli*

The American Motorcyclist Association

Founded in 1924, the American Motorcyclist Association (AMA) is a nonprofit organization that not only sanctions motorcycle competition in the United States, but also serves as a watchdog for motorcyclists' rights. Anti-rider discrimination comes in the form of mandatory helmet laws, land closures, and discriminatory insurance practices, each of which the AMA opposes vigorously. Also, its monthly *American Motorcyclist* magazine is highly informative and entertaining. While the AMA is on our side, it also takes a reasonable approach by advocating that motorcyclists ride safely and responsibly, use land with care, and stay aware that "Noise Annoys."

I have been an AMA member for more than 25 years, and I wish that everyone who rides were a member. For more information visit the AMA website at www.AMADirectlink.com, or call (800) AMA-JOIN.

6) I seem to be working really hard at riding, but can't keep up with my buddies who are riding easily on similar bikes.

Curves

We all learned in geometry class that the shortest distance between two points is a straight line. To ride more smoothly, quickly, and safely through a turn—or series of turns—you need to "straighten" the road. A car, which is a two-track vehicle, can't do that. It's stuck in its lane with little room to maneuver.

Because a motorcycle is a single-track vehicle, however, the rider can roam from side to side of the lane and position himself to take the most direct line through the turns. To do this, you first need to "read" the turn and identify the best line through it.

Those Stinkin' Apexes, and Tight Wide Stuff

First, a few terms. A turn is limited by its inside and outside edges. The apex is the tightest point on the inside of the turn. Before the apex the turn is tightening;

Target Fixation

While this is not a riding skills book, here's one aspect that needs to be addressed. Have you ever come around a curve, noticed a rock in the road, made a mental note to avoid it, and then run over the rock anyway? You feel really foolish when this happens—I know.

The reason you have run over the rock is a phenomenon known as "target fixation." Because we tend to go where we look, when we fixate on an object we tend to go to that object: See rock; run over rock. The antidote is to be aware of this situation and ride accordingly. Now when you come upon a rock in the road, mentally force yourself to locate a pathway around the rock. Got it? Fixate on the pathway, not the rock. Race car drivers use a similar philosophy to avoid a pileup in front of them: "look at the hole." If you see the hole, not the cars, that's where you'll go.

You can use target fixation to your advantage in another way. Have you ever entered a turn too hot, hit the brakes hard, and noticed the ditch looming in front of you? Again, tear your eyes away from the ditch and look at the road where you want to go.

beyond the apex the turn is opening up. In a constant-radius turn, the apex is the point at which the turn begins to open.

We say that a rider who enters a turn near its inside edge (near the apex) is going in "tight." Conversely, one who rides near the outside edge is entering "wide." Thus approaching a right-hand turn from the left side of the lane is going in wide and from the right side is going in tight.

Reading a Turn

Generally, so long as there is no problem with hazards on the pavement or oncoming traffic, you want to enter unfamiliar turns wide—near the outside edge. This not only allows you a better line of sight (view) into the turn, but also allows you to then take the straightest, shortest line through the turn.

Looking Through the Turn

Once you have identified the apex, look well past it down the road to see whether you need to come out of the apex tight or can let your momentum carry you wide to best set up for the next turn. Look where you want to go, as riders tend to go where they look.

The Proper Gear

Before entering a turn, shift down into the proper gear and begin braking so that you will be at the proper speed and rpm as you reach the apex. Then, you can begin accelerating through the apex and power out of the turn. Being in too high a gear causes all sorts of problems: you will have insufficient engine braking as you enter and insufficient power coming out; you'll have to use the brakes more; and you'll still have to downshift, but at a more awkward moment. By being in the proper gear going in you can use the throttle as a rheostat to fine-tune your speed and line through the turn, then accelerate out. So long as you're not exceeding redline, the extra rpm won't hurt your engine.

The proper gear also includes your riding gear. Because riding is risky business, always wear sturdy footwear, gloves, good leather or textile jacket and pants, and a high-quality helmet with good coverage that meets the requirements of the U.S. Department of Transportation (DOT).

Countersteering

If you happen to notice (many riders never do) what's happening during a turn, you will see that the handlebar is pointed in the *opposite* direction from which you're leaning—what!? In a left-hand turn the bar will be cocked slightly to the right. Another way of thinking about it is "push left/go left." This phenomenon is called "countersteering."

The rider initiates the turn with the hands while simultaneously leaning his body into the turn. Countersteering causes the contact patch of the front tire to shift rearward and to the side of the tire. The rider holds the line by balancing centrifugal force with speed and gravity, while using the throttle and perhaps the brakes. Don't force the handlebar; and remember that the same amount of pressure exerted will have a greater effect the slower you're going. Brake and downshift early, then steer and support the lean by bringing the bike back up with the throttle.

Since 1973, more than three million motorcyclists have graduated from the Basic or Experienced Motorcycle Safety Foundation RiderCourses. Some versions of these courses are geared specifically toward Harley riders. *Motorcycle Safety Foundation*

RiderCoaches use hand signals to communicate with students during the Motorcycle Safety Foundation's (MSF) Basic RiderCourse. If you're new to riding and have a Harley, your dealer can provide details about taking such a course. *Motorcycle Safety Foundation*

Learning to Ride:
The Rider's Edge and the MSF

Riding a motorcycle is an acquired skill. It takes time to become proficient, and there is a definite learning curve. To really speed up the process of becoming a safer street rider, the Motorcycle Safety Foundation (MSF) offers Basic and Experienced RiderCourses. These are available in every state, and Canada has its own version. And to help its customers, Harley-Davidson has a version of the course, called the Rider's Edge, that is specifically for riders of its bikes. They're similar to the MSF course and available through H-D dealers.

Both the Rider's Edge and the MSF Basic RiderCourse take place over a few days or consecutive weekends. However, some locations add additional modules of instruction/discussion that lengthen the class. Most locations issue a Completion Card to those who finish the course successfully, and some states will waive part or all of the motorcycle license test for those individuals.

The Basic Course begins with classroom instruction and progresses outdoors to a parking lot. There, students can suit up in safety gear and receive instruction on small bikes (usually a 125cc in the MSF, or the Buell Blast for the Rider's Edge). Students start with the basics by pushing the motorcycle around with the engine off, then riding it at very low speeds. They advance to braking drills, turning, braking in a turn, and all the useful riding skills that will soon become second nature. Once they have completed the basic RiderCourse, new riders can move out onto the public roads with a confidence born of an actual level of skill.

Once you've been riding awhile, you may take the Rider's Edge Skilled RiderCourse, which encompasses six to seven hours of instruction held entirely on the riding range over one or two days. It includes some enhancements developed by Harley-Davidson enthusiasts. You may ride own motorcycles or rent one for the course. This course concentrates on mastering control at low speeds, risk management, limited space maneuvers, cornering judgment, stopping quickly in a curve, swerving and stopping quickly, multiple curve maneuvers and surmounting objects.

The MSF also conducts three versions of its Experienced RiderCourse, which teaches experienced riders advanced skills. Here, riders use their own motorcycles. To learn more about the Motorcycle Safety Foundation and its RiderCourses, call (800) 446-9227, or go to www.msf-usa.org.

The MSF also offers dirt-bike training, which it bills as a fun, one-day, hands-on training session available to all riders six years of age and older in a low-pressure environment. It teaches basic riding skills, responsible riding practices, risk management, and environmental awareness. Call (877) 288-7093, or go to www.dirtbikeschool.com.

Canadian riders are directed to the Canadian Safety Council at (613) 739-1535, or go to www.safety-council.org.

Brake Control

You may have noticed that as you apply the brakes when leaned over, the bike wants to stand back up. This is one reason why it's not a good policy to roar into a turn and nail the brakes. Another is that hard braking injects layers of concerns (like suspension dive and the percentage of traction your front tire has to devote to braking versus turning) that you really don't want to have to deal with while you're approaching a corner's apex. Try to finish braking before you're deep into the turn.

However, there is a very useful concept called "trail braking" that can help you get through turns. Remember how the bike wants to stand up while braking? Well, put this concept to use by lightly braking up to the apex (longer than you normally would) as you're entering the turn. This will not only slow the motorcycle, but will also prevent it from destabilizing and trying to flop into the turn, while also compressing the suspension slightly. This series of events will slow the bike, help keep it stable through the turn, and when you get on the gas the energy stored in the compressed suspension system will help the bike to spring up out of the turn and away.

Use a similar technique in very tight turns (such as hairpins or in parking lots) if you feel that the bike is becoming

unstable; dragging the rear brake while staying on the throttle will help stabilize it at low speeds.

Late Apexing

We already understand that apexing a turn means to clip its inside edge in a line that maximizes flowing smoothness and efficiency. Late apexing means slowing down and delaying the turn and apex point. The rider chooses the point at which he will change his line (or his apex point), rather than taking that dictated by the turn.

For example, a rider in a blind right turn may late apex in order to give himself a better view through the turn. In a blind left-hand turn, if you apex at or near the centerline, your bike and body will be leaning out over the centerline into the oncoming lane—perfect placement if you wish to become a hood ornament on that approaching Peterbilt. In all cases, taking the proper line through a turn allows your riding to be smoother, faster, and safer.

SCARED STRAIGHT

Riders scare themselves because they don't know quite how fast to approach a turn, how to read it, or where to position themselves. The key is to look through the corner and work on lines and smoothness. Practice on quiet, winding roads.

The wisest words I've heard on the subject come from Reggie Pridmore, three-time national Superbike champion back in the '70s who, in the 1980s, instituted his CLASS motorcycle safety school and still conducts it. Sessions are held at racetracks nationwide, but teach performance riding rather than racing skills. He's trained thousands of students; I've taken his sessions a half-dozen times and can highly recommend them. Pridmore advises: "Don't go out there and try to be fast. Go out there and try to be smooth. When you become smooth, you will become fast." You can reach CLASS at www.classrides.com, or (805) 933-9936. Many other such track schools are also available.

A one-day riding skills tune-up aimed more toward the sporty rider is the Lee Parks Total Control Advanced Riding Clinic (ARC). The eight-hour program includes lunch and a workbook, and all students must have at least one year of prior riding experience. You provide your own bike and appropriate riding gear. Contact Lee Parks Design, Box 1838, Victorville, CA 92393, (800) 943-5638, (801) 760-8261 (fax), or www.leeparksdesign.com.

If you do get into a scary situation where you're in a turn too hot, remember

"Don't go out there and try to be fast. Go out there and try to be smooth. When you become smooth, you will become fast."

Though you probably don't intend to become a racer, learning to ride better will make you not only a quicker rider, but a safer one, too.

lean into turns, then it's something you expect. Still, what drags, and where and to what extent it does so, is important.

It's okay to drag the pivoting kind of floorboards that fold up. Problems can occur when you begin dragging hard, unyielding parts such as stands, exhaust systems, and frame members. As the bike rolls over onto these hard parts, they begin to take weight that was riding on the tires. Transfer too much weight onto a dragging part and it can lever your tire off the ground, causing you to slide out of control. Don't go there.

Even when you think you've got the lean angle dialed, hitting a pavement dip while leaned over can cause additional parts to hit or drag. This is irritating and can be dangerous. Also, the weight of a passenger and luggage will compress the suspension system more than if it's just you on the bike, and parts will drag more easily.

If your bike drags too easily, open your owner's manual and read the section on setting spring preload on the suspension. It usually involves turning a ramped collar on the shock absorbers, or sometimes sticking a screwdriver or drift into a hole in the shock cover and rotating the collar to increase spring preload and ride height.

If your bike has an air suspension system, pumping more air pressure into it will increase ride height. Follow the instructions in your owner's manual and do not use a high-pressure system (like a service station hose) to adjust the air pressure in your suspension. Too much pressure can blow out seals. It can also introduce oil into your suspension system.

If the bike still drags too easily, consider installing a longer set of aftermarket shock absorbers to raise the bike in the rear and provide additional cornering clearance. The tradeoff is that this can also speed up its steering and increase forward weight transfer during

that you tend to go where you look. Look down the road to where you want to be and brake smoothly. The same applies when you come upon rocks in the road. Don't look at the rocks, look for the pathway *through* the rocks.

CORNERING CLEARANCE

Part of a Harley's appeal is its long wheelbase and low seat height, but as a result cornering clearance is going to be a problem if you try to take corners fast. In motorcycling being cool is optional, but making turns is required. To make those turns you have to lean the bike over. If your bike tends to drag floorboards, your boots, or other yielding parts while you braking. To bring things back in balance you could then add longer fork springs to raise front ride height, but at this point see your dealer—we're getting beyond the scope of this book. Finally, keep in mind that raising the bike overall will raise seat height, which shorter riders may not appreciate and which will reduce the coolness factor.

One other approach is to adjust your line. To delay running out of cornering clearance, enter the turn a little slower and tighter than usual. Lean it over as far as you dare, then as things begin to drag give ground by standing the bike up gradually as you allow it to drift to the outside of the turn. While this is not a solution to the cornering clearance problem, it's a way of dealing with it until you can fix it.

Another method of getting through a turn quickly without dragging hard parts as much is to shift your body weight to the inside of the turn. Do this by sliding across the seat and hanging one cheek off to the inside, then pulling the bike toward you. This method allows you to ride through the turn with the bike more upright, yet with full control.

Or, maybe you can move or change parts that drag so they don't anymore.

In any case, follow these suggestions and you will become smoother, faster, and safer through the turns. And that's its own reward.

PICKING UP A FALLEN BIKE

If all else fails, despite your best efforts, and the bike falls over, here's how to get it back on its wheels. Keep in mind that 30 years ago, when most of us were riding bikes up to 500 or 650cc (and we were 30 years younger), picking up a fallen bike was not that difficult. Today, with dressers weighing 800 to 900 pounds or more, it can be a real problem. I recall the time I rode a Honda GL1200 Gold Wing out into a field of flowers to photograph it . . . then had to hike back out to the road and flag down a guy to

ask him to help me pick it up. That's before I learned the key to doing it myself if no one is around to help.

The key is to remember that legs are stronger than arms and that it all starts with a wedge. If you drop your bike, remove any dense items that can come off easily such as the camping gear on the seat, the case of wine in the saddlebags, and the anvil in the trunk. There's no big rush unless it's leaking gas or battery acid.

If possible, put the bike in gear so it won't roll. Get on the low side and turn the handlebar toward you. Now, lifting as much as possible with your arms, try to wedge your knee under some part of the frame or a part of the engine that isn't hot. This could be a footpeg, floorboard, or frame member. Yes, it will probably get your pant leg dirty, but the alternative is to hang around and wait for help.

Be sure you'll be able to deploy the sidestand if the bike has fallen on its left side; deploy the stand before you pick up the bike if it's fallen to the right. Then, through a process of lifting with your arms and legs, and wedging your leg deeper into the bike, work it up high enough so that you can deploy the stand.

Head up, eyes alertly on the road, sane, sober, and sure is a good way to ride. One way to help tune up your riding skills is to ride with others who are good riders. Don't be afraid to ask questions.

Really hooking into the road on a competent motorcycle is a great joy. This V-Rod rider is obviously having a good time! *Buzz Buzzelli*

TIP

An alternative method of picking up a fallen bike is to stand with your back to the bike, bend at your knees, keep your back straight and grab any solid part of the bike you can. Then lean into the bike and push up with your legs. Just be careful you don't go over the other way.

In matters in which the officer has discretion as to whether or not to issue a ticket, did I mention attitude counts?

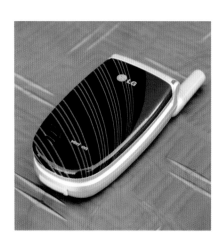

Cell phones have quickly become an indispensable tool when traveling; carry one for emergencies. Keep it handy, but don't try to answer it should it ring while you're riding.

If there are objects available such as rocks or chunks of wood, have them handy to slide under the bike as you work it up so it will not slip all the way back down if you cannot hold it.

ROAD STRATEGIES

Tank up the night before: You awake before the sun to get an early start, then waste an hour running around town looking for an open gas station. Prepare your bike the night before by tanking up late.

No matter when you get up, check tire pressure when the tires are still cold, and check the oil supply. The oil usually won't vary much from day to day, but I once was alerted to a nail in my tire by the fact it was a few psi low on successive mornings.

You need those stinkin' papers: If you get stopped by the law, you're going to have to produce your driver's license, registration, and possibly insurance papers. Make it easy on yourself by bringing them along and by being polite to the officer. Attitude counts, and if you get belligerent—trust me—he or she has dealt with your kind before. In matters in which the officer has discretion as to whether or not to issue a ticket, did I mention attitude counts?

And don't forget to bring your owner's manual. A shop manual can come in handy, too.

Contact information: Didja ever take a trip and become separated from others in your group? Before the trip, have everyone trade mobile phone numbers. If someone doesn't have a mobile phone, they still need to have the list of numbers of those who do and agree to call as soon as possible.

Also, I don't want to jinx anyone, but riding friends should share contact numbers for family members in case someone has an accident or medical problem. In some cases, a next-of-kin must give permission for medical treatment if the individual is not conscious, and in those situations time is critical.

ROAD EMERGENCIES

Here's how to deal with common road emergencies.

Service early: Stretching might be good exercise for you, but it's hell on your bike. Stretching that last tune-up, oil change, tire change, drive-belt adjustment, or tank of gas is just asking for it. Get your bike serviced early to handle delays or to work out the bugs. If there's something wrong with your bike at the start of the trip, I can guarantee it won't improve during the trip.

Flat tire: I covered this in detail in Chapter Eight, but here's a quick reference. Establish if your bike has tube-type or tubeless tires. For the past 20 years or so, most bikes with cast wheels have carried tubeless tires, while most with wire-spoke wheels have had tube-type. If it's a tube-type, you'll have to "break the bead," pull the tire away from the wheel (pack tire irons) far enough to expose the puncture in the tube. This will mean removing the wheel from the bike, and because Harleys do not have centerstands you may as well call the dealer.

Roughen the area around the puncture with the tool supplied in the patch kit and apply cement. Wait momentarily until the glue becomes tacky, then apply the patch.

For a tubeless tire, it's only necessary to remove the nail and insert the tool from the patch kit to enlarge and roughen the hole. Cover a plug with cement and insert. Cut off excess and add air with CO_2 cartridges, an electrical pump that runs off the battery, or a hand pump.

Tools: Toolkit, tire patch kit, tire irons, air supply.

Prevention: Inspect tire tread frequently for depth and foreign objects, and check pressure regularly. The last 10 percent of tire life results in 90 percent of the problems.

Low oil: Suddenly the oil light comes on. You're a quart low—oops! Rodney has a quart along, but your bike runs that expensive 20W50 synthetic bike oil and his is 40W cheapo car oil. Can you mix them?

The answer is yes. Considering that the alternative is either serious engine damage or sending someone on a 100-mile goose chase, mixing will not harm your engine, though it will dilute the properties of the high-quality oil. Change oil and filter at your earliest convenience.

Tools: Rag, funnel, extra quart of oil.
Prevention: Check oil.

Sudden engine stop; reason unknown: A sudden engine cutout usually boils down to fuel or electricity. Check fuel supply, check for a clogged gas cap vent (does opening the cap temporarily "solve" the problem?) or fuel filter. If there's fuel in the carburetor float bowl(s), the problem likely resides elsewhere.

Turn on the ignition and see if you have lights, horn, and starter. If not, check that the battery cables are tightly connected and clean. Is the battery properly topped up with distilled water? Spray WD-40 on the sparkplugs, wires, and coils to displace any water.

If you have strong lights and horn, check fuses (know your bike's fuse box location, and carry spares). With a clip lead and light, clip the lead to ground (a piece of bare metal on the engine) and place the point on either side of the fuse with the ignition on. If there's power on both sides, the fuse is good.

If the starter cranks but the engine does not start, use the clip lead to establish if there is juice at the coils. If so, pull

the spark plugs and establish if they're sparking. If not, trace the wires back to the last place where there was electricity, then inspect upstream for bare wires or breaks. Listen and watch for obvious stray sparks. Wrap broken wire with electrical tape to get you home.

Tools: Clip lead, electrical tape, fuses, WD-40.
Prevention: Pray.
And of course, whenever you travel, carry a mobile phone.

Riding in town requires a whole different strategy from riding the open road. Here, alertness is your first line of defense, as other motorists can (and will) come at you seemingly from out of nowhere.

Two-up riding doubles your fun when you reach your destination, but along with the fun comes additional responsibility. Be aware that the bike becomes heavier and harder to handle with two people aboard. The obvious message here is to slow down and enjoy the ride.

Go Along for the Ride

I've occasionally had passengers who actually gripped the bike with their legs and tried to stand it up as I gently leaned it into a turn . . . *not* a good practice! Remember, you want to allow the motorcycle to go where the rider wants it to go. To do otherwise is to invite disaster.

To help you go with the turn, look over the rider's shoulder in the direction of the turn. For example, if a left turn is coming up, look over the left shoulder. This will give you a better sense of what's happening on the bike, and the subtle weight shift will help the rider take the turn. Do not shift your weight drastically, however.

PASSENGERS

Whether you call them passengers, pillions, or co-riders (a much more active term), the person on the back of the bike really adds to the ride—especially when you've reached your destination. Here are a few words for the person on the back about getting there, the riding part of the experience.

Get the okay: Don't mount the bike until the rider says it's okay. Ask "Ready?" and wait for the affirming nod. It's really disconcerting for the rider to be pulling on a glove or strapping on a helmet when the passenger suddenly begins to mount, and the bike lurches to the side.

Mount from the left: Always mount a motorcycle from the left side, meaning your left when sitting astride the bike. That's the direction in which the bike leans on its sidestand, and that's where the rider expects you to be coming from.

Keep in balance: Disrupt the bike as little as possible when mounting. If you're tall enough, stand beside the bike, throw your right leg across the seat and slide on over. If you're not tall enough, allow the rider to straighten the bike, wait for his nod, step up onto the left footpeg, and throw your leg over. When mounting this way, place your hand on the rider's shoulder to steady yourself as you mount.

How to hold: If there's a backrest, lean against it. If there is no backrest, you'll have to lean forward and maintain muscle tension. Use the handholds (if any) on the sides of the bike if you must, but it's far better to place your hands on the rider's hips. Or, wrap your arms around the rider's torso. If that's too personal (or the torso is too large), you can grab the sides of his jacket. How chummy you get depends upon how well you know—or want to know—the rider.

Go with the lean: This is the second reason why it's best to hang on to the rider. I once took my sister for a ride, and she screamed every time the bike leaned over. Unfortunately, I had not sufficiently alerted her to the fact that leaning is how a motorcycle turns and is not necessarily the first step to a fall. The message to the co-rider is to go with the lean and trust that the rider knows what he or she is doing. If you don't trust them, don't get on the bike in the first place.

Become one with the bike: The best passenger is the one who's completely neutral, the one the rider can completely forget is even back there. Becoming one with the bike is the best way to ride. An easy rule to help do this is to keep your shoulders directly behind the rider's shoulders. That way, wherever he goes, you go. The weight transfer will be completely natural, and, best of all for the rider, predictable.

Keep your feet up: When the bike comes to a stop, keep your feet on the pegs. You don't need to "help" by putting a foot down. Not only is the rider perfectly capable of holding up the bike alone, but your major weight shift to get a foot down will severely unbalance the bike.

TIP

I know a guy who bought a neat intercom system for himself and his wife, and he decided to install the headsets the morning they left. It only took a few minutes to mount the headsets in the helmets, but when he tried to plug in the battery packs—oops, they were NiCads and had to be charged for four hours. Be prepared.

Anticipate: Do you find you sometimes click helmets with the rider? Learn to anticipate shifting and braking, a skill you'll develop with time. This situation will also be minimized if there's a backrest against which you can lean. If you expect to be riding with this person often, it's perfectly reasonable to request they install a backrest for your comfort.

No surprises: As you ride along, you will see things that surprise and delight you. However, if the rider is lost in reverie it's not a good idea to suddenly shout into his ear. This can startle the rider and take his attention away from the road. Instead, devise a signal (such as squeezing his arm) to let him know that you want to talk. Better yet, suggest to the rider that he pick up a rider/passenger intercom system that fits in the helmet and allows you to talk as you ride. In any case, resist the temptation to surprise the rider with nonessential information, or to shout in his ear unless there's an emergency. It can be frustrating and distracting to try to converse on a motorcycle.

WOMEN WHO RIDE

The sight of women riding their own bikes is becoming increasingly common, and women have their own special situations. Because they're usually smaller, women will tend to feel more comfortable on lighter, smaller bikes. All Harleys generally have a low seat height, and although they're heavy, the Big

The sight of women riding their own bikes is becoming increasingly common.

In 1979, grandmother Hazel Kolb rode her 80-inch Electra Glide around the perimeter of the United States—alone—to honor her late husband's memory. Her story was picked up by the news media all over the country, and she was a guest on *The Tonight Show with Johnny Carson*.

Though a high percentage of motorcycle operators are male, the riding community welcomes female riders. It's a good idea, however, for all riders to wear proper apparel at all times. *Buzz Buzzelli*

Twins are easy to ride because they carry their weight so low.

To say much more is to buy into the old stereotypes about women: they don't know much about mechanical things, they're too weak to hold the bike up, they would be prey to unscrupulous men—you know the rest. I would rather just give women the same advice I give all riders. A motorcycle is a tool for a job. Define the job accurately and that will help you choose the right bike. And of course, with an increasing number of companies now offering women's apparel, it's pretty easy to choose protective gear sized and cut for you.

Women are often leery of riding or traveling alone. However, as a means of encouragement I want to mention that I had the privilege of knowing Hazel Kolb, "The Motorcycling Grandma." In 1979, Hazel rode her 80-cubic-inch Harley-Davidson Electra Glide around the perimeter of the United States—alone. She spent her "80 Days on an 80" when she was in her 50s, partly as a tribute to her late husband and partly because she wanted to prove something to herself. During the course of her "Perimeter Ride" her story was picked up by the national news media, and she appeared on *The Tonight Show with Johnny Carson*, where she was interviewed by Carson himself.

I later helped Hazel write her autobiography, *On the Perimeter*, which is now out of print. Her attitude was "Other women talked about doing this sort of thing. I just went ahead and *did* it!" Good for her! Unfortunately, she passed away of cancer in 1990.

COMMUTING

Many commuters utilize motorcycles for getting to work because they use less gas than a car, slice through traffic jams, and are often easier to park. Of course, a bike can't carry nearly as much, and you'd better have some good riding gear for inclement weather. Still, offsetting all of this is the enjoyment factor—riding a motorcycle is just a lot more fun than driving a car or taking a bus or train.

A full weatherproof suit that goes on over your work clothes is a real plus. A briefcase will fit in most saddlebags, and lunch and other small items in a tank bag, the other saddlebag or TourPak. A laptop can be carried in a saddlebag, so long as it's well padded.

WILL A MOTORCYCLE REDUCE COMMUTING COSTS?

With the high cost of gasoline, some non-riders have asked about commuting to work by motorcycle to

Women Riders
By Genevieve Schmitt

One of the biggest shifts in the motorcycle industry in the last 30 years is the growth and impact of female motorcyclists. Women are taking up motorcycling in record numbers.

Why are so many women sliding onto the front of a motorcycle seat? Because they want the same excitement of riding one's own bike that men have enjoyed all these years. In society, more women are exercising their independence. They're asserting themselves and rising up corporate ladders and, as a result, have their own disposable income. Women are seeing other women on the road riding their own motorcycles, and they are inspired by that. Old stereotypes of the loose biker babe are gone. There are no more societal barriers for a woman who wants to ride her own motorcycle, other than the ones she imposes on herself.

And that is one of the areas where men and women differ in the two-wheeled world. Many women are holding themselves back from motorcycling by what they perceive as barriers. Those barriers are confidence, product knowledge, skills, and life stage.

Confidence: Sometimes a woman is intimidated by the thought of handling such a big machine. "What if I can't handle it on my own?" and "What if I drop the bike?" are some of the negative thoughts that run through her head. As with any sport or activity, there is a learning curve. As one gradually increases in skill level, confidence builds. There are many small women who can ride a motorcycle. One's size should not be a limitation.

In recent years, bike manufacturers have broadened their model lineups to include many different sizes. The aftermarket industry has responded by offering plenty of parts to modify a motorcycle to fit riders better. There are ways to lower a motorcycle, bring the handlebars closer to the rider, lower the seat, or adjust the footpegs—nearly any part of a motorcycle can be changed to accommodate a particular rider. Size is no longer a limitation.

Product knowledge: If a woman has never been exposed to motorcycling, she may be intimidated by a lack of knowledge on how to operate a motorcycle. Proper training takes students through every step of learning, starting with the basics. Contact your Harley dealer or the Motorcycle Safety Foundation for information on training.

Skills: For some, a barrier to pursuing the enjoyment of motorcycling is not knowing where to start. Fortunately, there are training classes in street and dirt riding in every state and in Canada. Most schools use a curriculum developed by the Motorcycle Safety Foundation, the industry standard in how-to-ride instruction. These classes are very popular among women, and one-third of all graduates are female. In some states, passing the riding test in the class satisfies the state motor vehicle licensing requirements. Taking the beginner class is also a good opportunity to see if motorcycling is something you might enjoy.

Motorcycling is like any other activity—the more you practice, the more proficient you become. No one can expect to be an expert rider right after graduating from the training class. Rather, some women and men will practice their newfound skills in a parking lot or in a quiet neighborhood before hitting the streets. Everyone learns at his or her own pace.

Life stage: Some women will use the excuse that they are too busy doing something else in their lives, so they don't have time to learn to ride a motorcycle. For example, "I just had a baby" or "I just started a new career." Women can always find an excuse not to ride. The question is how badly do you want to ride? So many female riders say they would have started riding earlier if they had only known how much joy it would bring to their lives.

For a woman, motorcycling is an expression of herself. Many say riding is very empowering, that the confidence they get from riding their own motorcycles spills over into other areas of their lives. It's that "you don't know what you're missing until you do it" kind of thinking.

So, if you've ever thought about donning a leather jacket, some cool black boots, and a pair of stylish shades and cruising along the open road in search of adventure, now's the time to do it. Motorcycle riding is the stuff dreams are made of, and so many women are living their dream right now. Isn't it time you did, too?

For more information on women riders, go to Genevieve Schmitt's website at www.womenridersnow.com.

Don't ever think that just because you don't have your ideal bike, you can't take that trip or go on that ride. Whether your ride is a Big Twin, Sportster, V-Rod, or something else, ride it and enjoy it now. There's time to get your ideal bike later, but the time to ride is *now*!

Riding a Harley gives the rider entrée to certain special events. Here's the crowd for the Harley Barbecue and Rodeo at the Americade Rally.

save money. I'm often asked how many miles a motorcycle can typically go on a gallon of gas, and if it would be a good idea to buy one for commuting.

To answer that first question, as a professional motorcycle test rider I have tested bikes from 250cc to more than 2,000cc, and I find that generally, under testing conditions (which means hard usage), new bikes will average from about 37 to 50 miles or more per gallon. Fuel mileage varies, depending upon the size and orientation of the bike (heavier and more powerful bikes tend to be thirstier- and how it's used. I have found that a

rider on a smaller bike trying to stay with aggressive riders on larger bikes will sometimes get fewer miles per gallon, as he has to ride the smaller bike so hard.

Professional testers tend to be aggressive riders; it's fun to go fast, and we're not paying for the gas, tune-ups, tires, or insurance! We probably use test bikes harder than the average person would use a personal bike. Therefore, I would estimate that a sane rider (that means someone *other* than a professional test rider) could probably improve my figures above by from 3 to 5 miles per gallon on the bigger bikes and 5 to 10 on

There's nothing like a custom Harley to garner attention and entice people to come on over and talk. Here's a colorful custom spotted at the Americade rally in Lake George, New York.

the smaller ones. In general, 40 to 55 miles per gallon is well within reason for the great majority of street motorcycles, including Harley-Davidsons. How much better mileage it will get than a car depends a lot upon the nature of the car, the bike, and the commute.

It's a complex question whether this mileage difference would convince someone who doesn't ride to buy a motorcycle, learn to ride it, equip themselves for riding, and then insure and maintain the bike. I can't tell you the answer, but I can tell you how to go about thinking about it.

Let's say, for example, that your car gets 20 miles per gallon, and gas costs $3.00 per gallon. A Sportster you might buy for commuting may get 45 miles per gallon. In every 1,000 miles, the car would require $150 in fuel costs, and the motorcycle would require $66.67. If you live 25 miles from work, your daily commute would be 50 miles, so, assuming 20 work days per month, you'd commute 1,000 miles a month, or approximately 12,000 miles per year. Let's cut that figure by a third, though, because you'll take the car during inclement weather, on days on which you had to carry bulky items to or from work, when you need to give someone a

ride, etc. Now you're commuting 8,000 miles per year on the motorcycle rather than taking the car. Your fuel costs for those 8,000 miles would be $533.33; had you taken the car you would have spent $1,200. Congratulations, you've have saved $666.67 in one year! Had you been diligent and taken the motorcycle *every single day*, your fuel savings over the 12,000-mile distance would have been $1,000!

However, for the first year at least, you've got to figure the minimal cost of outfitting yourself with a helmet ($50), jacket ($200), gloves ($50), boots ($100),

Rallies and events are great places to see and be seen, as well as have a little fun. In the world of Harleys, events like Daytona, Myrtle Beach, Sturgis, and others are becoming part of the lore.

If you ever get the chance, be sure to visit the Harley-Davidson Traveling Museum. It provides a compact view of The Motor Company's history.

I have good news and bad news. The bad news is that, all things considered, buying a motorcycle (in addition to keeping your car) for the sole purpose of saving money is not likely to work out. However, if you're doing it to save natural resources and energy, well, you've likely used at least 1,000 fewer gallons of gasoline, and possibly more than 1,600 gallons fewer. The other good news is that motorcycles are wonderfully fun, and a great many people happily ride even when they understand they're not saving any significant amount of money.

Personally, most of my closest friends are people I've met through riding, and they have enriched my life greatly. It has been said that motorcycling is the most fun a person can have fully clothed, and I cannot disagree with that statement.

MOTORCYCLE EVENTS, RIDES, AND RALLIES

There are many kinds of motorcycle rallies, and they're all fun. These gatherings run the gamut from highly organized to very loose affairs, and from family oriented to "biker" events complete with readily available alcohol and wet T-shirt contests. A rally is any kind of motorcycle event that tends to go on for a couple days or longer, while a ride is usually an event that starts at Point A and may end at the same place, or at a Point B. Rides are often among the major activities within a rally.

and Motorcycle Safety Foundation course ($100). In 8,000 miles you will likely have gone through at least one set of tires (bike tires don't last nearly as long as car tires), and that may cost $200 to $300 or more. You have already spent $700, not including the original cost of buying the motorcycle, insuring it, and tune-ups. If you ride the bike five years, your total fuel savings will be $3,333.20 to $5,000, which may just approach what you paid for a used bike five years ago that now has an additional 40,000 miles on it. Only it still doesn't include five years of insurance costs, tune-ups, and maybe four more sets of tires. Discouraged?

Motorcycle events, rides, and rallies come in all shapes and sizes. The largest events in the United States are Bike Week, held in Daytona Beach, Florida, every March, and the Sturgis Rally and Races, held in Sturgis, South Dakota, every August. More than 300,000 riders attend these events each year, and I've seen estimates of close to 400,000. They're huge! Most rallies are much smaller and consist of anywhere from a few hundred riders to a few thousand. The largest touring rally in the United States is Americade in Lake George, New York, each June (www.tourexpo.com).

At rallies you will find a wealth of activities that can include races, field events (bike games), vendors, door prizes, bike shows (with judging and trophies), live entertainment (usually bands), seminars, and much more. The larger rallies will attract demo teams from the major manufacturers, and you can take free rides on new motorcycles.

There are three general types of rallies: brand, club, and open. Brand rallies are intended for riders of certain brands of bikes, and a great percentage of them attract riders on Harley-Davidsons. If they're sponsored by a club, attendance may be restricted to members and guests only. Of course, if you show up at the gate and are not a member, there is usually someone who will cheerfully sign you up. You will not necessarily have to ride that certain brand or model to the rally, but if you don't you're kind of missing the point.

Club rallies are usually restricted to members only, or members and guests, and they cover a wide area of motorcycling interests. While some are formed around brands or models as above, others may be centered on a certain area of interest such as touring, vintage, or performance riding.

Open rallies are those that welcome all comers. These include Sturgis, Daytona, the Laughlin River Run, Myrtle Beach, and many more. Membership is not required, but an entry fee may be, at least for certain rally events. For example at Americade, anyone can ride into Lake George, New York, and hang around during the rally. However, if you wish to enter the grounds where the seminars are held, sign up for a tour, enter the area where most of the vendors and demo rides are located, you'll need a wristband that is available only at the registration booth for a fee.

Sane and Sober

We all know that drinking alcohol slows your reaction time, impairs judgment, and makes you more prone to take risks and that it's just plain stupid to drink and operate a motor vehicle. Be aware that drinking can also make you sleepy, especially when combined with a late dinner.

If you'd like to enjoy a nightcap, bring along a bottle and enjoy it once you've reached your destination and are in for the night. Pack a corkscrew and bottle opener—they may be on your multitool.

PARADES AND RIDES

Many rallies include a parade as part of the program, in which case you'll be introduced to formation riding. The idea is to ride two bikes to a lane, but staggered so you're not riding right beside the bike in the other wheel track. This formation allows the riders more space should they need to meander from their wheel track to avoid an obstacle or pothole, or to take a better line in a turn. Increase following distance as speed increases, and if the parade heads out into the country where the roads are winding, break formation and ride single-file.

Group rides should follow the same format as parades: Formation riding applies in town as well as on freeways, with appropriate spacing depending upon speed. Rather than riding in huge groups, rides should be broken into smaller groups led by a ride leader. In this way, more compact groups can usually be led intact through stoplights. In the more organized rides, each group has a leader and a sweep rider, connected by radio. When a small group is broken by a stoplight, the sweep rider will alert the lead rider by radio, who will pull the group over so that it can reunite. If this isn't practical, the sweep rider can ride to the head of the second-half group and conduct them until they join up with their front half.

TIP

The biggest problem with parades is stoplights. At larger events, the rally promoters will have arranged with local law enforcement to place officers at the lights to hold traffic and conduct the riders through.

The idea is to ride two bikes to a lane, but staggered so you're not riding right beside the bike in the other wheel track.

While some riders envision racetrack days as being exclusively for those who plan to race, that's far from true for the great majority of riders who take them.

CAMPING BY MOTORCYCLE

Motorcycle camping and backpacking have a lot in common. In both activities the main concerns are weight and finding enough room to pack everything. At least motorcyclists have the upper hand—we don't have to carry the weight on our backs!

Camping styles are quite personal, and you'll learn a lot more about camping or backpacking in books about those specific activities than you will here, but let's cover the basics of motorcycle camping.

As you know, carrying a passenger by motorcycle not only nearly doubles your luggage needs, but also takes up that valuable bit of carrying room on the rear portion of the seat. For that reason, riding two-up makes camping more difficult. I have done it, but found that it really puts a strain on packing and luggage capacity. You'll still only need one tent if it's a two-person or larger, but what you have to carry in terms of sleeping bags, pads and clothing will double.

Camp cooking requires a lot of packing space for cooking gear and food, so to compensate for the additional luggage needs of a passenger I have found it necessary to do away with any attempt to cook meals in camp. We eat in restaurants when packing double.

If you're riding solo, I suggest using the rear portion of the seat for a large nylon bag that will accommodate the tent, sleeping bag, pad, and camp chair. If the bag is not waterproof, line it with a sturdy bag that is. For more information on camping and travel by motorcycle, see Chapter Six on Touring.

TRACK DAYS

While some riders envision racetrack days as being exclusively for those who plan to race, that's far from true for the great majority of riders who take them.

The ABCs of Siphoning

When you run out of gas and someone produces a siphon hose, your first reaction is, "Aw, man, I'm not gettin' gas in *my* mouth!" Well, with the alternative being a long and inconvenient delay, that hose starts looking more delicious all the time.

If you do it right, siphoning doesn't have to mean raw gas in your mouth. Start with about five feet of thin, clear-plastic industrial hose available at any auto supply store. Arrange that the donor bike is sitting higher than the dry bike, such as up on a curb or rise. Stick one end of the hose into the fuel supply until just the end part you're holding is sticking out, then cap the end you're holding with your thumb. Now, slowly withdraw the hose from the fuel supply (the vacuum caused by your thumb will pull the gas with it), keeping the open end of the hose immersed in the donor bike's fuel supply. The hard part will be keeping the open end of the hose immersed, as the coiled hose tends to want to coil again when straightened.

Pull the capped end of the hose over the open tank of the dry bike. Once the fuel level in the hose is *below* that of the level in the donor tank (watch it through the clear hose), remove your thumb and the gas should flow. If this simply cannot be done, siphon by mouth only until the level in the hose reaches below that of the tank, then pull away and let 'er flow.

The better alternative is to buy a siphon hose with squeeze bulb that allows for easy siphoning without having to create a vacuum with your mouth. They're available in auto parts stores for $10 or less.

Road Food

Snackers: You ride, you get hungry, but a big, heavy meal (like a double bacon cheese fatburger) can make you sleepy. Some healthy, low-fat, easily packable snacks include raisins, trail mix, nuts, energy bars (check for the low-fat, low-calorie variety), apples, bananas, and many other fruits. Keep them handy in your tank bag or saddlebag. Wrap them in a plastic bag so they don't make a mess if they get smushed.

Eat first, ask questions later: It's late in the day, and you're tired, but you have a few hours to go yet. Stop. Rest. Get something light to eat, such as an energy bar or apple. The break and food will likely give you the needed energy to continue, and will make your ride enjoyable rather than an ordeal. The short rest will make you a more awake and energetic rider. Avoid a big meal, as that can make you sleepy.

Water, energy bars, sunscreen, notepads, a hat, shield cleaner and rag, and other incidentals... that's what a tank bag is for. *Buzz Buzzelli*

I took my first track school (which included instruction) after I'd been riding for 20 years, and nothing I've ever done improved my riding to such a degree so quickly. In a single day I learned how to read the lines in a turn, how to brake properly at high speed, how to match engine rpm when downshifting, how to move my body on the bike to enhance steering, how far my bike could lean, what happened when things touched down, how far I could trust my tires, and much more. I was led through the entire process by trained instructors who, at times, worked individually with the students.

The track school was an eye opener, and it enhanced my riding abilities immensely. Previous to the school I had been a typical uneducated rider. When I wanted to stay with other riders who were going fast I would wring the bike's neck to accelerate, brake in almost a panic mode for the next turn, then tiptoe through it and start the sorry scenario all over again. At the track school I learned, after 20 years, how to negotiate a turn properly at speed. That school, repeated periodically, did more for my riding ability than any mechanical device I ever added to a bike. I highly recommend taking high-performance riding schools, especially those conducted at racetracks.

Road Rags

Motels understandably hate it when riders use the motel's nice, clean towels to wipe down their dirty bikes, as this generally ruins the towels. Do everyone a favor by asking at the desk for rags. They often have a stash of worn-out or too-dirty towels (those used by previous bikers) just for the occasion.

One product I've found very useful on the road is Castrol's Waterless, Towelless Hand Cleaner. How does it work? Squirt some of this viscous goop into one hand, rub palms together briskly in a hand-washing motion, and the dirt rolls up and flakes off. It's amazing!

Don't limit yourself to just one H-D! Sure, you need a late-model Harley for reliability and travel, but you want several others to suit your moods. Here's a modern bobber for local rides. A bike like this is sometimes referred to as a "bar hopper." *Bob Clark*

Email and the internet have become indispensable, but when you're traveling how do you carry your laptop? One answer is with Roadgear's Multi-Tasker. It's a Cordura briefcase that can be carried on back with its three-piece harness. Or stow the harness and have a conventional briefcase. *Roadgear*

Just because Harleys aren't considered racetrack vehicles, and may suffer from a lack of cornering clearance, there is much to be learned by taking one to a track school with instruction, or a track day without. The trick is to learn at your own pace and within the limitations of your equipment so you can get the most out of each.

If you'd like to take a track school, get your bike tuned, have new tires mounted, and set your suspension to its higher preload settings to raise the bike farther off the track for greater cornering clearance. Set tire inflation pressures to the higher end of the scale, and check brake pads. Remove unnecessary weight. Have fun.

First-Aid Kit

While a mere first-aid kit won't be of much use in a serious situation, a basic kit will help a rider get through minor mishaps. The most common injuries from riding involve burns and scrapes, so plan your first-aid kit accordingly. Cover a minor burn with antiseptic cream, and tape a loosely wrapped gauze bandage over it.

Minor scrapes with the pavement (also known as "road rash") are a form of burn and can be treated similarly. Wash the skin trauma immediately with soap and water and cover it with the antiseptic cream and gauze. Have it checked by a physician as soon as possible.

Pack scissors, cleaning agents, aspirin, and a booklet of first-aid tips. More importantly, take a first-aid class; they're available through the American Red Cross.

For a century, men have found that cute girls just can't resist the allure of a big V-twin. Even at the age of four, my daughter Julia found something special about this Big Dog.

There is no motorcycle prominently displayed in this shot, which was taken on Main Street in Daytona. Who cares?

Pocket Pals

Some little gadgets are just indispensable. Carry a Swiss Army knife or other multitool for their mini screwdrivers, knife blades, bottle and can openers, scissors, and mini-pliers.

Other items to take along include a calculator watch with alarm.

Whenever you do a dirty job, like changing a tire or fooling with spark plugs or oil, you'll be a mess. For cleanup, bring along a rag and some dish detergent (it's formulated for getting grease off hands) in a film canister. An alternative is to pick up some Castrol Waterless/Towelless Hand Cleaner. I've tried it, and it works well.

Start 'em young and bring 'em up right! This young man, who happened to attend Daytona Bike Week, has his priorities straight.

The Most Important Part of Your Bike Is the Nut Holding onto the Handlebars

Some riders believe the money required of a track day would be better spent on a go-fast part, such as a new pipe, shocks, brakes, or whatever. In my case, before I took a track school, no matter how much better I could have made my bike perform, the choking point was my lack of cornering ability. The faster I could have made the bike go, the harder I would have had to brake to bring it back down to a speed I could comfortably control for the next turn. By tuning up my riding ability instead, I was able to extract the performance that was already built into my bike, and that's what made me a better rider—and capable of becoming a professional test rider.

MOTORCYCLE TERMS

Appendix

TECHNICAL DICTIONARY

While much of this information is presented throughout the book, here's a quick reference to some basic concepts and terms of motorcycling. This list is by no means complete, and of necessity repeats some topics listed elsewhere.

Words are defined as they apply to motorcycling specifically, and discussed briefly. Related words and concepts are grouped.

ELECTRICAL

Charging output, n: The amount of electrical power an engine's charging system is capable of producing. Modern bikes offer adequate charging output, but the addition of a couple of electric vests, auxiliary lights, and slow riding can strain some systems. Typical charging outputs will range from about 250 to 700 watts or more. Big dressers, those with anti-lock brakes and/or fuel injection, may have higher outputs. Note that maximum charging output is often achieved at rpm levels higher than normal cruising speeds. If your bike's charging output is barely able to handle the electrical draw, turn off unneeded items and/or shift to a lower gear so the engine will run at higher rpm.

ENGINE

Bore and stroke, n: An engine's bore is the diameter of any of its cylinders. Stroke is the distance any of its piston travels from top dead center (TDC) to bottom dead center (BDC). The total volume displaced by the piston(s) during their stroke(s) is the engine's displacement.

CV carburetor, n: A constant-velocity (sometimes called a constant-vacuum) carburetor. Long ago, before the Environmental Protection Agency became involved in emissions standards, the throttle cable was connected to the carburetor throttle plate. This

resulted in a load of raw gas being dumped into the carb whenever the cable was yanked, which led to excessive hydrocarbon emissions. Today, the cable is attached to a slide, which changes the vacuum in the carburetor.

Displacement, n: The total cubic volume displaced by the movement of the piston(s) from top dead center to bottom dead center. Engine displacement may be expressed in cubic centimeters (cc) or cubic inches (ci). Greater displacement generally indicates a more powerful engine, but not always. Some 600cc sportbikes produce more than 100 rear-wheel horsepower, while a typical stock Harley Twin Cam engine with 1,450cc puts out about 65 horsepower. A thousand cubic centimeters equal 1 liter, or 61.02 cubic inches.

DOHC, n and adj: Double overhead camshafts. Back in the 1960s, it was common for the camshaft to be located down by the crankshaft, which required that overhead valve gear be actuated via pushrods. But pushrods induce rpm limitations that are unacceptable on high-revving performance engines, so manufacturers began using an overhead cam driven by a chain. Dual overhead cams offer more positive valve actuation, and allow for a more optimal combustion chamber shape and port location. Larger, heavier rocker arms are required by a single overhead cam, but with DOHC the engineers are better able to put the valves where they need them. They can use bucket-and-shim actuators that offer less inertia, run lower valve-spring pressures for less wear and higher rpm, and require less frequent adjustment.

Dry sump, n: Harleys have a dry-sump engine lubrication system in which the engine oil is kept in a separate, external engine oil tank, circulated through the engine, then pumped back into the oil tank.

EFI, n: Electronic fuel injection, which takes the place of a carburetor and precisely meters fuel into the engine.

Engine type, adj: The arrangement and orientation of a motorcycle's cylinders, relative to the frame or each other. In addition to the number of cylinders, type also describes the manner in which those cylinders are configured. Examples: transverse, longitudinal, V, opposed, etc. In a transverse arrangement, the crankshaft is arranged across, or at a 90-degree angle, to the direction of the frame. On a longitudinal engine, the crankshaft runs parallel to the frame. A V engine has two or more cylinders arranged at less than a 180-degree angle to each other, joining a common crankshaft. The crankshaft of a V engine may run longitudinally (as with a Moto Guzzi), or transversely as with most cruisers. An opposed engine has its cylinders arranged in opposition to each other at 180 degrees, such as BMW flat twins and the Honda Gold Wing.

Four-valve head, n: A type of motorcycle head that utilizes two intake and two exhaust valves per cylinder. In motorcycling there are also two-, three-, and five-valve heads, the latter in the interest of freer breathing. Till the late 1970s, most motorcycle engines utilized the conventional single intake and exhaust valve per cylinder, but this arrangement reached its limits in terms of engine rpm. Multiple valves can be made smaller and lighter, reducing inertial stresses on the valvetrain and allowing the engine to flow more gases so it can be revved higher and more quickly.

Gearbox, n: What the British essentially call a box of gears, we Yanks call a transmission. It's called the latter because it transmits power from the engine to the rear wheels via a set of (usually) four, five or six reduction gears that provide a series of suitable ratios between engine rpm and road speed.

Horsepower, n: A unit of power equal to 746 watts, and nearly equivalent to the English gravitational unit that equals 550 foot-pounds of work per second.

OHC, n: Overhead camshaft, which is a camshaft located in the head where it can act upon the valves directly. This cuts down on the length of the valve train and its reciprocating mass relative to a pushrod engine, and allows for higher rpm.

OHV, n: Overhead valve; an arrangement that allows for more direct fuel flow into the combustion chambers

Oil tank, n: While automobiles and most other brands of motorcycle engines have integral oil reservoirs at the base of the engine, Harleys have a remote tank (also called an "oil bag") for engine oil. The main advantage to the oil tank is that the oil can be kept cooler by locating it away from the engine.

Primary drive, n: On bikes that have separate engine and transmission cases, such as Harley Big Twins, power is transferred through the clutch to the gearbox by a primary chain (a belt can also be used). On Harley Sportsters, the engine and gearbox are in a single unit so there is no need for a primary drive. The secondary (or "final") drive is what transfers power from the transmission to the rear wheel. Originally, Harleys used chain final drive, but all models began using belts in the 1990s.

Torque, n: A turning or twisting force. Horsepower and torque are different, but interrelated. Horsepower is a unit of work over time, but torque is instantaneous. In simple terms, torque is the twisting force that an engine generates, and horsepower is high-rpm maximum power. Horsepower equals torque (in pound-feet) times rpm, divided by 5,252. Because of this constant, the horsepower and torque curves on a dyno chart will always converge at 5,252 rpm.

Think of riding a bicycle. Torque is the twisting force you impart to the pedals that turns the crank at low speeds. At a certain point you're spinning the pedals so fast that the force diminishes; torque is dropping off. Beyond this point the only way to go faster is to shift to a higher gear or to extract more revs (which your body may not be able to provide). An engine can rev higher by utilizing more fuel. This carryover net effect of increased revs is more horsepower.

CHASSIS

Anti-lock braking system, n: A braking system that is engineered so that the brakes cannot lock and cause a skid. Pioneered on the BMW K100s in the late 1980s, ABS is now available on most BMWs and select models from various other manufacturers. The system includes a device for counting wheel revolution, and a computer that compares that figure with appropriate rpm. When wheel revs drop too suddenly, signaling imminent lockup, the computer signals the master cylinder to release braking force and reapply it immediately. This pulsing, which can happen 30 times per second or more and is constantly monitored by the computer, provides a safe, steady stop under most conditions. Note that ABS is not effective when the bike is leaned over.

Caliper, n: A device consisting of two plates, lined with a frictional material, that press against the rotating disc rotor on a brake system. Calipers commonly have one, two, three, four, or six pistons that push the frictional material outward against the rotor surface. Generally, additional pistons can result in improved braking force and "feel."

Damping, n: The degree to which the system of valves and orifices in a suspension system damp, or control and dispel, the energy fed into it. A suspension system works in two directions, compressing over bumps then rebounding, propelled upward again by the energy temporarily stored in the fork or shock springs. To control and dissipate that energy, suspension components utilize damping systems that force fluid through various orifices. Some suspension components have a series of damping controls that activate at various pressures. Some offer damping adjustment settings that allow the rider to select the amount of damping on the system. If a system has a single control, it will be for rebound damping. Some also offer a compression damping control.

Disc rotor, n: The round plate that rotates with the wheel, and which is gripped by the brake caliper when it is actuated. Rotors can be fixed or floating. A floating caliper is allowed some lateral movement, which allows it to slide between the caliper more freely when the brake is not in use.

Frame, n: The constructional system that gives shape and strength to a motorcycle. The frame is the structure (usually made of steel or aluminum tubing, or plates) that ties the motorcycle's various components together. It supports the engine (see "engine as a stressed member"), attaches to the swingarm, and its steering stem attaches to the fork via the triple clamps.

Gross Vehicle Weight Rating (GVWR), n: The maximum amount of weight that a vehicle can carry, including its own weight, luggage, and riders, and still meet certain design performance criteria. The GVWR figure is listed on a plate, usually affixed to the bike's steering head. Subtracting wet weight from GVWR results in the load capacity figure, which is the total weight of rider(s), luggage, and accessories the motorcycle can carry.

Hardtail, adj: A type of frame that has no swingarm, and no rear suspension. Because it was simpler to build, it was common until the late 1940s and 1950s, after which swingarm frames with rear suspension systems became common. Today, a number of aftermarket companies offer hardtail frames that give a bike a lower, cooler, more custom look.

Male-slider fork, n: A fork on which the lower slider is smaller and slips up into the larger stanchion. With a conventional fork, the slider is the larger-diameter lower unit that slides up over the smaller fork tubes. On a male-slider fork, which has become common on sportbikes, the slider is the smaller-diameter unit that slips into the larger stanchion. The main advantage to a male-slider fork is that the stanchions can be much thicker and stronger, leading to a more rigid fork.

Rake, n: The angle at which the steering stem is inclined from the perpendicular. Generally, the steeper the rake the quicker the bike will steer. A less-steep rake gives the bike greater stability at speed.

Spring preload, n: The amount a motorcycle's springs have been precompressed (preloaded); vt: The act of preloading a spring. If a motorcycle's suspension is sagging too much, or if it has inadequate cornering clearance and its hard bits are dragging in turns, preloading the springs can help raise it. This adjustment is accomplished by turning a ramped collar or a ring on the threaded shock body; some forks also have a preload adjuster at the top of the fork tubes. Precompressing (imparting a preload) on the spring(s) will raise the ride height, just as backing off the adjusters will lower it.

Spring rate, n: The resistance of a spring to being compressed. Common spring rates used on motorcycles are 80, 100, and 120 pounds of force required to compress the spring 1 inch.

Stiction, n: The amount of static friction, or drag, in fork operation. A combination of "static" and "friction," stiction refers to the relative amount of fork-seal drag as the sliders begin to slide up or down the fork tubes. In extreme cases, the fork seals will leave chatter marks on the tubes.

Swingarm, n: The swinging arm that supports the rear wheel and connects to the rear suspension. Until recent years, the swingarm was usually made of tube steel, like the frame, but higher-horsepower engines and modern cornering loads soon found the limits of contemporary frames and swingarms. On bigger, more powerful bikes, swingarms are now composed of welded-up steel or aluminum plates that form a much more rigid unit.

Tire: bias-ply, n: A tire on which the plies run at an angle (or bias) to the direction of travel.

Tire: radial, n: A tire on which the plies run essentially bead to bead, at a 90-degree angle to the direction of travel. A tire is defined by the arrangement of its plies. Belts run circumferentially around the tire, but plies run bead to bead. If those plies are arranged substantially straight across the tire, 90 degrees to the direction of rotation, it's a radial tire. If they run on a bias, it's a bias-ply. Because of their ply arrangement, bias-ply tires (all else being equal) tend to have a more rigid sidewall that can support a greater amount of weight. A radial has a much more pliable, shorter sidewall. As a result, touring bikes and cruisers tend to run on bias-ply tires, while sportbikes benefit from the radial's wider footprint. Because radials and bias-ply tires are designed to flex in opposite directions, don't mix them on the same motorcycle.

Trail, n: The distance that an imaginary line drawn straight down from the front axle of a motorcycle would trail behind an imaginary line drawn from the steering stem. Rake and trail are separate entities, but interrelated in explaining steering characteristics. First, draw a line continuing the angle of the steering head down to the ground and place a mark there.

Now draw a perpendicular line from the center of the front axle to the ground and place a second mark there. The distance between these two marks is trail. Rake figures on big streetbikes range from about 23 to 36 degrees, and common trail figures are from 3 to 6 inches. Generally, the greater the rake (larger numerical) the greater the trail. Bikes with greater rake and trail tend to steer more slowly but can be more stable at speed, while bikes with lesser rake and trail figures tend to steer more quickly but offer less of an "on rails" feeling at higher speeds. A big cruising bike, the Honda VTX1800 has lazy rake/trail figures of 32 degrees/6.5 inches. Honda's ST1300, a sport-tourer, offers medium figures of 26.0 degrees/4.0 inches. A sportbike needs to turn quickly, and Suzuki's GSX-R600 offers razor-sharp 24.0/3.7 figures.

Triple clamp, n: The upper and lower clamps (also called "triple trees") that connect the fork tubes to the steering head. They get their name from the fact that they clamp at three locations, two on the fork tubes and one on the steering head. The angle of these clamps also helps to determine the rake and trail.

Wheelbase, n: The distance between the front and rear axle centers of a vehicle. The wheelbase is the literal base upon which the motorcycle rests. All else being equal, bikes having a longer wheelbase tend to be more stable at speed, but are more reluctant to turn quickly. Bikes with shorter wheelbases will usually turn more quickly, but may tend to wander at higher speeds.

MISCELLANEOUS RIDING TERMINOLOGY

Aftermarket, n, adj: The aftermarket is all the companies that make parts and accessories for vehicles other than the companies that build the vehicles themselves. Any parts you install on your Harley that were made by a company other than the Harley-Davidson Motor Company are aftermarket parts, while those by H-D are Original Equipment Manufacturer (OEM) parts.

Apex, n: The tightest part of a turn; v: to ride across the apex of a turn. The apex is the tightest point of the turn. Before the apex, the turn is tightening; after the apex it's opening up. The preferred line through a turn is to enter it wide, tighten up and run in near the apex, then accelerate through and allow centrifugal force to bring you out wide.

Basket case, n: A bike that has been disassembled whose pieces have been put into boxes or baskets. Usually used to describe a bike that has become a project, and will be or, when used in past tense, has been restored.

Countersteering, n and v: The process of causing a single-track vehicle to go in one direction by turning its handlebar in the opposite direction. Huh? Probably the most misunderstood and indefinable concept in all of motorcycling, countersteering refers to the idea that when you lean left, the handlebar actually cocks slightly to the right. Which seems to make no sense at all. What happens is that as the rider cocks the bar away from the direction of the turn, the front wheel steers out from under the center of mass, changing the point on the tire that the motorcycle uses to steer. In essence, you steer counter to the direction in which you intend to go.

Cruiser, n, adj: A long, low, stylish bike with laid-back style usually (but not always) powered by a V-twin engine. In the US, this has been the most popular type of bike since the 1980s.

DOT, n: The United States Department of Transportation; often used when referring to a particular safety standard or mandate. It's frequently used when referring to the basic safety standard required for motorcycle helmets.

Dresser, n: A motorcycle that has been "dressed" for touring, with a fairing and saddlebags, and sometimes a trunk.

EPS foam, n: expanded polystyrene foam. This is the type of closed-cell foam that absorbs impact in helmets. EPS foam will absorb a great deal of energy by crushing.

Face plant, n: What you may do with your face if you screw up a wheelie, stoppie, or any other riding maneuver.

Fairing, n: A formed shell, usually of fiberglass or a plastic-based resin, that attaches to the front of the motorcycle and is designed to protect the rider from wind and the elements. It includes a windshield and may have lowers, which keep the wind off the legs. A fairing may

be mounted to the fork (so that it turns with the handlebar), or to the frame (so it does not).

High side/low side, n: When a motorcycle is leaned over, the high side is higher and the low side is, well, you get the idea; v: To experience a high-side or low-side crash. Stay away from the verb tense. To high side is a scary accident in which the bike's tires lose traction in a turn, begin to slide to the outside, then catch traction and snap the bike back upright and over. This throws the rider forcefully over the high side, often resulting in spectacular cartwheels and broken bones.

A low-side accident starts the same way, with the tires sliding out, but instead of regaining traction the bike continues to slide until it eventually falls over onto its low side.

Highway pegs, n: Extended footpegs mounted to the front of the bike that allow the rider to stretch his or her legs while riding. The downside is that, unless they're part of forward controls, highway pegs position the feet farther from the controls.

Hook and loop, n: 1. often used in articles about clothing or soft luggage, hook and loop refers to a fastening device composed of one half tiny hooks, and the other tiny loops that the hooks grip. 2. One type of such fastening device that goes under the trade name Velcro. 3. We get nasty letters from the people at Velcro if we don't call it "hook and loop."

Hygroscopic, adj: readily taking up and retaining water. If your owner's manual calls for using DOT 4 brake fluid in your bike, do not think you're doing yourself a favor by using DOT 5 instead. DOT 5 is much more hygroscopic than DOT 4, and tends to pick up moisture from humidity and condensation over time, which contaminates the brake fluid.

Late apex, n and v: A riding strategy in which the rider enters a turn wide and stays wide longer, apexing much later than usual. Late apexing is a good strategy to use in situations when your line of sight is diminished, such as on a road with many blind turns. The rider stays wider longer so that he can see farther into the turn, rather than zapping across the apex.

MSF, n: Motorcycle Safety Foundation; an association devoted to safe riding practices

that offers training for both beginning and experienced riders.

OEM, n: original equipment manufacturers. Probably the most used and least understood abbreviation in all of road testing, it simply refers to the companies that originally built the bikes. You know, like Honda, BMW, Harley-Davidson, Kawasaki—those guys.

Poker Run, n: A ride during which riders stop at various checkpoints along the way to draw a playing card. At the end of the ride, the best poker hands win prizes.

Rally, n: A gathering for motorcycle riders. They can center upon a particular bike brand or club, or they can be open to all.

Range, n: A figure expressed in miles that is average miles per gallon multiplied by fuel capacity. Range depends upon fuel mileage, and will vary with each tank.

Rat Bike, n: A particularly well-used bike that not only is rarely cleaned, but may also be extravagantly personalized to look unusually road weary.

Sissy bar, n: If you've ever ridden on the back of a bike and were noticeably paranoid about falling off, you may have been called a sissy. To appease their passengers, some bike owners add a nearly vertical tube-steel "sissy bar," a framework against which the passenger can rest. The more considerate bike owners add a pad for the passenger's comfort.

Softail, n: A Harley model that appears to be a hard-tail, but actually conceals its rear suspension under the engine. The name "Softail" is trademarked by The Motor Company.

Stoppie, n and v: To stop a motorcycle so hard that the rear wheel lifts off the ground as the rider balances on the front.

Two up, adj: Riding two on a bike, with a passenger.

Wheelie, n and v: To accelerate so hard that the front wheel of the motorcycle lifts off the ground. On a horse, a wheelie-type maneuver is called a hoofie.

Index

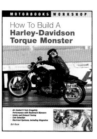

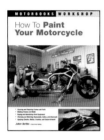

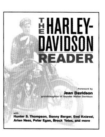
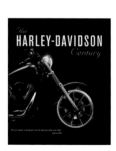